MULTICULTURALISM AND LEARNING STYLE

MULTICULTURALISM AND LEARNING STYLE

Teaching and Counseling Adolescents

Rita Dunn & Shirley A. Griggs

Westport, Connecticut
London

Library of Congress Cataloging-in-Publication Data

Dunn, Rita Stafford.
    Multiculturalism and learning style : teaching and counseling
adolescents / Rita Dunn and Shirley A. Griggs.
        p.   cm.
    Includes bibliographical references and index.
    ISBN 0–275–94762–9 (alk. paper)
        1. Minority students—Education—United States.   2. Learning,
Psychology of.   3. Minority students—Counseling of—United States.
I. Griggs, Shirley A.   II. Title.
LC3731.D85   1995
371.97′00973—dc20   94–36775

British Library Cataloguing in Publication Data is available.

Library of Congress Catalog Card Number: 94–36775
ISBN: 0–275–96480–9 (pbk.)

First published in 1995

Praeger Publishers, 88 Post Road West, Westport, CT 06881
An imprint of Greenwood Publishing Group, Inc.

Printed in the United States of America

The paper used in this book complies with the
Permanent Paper Standard issued by the National
Information Standards Organization (Z39.48–1984).

10 9 8 7 6 5 4 3 2 1

Contents

Preface

In recent years, the costs and consequences of the high number of at-risk and dropout minority students in the United States and throughout the world have been major concerns of educators and parents. They are also concerns of governments and communities faced with exorbitant welfare and crime rates.

Analyses of the learning styles of many at-risk and dropout students have revealed that such students learn in a processing style and with instructional strategies that differ significantly from those of adolescents who tend to perform well in conventional schools (Dunn & Dunn, 1992, 1993; Dunn & Griggs, 1988b; Dunn, Dunn, & Perrin, 1994). In addition, dropouts are more likely to be African Americans, Native Americans, and Hispanics than whites or Asian Americans (Paulu, 1987), and they are overrepresented in vocational and general tracks and in special education (Oakes, 1985). Indeed, the high rate of underachievement among minorities prompted suggestions that teachers should "teach to the learning styles of black children" (Hale-Benson, 1982, p. 196).

Allegations that minorities may learn differently from majority Caucasians led to the establishment of a New York State Board of Regents panel to investigate that concept (D'Antonio, 1988). Ultimately, that panel of representatives from diverse disciplines reported that no evidence supported the controversial theory that African Americans shared distinctly different learning styles from those of Caucasians (Gordon, 1988). The panel's conclusions, however, were based solely on examination of a limited number of published studies at that time, selected articles, and personal testimony. Its budget permitted the panel of a dozen authorities to meet for a total of only two full days.

Since that time, at least 35 independent studies have compared the learning styles of multicultural students both in the United States and abroad. Some of these compared various age and academic-achievement groups (Dunn & Griggs, 1989b, 1990). Others concentrated on the learning styles of gifted minority youngsters in Illinois (Ewing & Yong, 1992) and underachieving Cajun and Native American students in Louisiana (Drew, 1991). Dunn, Griggs, and Price (1993a) differentiated among the styles of adolescents gifted in art, athletics, dance, literature, mathematics, music, and science across the United States and also compared those of Mexican American and Anglo American elementary school males and females (1993b). A series of international studies examined the learning styles of gifted and talented adolescents in nations as diverse as Brazil, Canada, Egypt, Greece, Guatemala, Israel, Korea, the Philippines, and the United States (Milgram, Dunn, & Price, 1993a).

Other researchers compared the learning styles of underachievers regardless of their ethnicity (Andrews, 1990, 1991; Dunn & Griggs, 1988b; Dunn, Bruno, Sklar, & Beaudry, 1990; Gardiner, 1986; Hodges, 1985; Wittenberg, 1984). Some examined the learning styles of various special education populations (Bauer, 1991; Brunner & Majewski, 1990; Dean, 1982; Lux, 1987; Snider, 1985). Reid (1987) identified the style preferences of English-as-a-second-language (ESL) students without regard to cultural differences.

Underachievers in each group revealed essentially similar learning-style traits, and those differed significantly from the learning styles of gifted students. Indeed, in the Milgram, Dunn, and Price (1993b) findings, the learning styles of gifted adolescents in mathematics were essentially similar across cultures, as were the learning styles of the gifted in literature, and the gifted in art, music, dance, drama, or sports. Although gifted adolescents within each talent area tended to reveal essentially similar styles, the learning styles of each gifted group was significantly different from the learning style of every other gifted group.

Thus, this book, the first of its kind,

1. analyzes and synthesizes the research that reveals the similarities and differences among the learning styles of culturally diverse populations;
2. clarifies the implications of multicultural students' varied learning styles for both teaching and counseling;
3. describes how to teach and counsel adolescents with different learning styles through their identified individual strengths;
4. reports on schools that have successfully reversed underachievement among culturally diverse students; and

5. guides readers toward teaching and counseling multicultural adolescents with diverse learning styles so that the students can achieve better, enjoy learning more, develop confidence in their ability to master new and difficult information, and discipline themselves while learning.

Acknowledgments

This book is an outgrowth of almost three decades of research concerned with the learning styles of multicultural populations throughout the United States and abroad. These investigations involved the commitment and expertise of more than 18 professors and 60 doctoral students working cooperatively at St. John's University in New York—the largest Catholic University in the United States.

We are deeply appreciative of the support and encouragement given to us by our university's administrators who foster a climate "based on respect for all persons" and support "cultural diversity in an interdependent world" (Harrington, 1994, p. 2). In keeping with this commitment, which has been endorsed by all segments of our community, we were granted a six-month research leave to complete this text.

We also express our gratitude to Mrs. Madeline Larsen, secretary, Division of Administrative and Instructional Leadership, who assisted in the typing of this manuscript.

Harrington, D. (1994, January). Mission Statement. *Strategic Planning*. New York: St. John's University.

MULTICULTURALISM AND LEARNING STYLE

Chapter 1

Examining Your Knowledge
of Multiculturalism and
Learning Styles

Beginning with the first one-room schoolhouse established in the colonies, American teachers have always taught students from widely diverse backgrounds. For almost 200 years, we successfully absorbed immigrants into our classrooms, but during most of that period they comprised only a small percentage of the total school population. Then, as the birthrate among Caucasians in the United States declined, the proportion of minority children increased. By 1987, Edelman calculated that nearly one-quarter of all children under age 15 were black and Hispanic. In that same year, Paulu (1987) reported that black and Hispanic students were more likely than others to perform poorly in school, become at risk, and drop out.

Changing demographics in U.S. schools reveal that within the next five years the current "minority" population will have become the majority population in 53 major U.S. cities (Rodriguez, 1988). Although government and industry grants have provided extensive funding for a variety of new programs for underachieving minority students, few of those programs have succeeded in improving the students' standardized achievement test scores.

In schools that have evidenced statistically increased achievement gains among African-American youth, instruction had been changed to respond to how those students most preferred to learn—their "learning styles" (Andrews, 1990, 1991; Brunner & Majewski, 1990; Nganwa-Bagumah & Mwamwenda, 1991; Perrin, 1990; Quinn, 1994; Stone, 1992; *The Bridge to Learning*, 1993). For example, in 1985 and 1986 students in the Brightwood Elementary School, Greensboro, North Carolina, had achieved only in the 30th percentile on the California Achievement Tests of Basic Skills

(CATs). Principal Roland Andrews then identified the youngsters' learning styles with the Learning Style Inventory (LSI) (Dunn, Dunn, & Price, 1979) and found that

- 126 were global, 119 were analytic, and only 9 could learn difficult academic information either way;
- 61 needed low light, 36 needed bright light, and 167 could work in either illumination;
- 29 preferred conventional seating, but 91 could not sit in a wooden, plastic, or steel chair for more than 10–12 minutes;
- 147 required a great deal of structure, but 10 required options when learning; 108 required structure when not interested in the curriculum content, and choices when they were;
- 26 could achieve better in a structured situation when learning alone than with a teacher or with classmates; 56 were peer oriented and could learn well in either pairs or small groups;
- 182 could learn neither alone nor with classmates; of those, 94 required an authoritative teacher whereas 27 required a collegial teacher;
- 98 needed a variety of instructional strategies and became bored with repetition; conversely, 34 needed routines and patterns and felt uncomfortable when new strategies were introduced;
- whereas 90 *were* auditory, 21 could not remember much of what they heard and 147 only could retain well by listening when they were interested in what they were learning;
- all 54 fifth and sixth graders were visual; 33 others in the school were not; 176 could remember three-quarters of what they read or observed only when interested in the topic;
- 165 were tactual learners—a group substantially larger than either the auditory or visual learners; only 5 percent were low tactual, and 94 additional youngsters could learn tactually only when interested in the material;
- 175 were kinesthetic learners—children who learn while actively engaged in activities related to what they are learning, such as role playing, trips, making and doing things, and educational floor games; indeed, kinesthetic and tactual learners comprised the majority of Brightwood's students;
- 64 required some form of snacking or liquid while learning; 84 did not; 116 did at times;
- 55 were "early-morning birds"; 70 were "night owls"; 41 were late-morning preferents; 100 were virtually nonfunctional in the early morning but "came alive" in the afternoon; thus, the majority should have been taught basic required subjects in the afternoon and/or late morning; "night" children should have been taught how to study at home in the evening;
- 102 required frequent mobility; only 53 could sit passively for any length of time; 109 could remain in their seats only when interested in what they were learning; when not, they needed mobility;

- only two children were neither parent nor teacher motivated; most wanted to please the adults in their lives but were incapable of doing so while learning conventionally (Klavas, 1993).

In 1987, after only one year of teaching the children about their learning-style strengths, adjusting the environment to permit alternative illumination and seating, and introducing tactual instructional resources to those with tactual preferences, teachers found that students' test scores on the CATs escalated to the 40th percentile. In 1988, the second year of the learning-styles program, when reading and mathematics were taught in the afternoon and small-group strategies were introduced, the school's CAT scores in both subjects jumped to between the 74th and 76th percentile. In 1989, the third year of Brightwood's learning-styles program, CAT scores reached the 83rd percentile. One year later they reached the 89th percentile (Andrews, 1990, 1991). During that period African-American youth in North Carolina consistently performed between the 20th and 30th percentiles nationally. In Brightwood, black students performed at the 70th percentile or better (Andrews, 1990, 1991).

Essentially similar gains were reported by the Buffalo City schools. Under the supervision of a team of researchers from the State University at Buffalo, learning-disabled (LD) and emotionally handicapped (EH) students (K–6) were randomly selected and randomly assigned to two groups. The experimental group was taught through its students' learning-style preferences, whereas the control group was taught with the methods its special education teachers had used traditionally. Results at the end of the first two-year period revealed that the experimental group had achieved statistically higher test scores than the control group in both reading and mathematics on two different standardized achievement tests—the Woodcock-Johnson and the CATs. In contrast, the control group had evidenced academic losses between the pretest and the posttest (see Table 1.1).

These findings suggest that students whose instruction is not responsive to their learning styles achieve significantly less well than children whose instruction is responsive to their learning styles. Nothing differed between either (1) the experimental group and the control group in Buffalo or (2) pre-1987 test score and the post-1987 test score in Brightwood other than the introduction of learning-style-based instruction. That single factor contributed to the significantly higher test scores in the two school systems.

Brightwood Elementary School in North Carolina and the Buffalo City schools in New York were comprised of culturally diverse students who had not been achieving well with conventional teaching. Does the fact that their students achieved statistically higher test scores only *after* learning-style-responsive instruction suggest that they had previously not been taught correctly—for them? Do the changes in their students' performance

Table 1.1

Comparison of SAT Scores

Report from the Independent Research Team of the University of Buffalo: Results of Standardized Achievement Test Scores in Reading and Mathematics for Students in the Buffalo City Schools' Learning Styles Program (Experimental Group) in Contrast with the Results of Students in its Non-Learning Styles Program (Control Group) for the First Two Years of Program Implementation.

Test Name	Group	Pre-Test	Post-test	Net Difference
WJ* Reading	Exper.	72.38	79.1	+ 6.72
	Control	76.48	71.52	- 4.96#
WJ+ Math	Exper.	69.67	84.2	+ 14.53
	Control	73.52	69.09	- 4.43#
CTBS+ Reading	Exper.	18.76	31.33	+ 12.57
	Control	24.83	21.25	-3.58
CTBS+ Math	Exper.	15.83	18.61	+2.78
	Control	23.44	16.95	-6.49

*WJ: Woodcock-Johnson   +CTBS: California Test of Basic Skills

#Loss

further suggest that how their students learn may be different from how other students in U.S. schools learn?

Another issue to consider is that of Asian or German students achieving better than U.S. students. Does such achievement imply a difference in the learning styles of one group in comparison with the other? Is instruction in one system less responsive to individual differences than in another? Or are other factors at work here?

Before providing answers to these questions, we would like you to consider and confront your own beliefs about how students learn and why some succeed when others fail. Do most people learn in the same way? Do people from different cultures, races, religions, and/or nations learn similarly to each other? Should we alter the instructional delivery system for different students based on their learning styles? Is it important to change instruction at all? Do IQ, motivation, school expectations, family background, or cultural heritage influence learning so much that certain children can, whereas other children cannot, learn easily? What do you believe about how culturally diverse students learn?

YOUR BELIEFS ABOUT HOW DIVERSE STUDENTS LEARN

Questionnaire on Learning Style and Multiculturalism

Directions

Consider the following questions carefully. At the end of each sentence, circle or write what you believe is the most accurate answer. After answering all the questions, compare your answers with those at the end of the chapter. The references at the end provide the research support for the answers.

In this questionnaire "learning" refers to how individuals concentrate on, process, and remember new and difficult information, and "significantly" refers to statistically measurable differences.

Questions

1. Do most people in one culture learn differently from most people in another culture? Yes _____ No _____

2. Do most people in the same culture learn in basically the same way? Yes _____ No _____

3. Do boys and girls learn differently from each other? Yes _____ No _____

4. Do high and low achievers learn differently from each other?

5. Is there a relationship between how someone learns and being gifted? Yes _____ No _____

6. Does learning style contribute to underachievement? Yes _____ No _____

7. Do children and adults learn differently? Yes _____ No _____

8. Do the *majority* of students (K–12) learn best by listening? _____ by reading? _____ by taking notes? _____ by experiencing? _____

   How large is the largest group that learns best through any of the above modalities? _____

9. Can a low auditory and low visual student become an A, B+, or B student in conventional schools? _____

10. (a) Do a *majority* of students (K–12) learn best through cooperative learning? (b) Who does? _____ (c) Who doesn't? _____ (d) How do we know? _____

11. (a) Do a *majority* of students learn best in early morning? _____ (b) Who learns best in early morning? _____ (c) Who learns best at night? _____

12. Are people with one learning style more or less intelligent than people with another learning style? Yes _____ No _____

13. (a) Are the majority of students "analytic" (step-by-step sequential) learners? Yes _____ No _____ (b) What is the opposite of being analytic? _____

(c) Name another processing style. _____ (d) Are people with one processing style more or less intelligent than people with another? Yes _____ No _____

14. Are the majority of teachers "analytic" (step-by-step sequential) instructors? Yes _____ No _____

15. Are there differences among cultures concerning attitudes toward school and teachers? Yes _____ No _____

16. How do selected learning-style elements change based on growth and development?

17. Is it necessary to consider an adolescent's learning style when selecting various counseling techniques and interventions? Yes _____ No _____

18. Identify a counseling approach that accommodates analytic students and another that accommodates global students.

Answers to Questionnaire on Learning Styles and Multiculturalism

1. No. Within every family in each culture, people learn differently from each other (Dunn & Griggs, 1990).

2. No. Most people *within* each culture learn differently from other people in the same culture. Therefore, most people in any culture learn differently from the people within the same culture and from people in different cultures.

3. Yes. Particularly during the primary school years, there are more differences between the learning styles of boys and girls than between the learning styles of people in different cultures. For example, girls develop comparatively strong auditory memory and small-motor coordination earlier than boys. Thus, they remember what they hear better and write more neatly than their male classmates. We rarely say to girls, "Why can't you remember!" or "How many times must I tell you that!" We frequently admonish boys for either forgetting, "not hearing," or not "concentrating"—because many of them cannot remember a great deal of what has been said to them. Girls are also better able to sit passively for a longer amount of time in conventional seats and desks, whereas most boys require mobility and an informal design significantly more than girls. That is why boys are repeatedly reprimanded for squirming in, or falling out of, their seats. Conversely, boys develop large-motor coordination earlier and excel in physical activities such as sports, in contrast with girls' ability to write more neatly, cut with a pair of scissors more precisely, and draw within lines better than boys. Too, boys remain tactual and kinesthetic learners longer than girls. Girls are more authority oriented, whereas boys tend to become peer oriented earlier and remain that way longer. In addition, girls need significantly more quiet while learning whereas boys tolerate noise in the environment better; few males are distracted by sound because most are not very aware of it.

4. Yes. The learning styles of high-academic achievers and low-academic achievers differ significantly. The former generally have preferences that respond to conventional schooling; for example, they are (a) auditory or visual learners; (b) self-motivated, parent motivated, or authority motivated (rather than unmotivated or peer motivated); (c) not in need of mobility or food while learning; and (d) conforming rather than nonconforming. Underachievers tend to be tactual/kinesthetic learners who often require sound, soft lighting, an informal design, intake, and mobility while learning. They often are peer motivated or motivated only when interested in what they are learning. Underachievers also require a variety of resources, methods, or approaches while learning and become bored with routines. During the period in which adolescents may be experiencing nonconformity, achievers as well as underachievers may become temporarily anti-authoritarian; they may, for example, prefer collegial to authoritative teachers and other adults.

5. Yes. When students (a) are taught in ways that complement either their interests or natural talents, (b) feel a sense of accomplishment or pleasure, (c) reap benefits that respond to their emotionality, and (d) have the opportunity to engage in activities in which they can excel, over time their talent often develops into exceptional ability—which society views as giftedness (Dunn, Dunn, & Treffinger, 1992; Milgram, Dunn, & Price, 1993a).

6. Yes. When adolescents do not learn because of the way they are being taught, learning becomes difficult, boring, tension provoking, and frustrating. Some students give up, some give in, and others withdraw. Any one of these three conditions may lead to poor school achievement.

7. Yes. Many elements of style change as children grow older, mature, and spend time in school. We do not know whether those changes are maturational or an outgrowth of students' ability to respond to conventional schooling. Elements that tend to change developmentally include responsiveness to sound, light, seating designs, motivation, responsibility (conformity-nonconformity), need for structure and intake, social groupings, perception, and chronobiological highs and lows (Price, 1980). Some elements change in some people and not in others (e.g., global versus analytic inclinations and motivation). Temperature preferences rarely change, and persistence changes only slowly over time, if at all. Although some change can be predicted based on general patterns at various age levels, individual cycles are established because of biological and developmental uniqueness.

8. No. Less than 30 percent of adults learn best through auditory means, and among school-age youth the percentage is closer to 10–12 percent. Visual learners comprise up to 40 percent of adults, but many of these are graphic-photographic learners; among K–3 children, the percentage is closer to 15–20 percent, varying by gender and achievement. Note-takers tend to be visual/tactual students who cannot remember much of what they hear without writing it. Kinesthetic learners master what they learn through experience, involvement, and movement while learning; usually they do not learn through someone else's experiences or by listening or reading.

   The percentage of modality preferences varies with age, gender, and achievement, but there are more tactual and kinesthetic school-age youth than auditory learners everywhere we have tested students during the past quarter of a century.

9. Yes. Most students can learn anything when they (a) begin learning with their preferred perceptual strength, (b) reinforce through their secondary or tertiary modality, and then (c) apply the new information they have been exposed to by using it to develop a new instructional resource (e.g., explaining information by writing a poem; creating a play, film, book, or game; or making a set of task cards, an electroboard, a pic-a-hole, or a flip chute). The ability to learn is also based on the individual's interest in the topic or subject.

10. No. In the general population approximately 13 percent of most students learn best alone; approximately 28 percent learn well with peers, but within this group are students who learn only with one classmate and others who learn in a small group. Another 28 percent need an adult; within this cluster are some who need a collegial adult and others who need an authoritative adult. Some can learn well in two or more groupings, and many learn best only in one (Cholakis, 1986; DeBello, 1985; Dunn, Giannitti, Murray, Geisert, Rossi, & Quinn, 1990; Miles, 1987; Perrin, 1984). However, those percentages vary with academic achievement and age. For example, gifted adolescents in at least nine diverse nations strongly preferred to learn independently, that is, by themselves. Their second most-preferred sociological preference was learning with an *authoritative* adult. Young gifted children also preferred learning alone, unless they could not complete their tasks alone, at which point they preferred learning with other *gifted* children (Perrin, 1984). In U.S. schools sociological preferences appear to be substantially influenced by age, grade, and achievement levels (Dunn & Dunn, 1992, 1993; Dunn, Dunn, & Perrin, 1994).

11. No. Time-of-day energy levels vary widely, particularly with age. At best only between 30 and 40 percent of adolescents are most alert in the morning. A majority first "come alive" between 10:00 A.M. and 10:30 A.M., and their highest energy levels are between then and 2:30 P.M., during which time we give them a one-hour lunch period (Dunn & Dunn, 1993; Lynch, 1981).

12. No. Because most teachers teach either by talking (which requires students to learn well by listening) or by reading (which requires students to learn well by seeing), students who remember well by listening or seeing tend to become comparatively high achievers in school. Most young children are tactual and/or kinesthetic preferents but are taught through lectures or readings, so that it is difficult for them to remember at least 75 percent of what they need to learn. When tactual and kinesthetic students are (a) introduced to difficult materials with tactual or kinesthetic instructional resources, (b) reinforced with a *different* modality resource, and (c) required to apply the new information creatively, they learn significantly more than when they are taught incorrectly (for them) (Andrews, 1990, 1991; Ingham, 1991; *The Bridge to Learning*, 1993; Carbo, 1980; Garrett, 1991; Ingham, 1991; Jarsonbeck, 1984; Martini, 1986; Stone, 1992; Weinberg, 1983; Wheeler, 1980, 1983).

13. No. Based on correlations between at least three different instruments and learning-style characteristics, the majority of young children and students who

do not perform well in school appear to be global, that is, they are people who (a) need to understand a concept before they can focus on the details, (b) learn best when interested in the subject, (c) often learn informally, with music, intake, and others nearby, (d) may learn better in soft light than in bright light, and (e) prefer to work on several tasks simultaneously rather than on one at a time (Brennan, 1984; Cody, 1983; Dunn, Bruno, Sklar, & Beaudry, 1990; Dunn, Cavanaugh, Eberle, & Zenhausern, 1982; Trautman, 1979). Neither cognitive processing style is better, nor are analytic students more intelligent than global students. However, analytics tend to be higher academic achievers—because most teachers teach analytically.

14. Yes. Of the teachers we have tested during the past 20 years, 65 percent tend to be analytic, whereas in the overall population 55 percent of adults are global and only 28 percent of adults are analytic. In a study of gifted and talented adolescents in nine diverse cultures, 18 percent of the gifted students were analytic and 26 percent were global (Milgram, Dunn, & Price, 1993a). Students appear to be equally intelligent when they are taught in ways that respond to their learning-style preferences. Cody (1983) found that with an IQ of 125 and in the 94th percentile in reading or math, eight of ten students were analytic. With an IQ of 135, that statistic reversed and eight of ten students were global. With an IQ of 145 or above, nine of ten students were global.

15. Yes. Different cultures express different attitudes toward teachers, education, and what comprises valuable learning. It appears to be common knowledge that in the United States it is considered polite for students to look squarely into the eyes of a teacher when being addressed, whereas in certain cultures, as in Japan, looking directly at an adult is thought to be rude. Being on time, passively or actively participating in learning, studying theoretical versus practical matters, and many subtle behaviors vary extensively from one group to another. A culture's values, the opportunities it provides to individuals, and each student's interests, talents, and learning style contribute to the development, maturation, and expression of intelligence.

16. The need for sound and intake can be observed by second or third grade and for many remains fairly consistent until about sixth grade. At that time, the two preferences "explode," and during adolescence the need for sound and intake becomes stronger than before. For many, at about ninth or tenth grade the two elements begin to return to their previous "normal" level (for that individual). Among older adults the need for quiet appears to increase, and the need for intake appears to decrease.

Temperature inclinations tend to remain the same throughout childhood and adulthood but may gradually change toward the need for more warmth particularly among the aging. Design preferences tend to remain the same during elementary school, gradually lean toward becoming more informal as students reach adolescence, and then may change on an individual basis.

Responsibility tends to correlate with conformity versus nonconformity (Dunn, White, & Zenhausern, 1982). People tend to undergo three periods of nonconformity. The first occurs at approximately two years of age, the second during "adolescence," and the third in middle age, sometimes called the "midlife crisis." Motivation varies with interest and the degree to which the teaching matches the student's learning-style preference. Nothing holds true across the board, of course, but persistence tends to be an analytic quality. Analytic processors, more than global processors, tend to stay on task while learning. Their counterparts often require "breaks" for intake, interaction, changing focus, and so forth. The older students become, the less structure they need, although under pressure of exams or multiple study assignments, for example, many college students require structure (Napolitano, 1986). Sociologically, many young children come to school wanting to please the adults (parents and teachers) in their lives. Somewhere around third grade many start becoming peer motivated. Whereas students rarely used to become peer motivated before seventh or eighth grade (Dunn & Dunn, 1972), they have become peer motivated at younger ages during the past three decades. Many adolescents are peer oriented.

Gifted children also come to school wanting to please the adults in their lives, but early, by first or second grade, most become learning-alone preferents and do not seem to experience a peer stage. Underachievers remain peer oriented longer than either gifted or average achievers. Usually by ninth or tenth grade most average students have emerged from wanting to learn with classmates and become self-motivated. At no time have we ever found more than 28 percent of students in the peer stage, and among that group many learn better with just one other classmate than in a small group. Those who work well with one other classmate are pair-motivated; others need to learn with a teacher, although some need a collegial adult and others need an authoritative adult. In three studies of dropouts, at-risk students required a collegial adult but had been assigned to an authoritative adult (Gadwa & Griggs, 1985; Johnson, 1984; Thrasher, 1984).

Perceptually, the younger the children, the more tactual and/or kinesthetic they are. In elementary school less than 12 percent appear to be auditory (able to remember three-quarters of what they are taught through lecture or discussion) and less than 40 percent are visual (able to remember three-quarters of what they are taught through reading). The older children become, the more visual and, eventually, the more auditory they become. However, females are generally more auditory than males, and males generally become more visual and remain more tactual and kinesthetic than females. Time-of-day preferences change with age (see Chapter 2 for a more complete reference). Many students require mobility, learning more, more efficiently when permitted to move *while* learning (Della Valle, 1984; Miller, 1985).

17. Yes, it is important to design counseling interventions that respond to adolescents' learning-style preferences for structure, sociological needs, perceptual strengths, and cognitive styles. For example, (a) auditory learners are well accomodated by traditional "talking" counseling approaches, (b) visual learners respond to bibliotherapy and modeling, (c) tactual adolescents need hands-on strategies such as serial drawing or creative writing, and (d) kinesthetic students respond well to game therapy and experiential interventions.

18. Most cognitive behavioral counseling theories are designed for use with analytic students because they employ a rational, sequential approach to problem solving. Conversely, many affective counseling theories, such as Gestalt therapy, are compatible with the holistic, intuitive orientation of global adolescents (Griggs, 1991a).

Chapter 2

Understanding Learning Styles and the Need for Teaching to Individual, Rather than Group, Characteristics

INTRODUCTION TO LEARNING STYLE

Many people prefer to learn in ways that are sometimes slightly different, and often extremely different, from how other people of the same age, class, culture, grade, religion, or nationality prefer to learn. How people prefer to learn is called their learning-style preference.

Although some people may learn without using their learning-styles preferences, students achieve significantly better when they do, rather than when they don't, capitalize on their preferences. Because students achieve significantly higher standardized achievement and attitude test scores when they learn through their learning-style preferences, those preferences are called "strengths" (Sullivan, 1993).

Conventional schooling often requires that adolescents sit quietly at their desks for long periods of time. They need to learn by either listening to their teachers or reading assigned materials. Students usually show how much they have learned by answering questions on a paper-and-pencil test. Sometimes the entire class learns in small groups, by taking a trip, or by seeing a movie. Occasionally everybody is assigned to develop a project. However, regardless of the activity, the classroom environment and how students are taught is identical for each learner. Everyone is expected to learn in exactly the same way that everyone else learns (Goodlad, 1984).

In learning-style classes, students' strengths are identified and then transferred into a computer software package. That "Homework Disc" generates a personalized, printed prescription for each student describing how that student is to study and concentrate given his or her strengths. Practitioners reported statistically higher test scores and/or grade-point averages for students taught through their learning-style strengths at the elementary level (Andrews, 1990; Lemmon, 1985; Stone, 1992; Turner, 1993), at the secondary level (Brunner & Majewski, 1990; Elliot, 1991; Gadwa & Griggs, 1985; Orsak, 1990b), and at the college level (Clark-Thayer, 1987; Lenehan, Dunn, Ingham, Signer, & Murray, 1994; Mickler & Zippert, 1987; Nelson, Dunn, Griggs, Primavera, Fitzpatrick, Bacilious, & Miller, 1993).

Differences in how individuals learn explain why certain children perform well in school whereas their siblings may not. Those differences also explain why no one instructional method or resource "works" for all students. Any one approach may help certain adolescents perform well and enable others to perform only marginally, but may also contribute to the poor performances or failure of other individuals.

The research on learning styles provides clear directions for teaching individuals through their learning-style strengths or enabling individuals to teach themselves by capitalizing on their learning-style strengths.

WHAT IS LEARNING STYLE?

Learning style is the way in which each person begins to concentrate on, process, and retain new and difficult information. Concentration occurs differently for different people at different times. It is important to know many things about *individual's* traits to determine what is most likely to trigger each adolescent's concentration, energize his or her processing style, and intervene to increase long-term memory.

To identify the individual's learning-style traits, it is necessary to use a "comprehensive" instrument—one that diagnoses many different traits. A reliable and valid comprehensive instrument reveals which people are affected by which traits. Only three comprehensive models exist, and each has a related instrument designed to reveal individuals' styles based on the traits examined by that model (DeBello, 1990).

It is impossible to obtain reliable and valid data from an unreliable or invalid assessment. The instrument with the highest reliability and validity and the one used in most research on learning styles is the Dunn, Dunn, and Price Learning Style Inventory (LSI) (*Research on the Dunn and Dunn Model*, 1995).

Educators cannot identify students' learning-style traits correctly without an instrument (Beaty, 1986; Dunn, Dunn, Price, 1977; Marcus, 1977); some traits are not observable, even to the experienced educator. In addition, teachers often misinterpret adolescents' behaviors and misunderstand their traits and preferences.

THEORETICAL CORNERSTONE OF THE DUNN AND DUNN LEARNING-STYLE MODEL

Brain lateralization theory emerged in the 1970s and demonstrated that the left hemisphere appeared to be associated with verbal and sequential abilities whereas the right hemisphere appeared to be associated with emotions and with spatial, holistic processing. Although those particular conclusions continue to be challenged, it is clear that people concentrate, process, and remember new and difficult information under very different conditions. For example, auditory and visual perceptual strengths, passivity, and self-oriented or authority-oriented motivation often correlate with high academic achievement, whereas tactual and kinesthetic strengths, a need for mobility, nonconformity, and peer motivation often correlate with school underachievement (Dunn & Dunn, 1992, 1993).

Cognitive-style theory suggests that individuals process information differently based on either learned or inherent traits. Many previous researchers investigated the variables of field dependence/independence, global/analytic, simultaneous/successive, and/or left- or right-preferenced processing. The Dunns and researchers throughout the world conducted studies to determine whether relationships existed between these cognitive dimensions and students' characteristics that appeared to be more or less responsive to environmental, emotional, sociological, and physiological stimuli. They found that selected variables often clustered together. Relationships appeared to exist between learning persistently (with few or no intermissions) in a quiet environment and bright light, in formal seating, and with little or no intake, and being an analytic-left processor (Dunn, Bruno, Sklar, & Beaudry, 1990; Dunn, Cavanaugh, Eberle, & Zenhausern, 1982). Similarly, adolescents who often requested "breaks" while learning and who preferred concentrating in an informal, softly lit, and sound-packed environment with snacks revealed high scores as global-right processors. In many ways, field dependence versus field independence correlated with a global versus an analytic cognitive style and yielded similar traits to those of right- and left-preferenced students. In some instances, more attributes allied themselves with global-right processors than with analytic-left processors. Thus, although global-rights often enjoyed working with peers and using tactual strengths, analytic-lefts revealed neither sociological nor perceptual preferences.

The Dunn and Dunn learning-style model is based on the following tenets:

1. Learning style is a biological and developmental set of personal characteristics (Thies, 1979) that makes the identical instructional environments, methods, and resources effective for some learners and ineffective for others.

2. Most people have learning-style preferences, but individuals' learning-style preferences differ significantly.

3. Individual instructional preferences exist, and the impact of accommodating these preferences can be measured validly.

4. The stronger the preference, the more important it is to provide compatible instructional strategies.

5. Accommodating individual learning-style preferences through complementary educational, instructional, teaching, and counseling interventions results in increased academic achievement and improved student attitudes toward learning.

6. Given responsive environments, resources, and approaches, students attain statistically higher achievement and attitude test scores in congruent (matched) rather than dissonant (mismatched) treatments.

7. Most teachers and counselors can learn to use learning styles as a cornerstone of their instructional and counseling programs.

8. Most students can learn to capitalize on their learning-style strengths when concentrating on new or difficult academic material.

9. The less academically successful the individual, the more important it is to accommodate learning-style preferences (Dunn, Beaudry, & Klavas, 1989).

ADOLESCENTS AND INFORMATION PROCESSING

The terms *analytic/global, left/right, sequential/simultaneous*, and *inductive/deductive* have been used interchangeably in the literature. Descriptions of these variables tend to parallel each other—with the exception that inductive/deductive processing is identified by a visual ability to discern between the whole and its parts. The other paired constructs require mental differentiation that may use the perceptual modality as its cornerstone.

Analytics learn most easily when information is presented step by step in a cumulative sequential pattern that builds toward a conceptual understanding. Globals learn most easily either when they understand the concept first and then can concentrate on the details or when they are introduced to the information with, preferably, a humorous story replete with examples, applications, and graphics. Both types reason, but by using different strategies (Levy, 1979; Zenhausern, 1980); each strategy "is a reflection of a trend toward optimalization of efficient use of neural space" (Levy, 1982, p. 224).

For the most part, whether adolescents are analytic or global, left or right, sequential or simultaneous, or inductive or deductive processors, they seem capable of mastering identical information or skills when they are taught with instructional methods or resources that complement their styles. That conclusion was documented in mathematics at the elementary level (Jarsonbeck, 1984), high school level (Brennan, 1984), and community college level (Dunn, Bruno, Sklar, & Beaudry (1990); in high school science (Douglas, 1979) and nutrition (Tanenbaum 1982); and in junior high school social studies (Trautman, 1979). Processing style appears to change: The majority of elementary school children are global; however, the older children become and the longer they remain in school, the more analytic some become.

Analytic and global youngsters appear to have different environmental and physiological needs (Cody, 1983; Dunn, Bruno, Sklar, & Beaudry, 1990; Dunn, Cavanaugh, Eberle, & Zenhausern, 1982). Many adolescent analytics tend to prefer learning in quiet, well-illuminated, formal settings; they often have a strong emotional need to complete the tasks they are working on, and they rarely eat, drink, smoke, chew, or bite on objects while learning. Conversely, adolescent globals appear to work with what teachers describe as distractors; they concentrate better with sound (music or background talking), soft lighting, an informal seating arrangement, and some form of intake. In addition, globals take frequent breaks while studying and often prefer to work on several tasks simultaneously. They begin a task, stay with it for a short amount of time, stop, do something else, and eventually return to the original assignment.

Neither study procedure is better nor worse than the other; the procedures are merely different. Globals often prefer learning with their peers rather than alone or with their teacher; they also often prefer to structure tasks in their own way and thus tend to dislike imposed directives. With an IQ of 145 or higher, most gifted children are global (Cody, 1983). On the other hand, most underachievers are global. The learning-style differences between the high IQ and underachieving global students tend to involve motivation and perceptual preferences.

That the motivation level of underachievers is lower than that of achievers is understandable. What may separate the two groups is the biological development of their auditory, visual, tactual, and kinesthetic senses and the decreasing amount of motivation global students evidence the longer they remain in traditional classes. Although we do not currently know how to intervene in their biological development, we have been successful in teaching them through their existing perceptual preferences (Carbo, 1980; Gardiner, 1986; Ingham, 1991; Jarsonbeck, 1984; Kroon, 1985; Martini, 1986; Urbschat, 1977, Weinberg, 1983; Wheeler, 1983).

Teachers need to teach both analytically and globally. Global students often require an environment different from the conventional classroom. They also appear to need more encouragement than analytic students and short, varied tasks because of their lower motivation and persistence levels. Many adolescents learn more easily when lessons are interesting to them than when they are not, but globals require that difficult information be interesting, be relevant to their lives, and involve experiential activities.

ADOLESCENTS AND THE CLASSROOM ENVIRONMENT

Although many students require quiet while concentrating on difficult information, others literally learn better with sound (Pizzo, Dunn, & Dunn, 1990). For these adolescents, music without lyrics provides a more conducive-to-concentrating atmosphere than melodies with words (DeGregoris, 1986). Similarly, although many people concentrate better in brightly illuminated rooms, others think better in soft light than in bright light. Fluorescent lighting may overstimulate certain learners and cause hyperactivity and restlessness (Dunn, Krimsky, Murray, & Quinn, 1985).

Temperature variations affect individual students differently. Some adolescents achieve better in a warm and others in a cool environment (Murrain, 1983). Similar differences are evidenced with different seating arrangements. Some prefer studying in a wooden, plastic, or steel chair, but many others become so uncomfortable in conventional classroom seats that they are prevented from learning (Hodges, 1985; Nganwa-Bagumah, 1986; Nganwa-Bagumah & Mwamwenda, 1991; Shea, 1983).

Few teachers are aware that when a student is seated in a hard chair, fully 75 percent of the total body weight is supported by just four square inches of bone (Branton, 1966). The resulting stress on the tissues of the buttocks causes fatigue, discomfort, and frequent postural change—for which many young people are scolded on a daily basis. Only students who happen to be sufficiently well-padded exactly where they need to be can tolerate conventional seats and desks for long periods of time.

Males tend to be more hyperactive and restless than females, and seating arrangements contribute to this phenomenon. However, when students were permitted to learn and/or take tests in seating that responded to their learning-style preferences for either a formal or an informal design, they achieved significantly higher test scores when matched with their design preferences than when mismatched. That occurred in high school English (Nganwa-Bagumah, 1986; Shea, 1983), high school mathematics (Orsak, 1990b), junior high school word recognition (Della Valle, 1984), and junior high school mathematics (Hodges, 1985).

Teachers should permit students to redesign the conventional secondary school classroom with bookcase-type dividers placed perpendicular to the walls to permit quiet, well-lit areas and, simultaneously, sections for controlled interaction and soft lighting. Dividers can be made from cardboard boxes obtained without cost from a local supermarket or appliance store. Students should be permitted to do their work seated on chairs, carpeting, bean bags, or cushions or on the floor leaning against a wall—as long as they pay attention and perform as well or better than they have previously.

Illumination in sections of the classroom should allow students to read in natural daylight, in bright light, or in dim light. Reduced lighting is often a positive influence with underachievers or hyperactive youngsters. Specific rules should be established to maintain classroom decorum; for example, (a) neither feet nor shoes may be placed on chairs or desks; (b) no one's learning style may interfere with anyone else's learning style, or the offender relinquishes his or her privilege; and/or (c) better test performance and better behavior than ever before is required. These suggestions for making classrooms responsive to students' varied learning styles cost nothing and require only minimal teacher time and energy, but they contribute substantially to improved student attitudes and behavior. The results are often evident within the first six weeks of experimentation.

ADOLESCENTS' SOCIOLOGICAL PREFERENCES

Certain students are incapable of learning new and difficult information directly from an adult. These young people are uncomfortable under pressure to concentrate in either teacher-dominated or authoritative classes. Some are fearful of failing, embarrassed to show inability, and/or often become too tense to concentrate. For such adolescents either learning alone or with peers may be more effective than learning directly from their teachers. Many studies reveal that it is important to identify students' sociological preferences. When individuals' preferences for learning alone, in pairs, in a small group, or with the teacher were identified, students were taught in several different treatments—congruent as well as incongruent with their learning styles. Each achieved significantly higher test scores in the congruent treatments (Dunn & Dunn, 1992, 1993). Four studies also examined the effects of sociological preferences on attitude toward learning and found statistically higher attitudinal scores when students were taught in the congruent treatments (DeBello, 1985; Dunn, Giannitti, Murray, Geisert, Rossi, & Quinn, 1990; Miles, 1987; Perrin, 1984). Although all gifted students do not necessarily have the same learning-style characteristics, gifted adolescents tend to prefer learning alone more than with others (Cross, 1982; Griggs & Price, 1980; Kreitner, 1981; Milgram, Dunn, & Price, 1993a; Price, Dunn, Dunn, & Griggs, 1981).

Teachers need to try posting assignments with specific objectives and/ or tasks. They then should establish clear rules for students learning as they prefer sociologically. For example, "Your learning style may never interfere with someone else's; if it does, *you* lose the privilege. That means we all work quietly so that no one can actually hear the words we are saying. I expect to hear a low hum of voices, but no one should actually be able to tell me the words you are saying. If they can, you are speaking too loudly!" The class then can be told:

You may work on this project alone, in a pair, in a team of three or four, or with me. If you wish to work alone, sit wherever you feel comfortable in the room. If you wish to work in a pair, decide where the two of you want to work, speak quietly, and allow privacy to classmates who need to be by themselves. Work conscientiously because your grades have to be better than they have ever been before—or this is not working and there is no reason to continue.

After a pause, students who want to work together may move to wherever they agree to work in the room. When those students are settled, the adolescents who wish to work directly with the teacher or an aide may move to a specifically designated section of the room.

ADOLESCENTS AND PERCEPTUAL STRENGTHS

When adolescents were introduced to new material through their perceptual preferences, they remembered significantly more than when they were introduced to similar material through their least-preferred modality (Garrett, 1991, Kroon, 1985; Martini, 1986). Furthermore, when new material was reinforced through students' secondary or tertiary preferences, they achieved significantly more than when they were merely introduced once through the preferred modality. (Kroon, 1985).

Most adolescent males are not auditory. Few males remember at least three-quarters of what they hear in a normal 40–50 minute period. As a result, lectures, discussions, and listening are the least effective ways of teaching males. Thus, it is not surprising that although females comprise the majority of the population, males comprise the majority of remedial reading and math students.

Few teachers introduce difficult new material tactually or kinesthetically—the sensory preferences of many male students. Tactual and kinesthetic resources, described in Chapter 7, should be developed by students and used to introduce new and difficult academics prior to class discussions of new content:

1. Using all four modalities in sequence does not ensure that each student is introduced to difficult material correctly (i.e., through his or her perceptual strength/preference); neither does it ensure that each student will be reinforced correctly.
2. Many male adolescents or underachievers are almost exclusively tactual or kinesthetic learners (Dunn & Dunn, 1993; Milgram, Dunn, & Price, 1993a). Teach-

ing them new and difficult information auditorially at the onset produces confusion and/or difficulty for many. It is best to teach tactual students and underachievers tactually first and then use their secondary or tertiary modality to reinforce what was introduced through their strengths. In many cases, speaking about the material should be used to emphasize and reinforce what was already taught.

3. Underachieving, at-risk, and dropout students are almost exclusively tactual and/or kinesthetic learners. Auditory preference is usually their tertiary modality. Often students are either tactual/kinesthetic or tactual/auditory but low visual. Introducing tactual students to new material with flip chutes, pick-a-holes, multipart task cards, and/or electroboards and then reinforcing what was introduced with kinesthetic-visual resources is likely to help many of them to achieve better than they have previously (see Chapter 7).

ADOLESCENTS AND TIME OF DAY

Task efficiency is related to each person's temperature cycle (Biggers, 1980); thus it is related to when each student has the most energy to concentrate on difficult material. For example, junior high school math underachievers became more motivated, better disciplined, and produced a trend toward statistically increased achievement when they were assigned to afternoon math classes that matched their chronobiological time preferences; they had failed during their energy lows (Carruthers & Young, 1980). One year later Lynch (1981) reported that time preference was a crucial factor in the reversal of chronic initial truancy patterns among secondary students.

Later the matching of elementary students' time preferences and instructional schedules resulted in significant achievement gains (.001) in reading and math (Dunn, Dunn, Primavera, Sinatra, & Virostko, 1987). The following year teachers' time preferences were identified and inservice sessions were conducted in both matched and mismatched sessions (Freeley, 1984). The adult teachers used information they had learned significantly more often (.01) when they were taught during their most-preferred time of day than when taught during their nonpreferred times. Then Lemmon (1985) administered the Iowa Basic Skills Achievement Tests in reading and math to elementary school students whose time preferences matched their test schedule—either morning or afternoon. She reported significantly higher test gains in both subjects compared with each youngster's previous three years' growth as measured by the same test. Five years later Cramp (1990) reported similar results.

Most students are not alert early in the morning. Primary school children experience their strongest energy highs between 10:00 A.M. and 2:00 P.M.: Only approximately 28 percent are "morning" people (Price, 1980). Only one-third of junior high schoolers are alert in the early morning when academics are accented. Again, the majority "come alive" after about 10:00 A.M. In high school almost 40 percent of students are "early birds"; the majority continue to be late-morning or afternoon preferents; 13 percent are "night owls" (Price, 1980). There are exceptions to these patterns, of course. The teacher should test pupils to determine their individual patterns.

Teachers need to advise students to study during their energy highs at their best time of day. Required subjects should be scheduled at different times of the school day, and underachieving students and those at risk of dropping out of school should be assigned to their most important subjects when they are most alert. Time is a crucial element of learning style and requires knowledgeable scheduling, particularly for potential underachievers for whom learning during energy highs increases achievement (Gadwa & Griggs, 1985; Gardiner, 1986; Griggs & Dunn, 1988; Johnson, 1984; Thrasher, 1984).

ADOLESCENT RESTLESSNESS AND HYPERACTIVITY

Most students referred to psychologists are not clinically hyperactive; instead, they often are normal youngsters in need of mobility (Fadley & Hosler, 1979). In addition, the less interested students are in what they are being taught, the more mobility they need. A disquieting point is that such adolescents are "almost always boys" (p. 219).

Restak (1979) substantiated that "over 95 percent of hyperactives are males" (p. 230) and that the very same characteristic in girls correlates with academic achievement. He deplored that boys are required to be passive in school and are rejected for aggressive behaviors there but are encouraged to engage in typical male aggressions in the world at large— a situation that might, Restak suggested, lead to role conflict. He added that conventional classroom environments do not provide male students with sufficient outlet for their normal movement needs and warned that schools actually conflict with society's expectations that boys not be timid, passive, or conforming.

Tingley-Michaelis (1983) corroborated Restak's warnings and affirmed that boys labeled hyperactive in school often were fidgety because their teachers provided experiences for them "to think about something"; instead, those adolescents needed "to do something" (p. 26). Tingley-Michaelis also chastised educators for believing that activities prevented, rather than enhanced, learning!

When researchers originally began equating hyperactivity with students' normal need for mobility, they experimented with providing many opportunities for learning while engaged in movement. Reports then began to document that when previously restless youngsters were reassigned to classes that did not require passivity, their behaviors were rarely noticed (Fadley & Hosler, 1979; Koester & Farley, 1977). Eventually teachers began reporting that although certain students thrived in an activity-oriented environment that permitted mobility, others remained almost exclusively in the same area despite frequent attempts to coax them to move (Hodges, 1985; Miller, 1985). This observation led to Fitt's (1975) conclusions that no amount of persuasion increased selected students' interest in movement, whereas others found it impossible to remain seated passively for extended periods. "These are cases of a child's style . . . governing his interactions with and within the environment" (p. 94).

Add to these early reports the knowledge that between 40 percent and 50 percent of many adolescents require informal seating while concentrating (Hodges, 1985; Nganwa-Bagumah, 1986; Shea, 1983), and it is not difficult to understand why so many—particularly boys—squirm, sit on their ankles and calves, extend their feet into aisles, squirrel down into their seats, and occasionally fall off their chairs.

Della Valle (1984) documented that almost 50 percent of a large urban junior high school's students could not sit still for any appreciable amount of time. If interested in the lesson 25 percent could remain immobile; the remaining 25 percent preferred passivity. Della Valle demonstrated the importance of the mobility/passivity dimension of learning style. When students' preferences and their environment were matched, they achieved significantly higher test scores (.001) than when they were mismatched. Students who required mobility moved from one part of the room to another in order to master all the information in the lesson and performed better than when they sat for the entire period. On the other hand, students who did not wish to move while learning performed worse when required to walk about the classroom to gather information and significantly better when permitted to sit quietly and learn.

Teachers need to establish several different instructional "centers" or areas in each classroom so that mobility-preferenced adolescents who complete one task may move to another section to work on the next. Involving the students in redesigning their classroom is also wise. After identifying each student's mobility, light, sound, and seating design needs, students should be encouraged to plan how to move available items into alternative configurations to respond to the many different learning-style characteristics evidenced among the group. These plans can be drawn or outlined by individuals, pairs, or small groups and then presented to the class. Parts of several plans may be combined into the first experimental plan in which the students try different choices for a week to determine how they function in different-from-the traditional design. Changes can be suggested and further tried as better suggestions are offered based on the trial period. As long as the students behave responsibly based on the clearly established and discussed rules, they should be permitted to work comfortably. Should rules be broken, only the transgressor loses privileges.

Whenever possible incorporate kinesthetic activities into each lesson so that students may move. Such activities might include acting, role-playing, brainstorming, interviewing, whether simulated or real, or demonstrations. Permit students who show they can be trusted to behave and who require mobility to work in one or more of the varied instructional centers you establish. Some may need only the space available in their own "office" or "den," whereas others may require movement from one area to another—thus the purpose of a library corner, an interest center, a media section, or a partitioned hall space near the classroom door. One or two responsible students might be permitted to work in the corridor immediately outside the classroom. Young people become increasingly trustworthy when they see you recognize their needs and are aware they will lose a privilege if they abuse it. Many of the most difficult-to-contain adolescents are the ones who cannot sit and require opportunities to stretch (Dunn, Della Valle, Dunn, Geisert, Sinatra, & Zenhausern, 1986; Miller, 1985).

In addition, do not forget to experiment with a form of independent study such as contract activity packages (CAPs), discussed in Chapter 9, or programmed learning sequences (PLSs), discussed in Chapter 8, with which students may move as they concentrate without disturbing others. Finally, be certain to experiment with small-group techniques such as team learning for introducing new and difficult material and circle of knowledge for reinforcing it (see Chapter 6). Peer-oriented learners who need mobility will function well with these instructional strategies because of their responsiveness to students' sociological and physiological characteristics.

ADOLESCENTS AND SOME IMPORTANT RAMIFICATIONS OF STYLE

Based on the writings of Restak (1979) and Thies (1979), it is evident that at least three-fifths of learning style is genetic. The remainder, apart from persistence, develops through experience. Individual responses to sound, light, temperature, seating arrangements, perceptual strengths, intake, time of day, and mobility are biological. Sociological preferences, motivation, responsibility (which correlates with conformity/nonconformity), and structure (versus the need for permitting individuals opportunities for self-direction) are thought to be developmental. The similarities and the differences among the learning styles of students at different achievement levels in diverse cultures tend to support this theory (Dunn, 1990d; Dunn, Gemake, Jalali, & Zenhausern, 1990; Dunn, Gemake, Jalali, Zenhausern, Quinn, & Spiridakis, 1990; Dunn & Griggs, 1990; Guzzo, 1987;

Jacobs, 1987; Jalali, 1988; Lam-Phoon, 1986; Mariash, 1983; Milgram, Dunn, & Price, 1983a; Roberts, 1984; Sims, 1988; Vazquez, 1985).

The one variable with which there may be disagreement concerning its origin is persistence. Whether it is biological or developmental remains in question. Analytics tend to be more persistent than globals. Globals tend to concentrate on difficult academic studies for relatively short periods of time. They often need frequent breaks and work on several different tasks simultaneously. Once strongly analytic students begin a task, they appear to have an emotional need to complete it.

HOW TO BEGIN WORKING WITH ADOLESCENTS' LEARNING STYLES

Experiment with several beginning steps to see whether you and your students feel comfortable with a few learning-style procedures. Even these beginning steps should improve students' attitudes and behaviors. If they work, you and your students will gain in many ways; if they are not effective, do not continue them!

1. As each lesson begins, write the objectives on the chalkboard, overhead transparencies, or paper to make the students aware of what in this lesson is important for them to learn. Then as you are teaching, prompt students. As you cover the information you want them to remember, provide clues: "Make note of this!" "Be certain to write this in your notes!" "This is important" or "This could be on your test!" Such prompting provides structure for those who need it.

2. As you are teaching and mentioning the important information related to the lesson's objectives, walk to the chalkboard or overhead projector and in big print write a word or phrase that synthesizes the content so that visual learners can see it and others can copy it into their notes.

3. When you write on the chalkboard, illustrate important information; stick figures will do. If you can't draw, ask students to do it for you. Encourage global students to illustrate their notes. Visual-left processors seem to respond to words and numbers; visual-rights pay attention to drawings, symbols, and spatial designs. Both groups may profit from using colored pens, but global students seem to need the color to attract and keep their attention. Global-right adolescents are strongly tactual; they are the doodlers who pay attention better when they use their hands while they are listening. Permit these students to use colored chalk on blackboards or colored pens on the overhead transparencies.

4. Give strongly visual students a short assignment to read to introduce new and difficult material. They then should listen to you lecture or participate in a discussion of the topic. Strongly auditory students should hear your explanation first and then read materials that will reinforce it. Visual adolescents should take or copy the notes you are writing on the chalkboard while they

listen. Auditory learners should take notes while they read.

When you become acquainted with the tactual resource called task cards, provide tactual students with multiple copies of task card outlines (see Chapter 7) and encourage them to take their notes directly onto those outlines. Then for studying at home they merely need to cut each task card set into irregularly separated parts. They will automatically have a good tool that responds to their tactual need for reinforcing the information you presented.

When working with youngsters who read poorly, permit them to read in natural daylight. If you have windows, experiment a few times with turning off the classroom lights or darkening a section of the room. Low light relaxes many global students and permits better concentration for approximately eight of ten who do not read well.

5. Write a brief illustrated outline of the lesson on the chalkboard at the beginning of each period. That overview helps visual learners who cannot focus and keep track of the lesson's emphasis when only listening. From time to time, draw attention to the outline and say, "Now we're moving into this part of the topic."

6. Laminate 30–40 numbered, colored footprints and 6–8 hand prints. With masking tape folded against itself to provide two sticky surfaces, place the prints into a twister game pattern in a less busy part of the classroom so that walking on it in sequence requires body contortions. When youngsters with short attention spans lose interest in a task they should be doing, give them one minute, one at a time, to "walk the footprints"; kinesthetic youngsters, or those in need of mobility, will benefit greatly. After just one minute they will be able to return to their seats and concentrate—for another ten minutes or more. This type of kinesthetic activity can be designed to incorporate educational resources such as floor games (see Chapter 7).

7. Encourage highly kinesthetic students to walk back and forth while they are reading or doing their assignments. Whereas for low kinesthetics and analytic learners moving while learning is negative, for kinesthetic students, those in need of mobility, and many globals who enjoy doing several things simultaneously movement facilitates understanding and memory.

8. Encourage students to study at their best time of day, either early in the morning before they leave for school, during lunch or free periods, immediately after school, or in the evening before they go to bed.

9. Permit students who need to eat while concentrating to bring raw vegetables to school. Establish firm rules; for example, they cannot make noise while eating, since many students need quiet; the custodian must not learn that you are conducting this experiment; no leftovers should remain in the classroom when the students leave; the unwanted food must be placed into waste baskets; and students must get better test grades than they ever had before or they forego the privilege of learning in their learning style.

10. Permit limited choices in each assignment you give. Nonconforming students, that is, those low on the LSI element of responsibility, thrive on options and develop positive attitudes toward learning when they are available.

Chapter 3

Understanding Learning-Styles Counseling and the Adolescent Stages of Development

Like education, school counseling programs are in a state of crisis. Many school districts across the nation are experiencing fiscal cutbacks due to decreased federal allocations to education, economic recession, and urban finance deficits. As superintendents of schools and local school boards of education review budgets, frequently the first area reduced is student personnel services. Increasingly, school counselors are facing accountability issues: They need to demonstrate that their programs and services make a difference in the lives of the young people they service.

The paradox is that fewer school counselors are faced with a rapidly increasing number of student crises and problems. Rapid and often unpredictable societal changes, disintegration of the family as we have known it for decades, economic uncertainty and recession, conflicts that have escalated into military confrontations in many areas of the world, and increased crime and hostility among many adolescents have been translated into extensive student unrest, frequently in the form of undisciplined behavior, alienation, violence, pregnancy, depression, suicide, substance abuse, and dropoutism.

Futurists predict that as the rate of societal change escalates, the complexity of the individual's problems will increase. Futurists perceive that there will not be an adequate number of helping professionals to handle these crises. To ameliorate this problem, tomorrow's counselors will serve predominantly as consultants, identifying and training peer helpers. Thus, it is likely that adolescents who have abused alcohol or other substances and have effectively worked through their problems to become drugfree will be trained by counselors to assist adolescents who are currently experimenting or involved with abuse. On a societal level, many of these peer-help groups are already operative. These include Alcoholics Anonymous, Recovery Incorporated, and suicide prevention hotlines. In addition, many school counselors have prepared peer leaders to work in groups with other students in areas such as conflict resolution, under-achievement, and career decision making.

LEARNING-STYLES COUNSELING

Increasingly, educational leaders are recognizing that the *process* of learning is critically important. Glines (1989) observed that all students can learn if their program needs are appropriately diagnosed and pre-scribed and their affective development is addressed. The major mission of school counselors is to help students learn to love learning (Krum-boltz, 1988) and to support the process of learning by nurturing students' self-concept, independence, locus of control, and positive attitudes to-ward school (Selden, 1989).

Traditional Approaches to Counseling

Counseling is an interactive learning process between a professional counselor and a counselee. It should facilitate the counselee's under-standing of self, others, and his or her environment and result in increas-ingly positive changes in attitudes and behavior.

New counseling theories are proliferating at a rapid rate. One count revealed over 250 conceptually distinct approaches to counseling, all vy-ing for distinction as the most effective method (Parloff, 1980). These theories differ in terms of assumptions, philosophy, major personality constructs, counseling goals, relative importance of diagnosis, counseling techniques and strategies, and targeted clientele. Instead of strict adher-ence to a single theory, the majority of counselor practitioners use sys-tematic eclecticism in counseling—the application of a psychodynamic, humanistic, cognitive, or behavioral counseling system ostensibly respon-sive to the individual counselee and to the problem. However, the ma-jority of approaches, including systematic eclecticism, are verbal therapies designed for mature, verbally proficient, and cognitively aware people with insight and the ability or desire to change. Relatively few counseling theories and techniques have been designed for use with children and adolescents whose developmental needs are different from those of adults and who, consequently, require approaches congruent with their particular abilities to absorb, process, and retain information. Counseling based upon individual learning-style preferences is such an approach. It provides an eclectic model for assessing learning styles and using existing theories, techniques, and interventions compatible with unique individ-ual needs and differences.

Basic Tenets of Learning-Styles Counseling

In addition to the tenets presented in Chapter 2, the following basic assumptions apply to learning-styles counseling:

1. Counseling is fundamentally a *learning* process in which a professional counselor works with an individual to explore aspects of self—including values, goals, aspirations, and personality traits—toward the end of achieving increased autonomy and developing that person's full potential.

2. No single counseling theory or approach can be responsive to all counselees. Hence, an eclectic background in counseling, from which selections are made to appropriately accommodate the learning-style characteristics of each counselee, is critical to achieving positive behavioral changes. The need to choose a counseling approach responsive to highly diversified individual traits is particularly crucial when counseling adolescents, who experience extensive biological change and varied societal pressures based on their unique home, school, and living styles during this stage of their maturation.

3. Counselee resistance is partially due to the mismatch between the counseling interventions, strategies, and techniques used by the counselor and the learning-style preferences of the counselee.

4. When counselees are made aware of their learning-style strengths and advised how to accommodate these strengths in the learning and counseling processes, they are given a tool not previously available to them. They become empowered to achieve better academically and to make positive changes that can affect their life satisfaction and adjustment.

Relating Learning Styles to Effective Counseling

The role of the school counselor is comprehensive and multifaceted. It encompasses individual and group counseling with students; testing and interpreting assessment data in educational-vocational areas; developing, conducting, and evaluating programs in career and psychological education; training and then supervising peer helpers; and consulting with teachers, parents, and administrators concerning student progress and adjustment.

Counseling students for their individual learning styles involves the following steps:

1. Assessing the developmental needs of students.

    Awareness of and responsiveness to the developmental needs, psychosocial crises, and developmental tasks that are stage related and common to adolescents overall.

    Determination of the special concerns related to each school population's economic, social, and family situations. At the same time, consideration of the unique needs of special education youngsters, low-income, single-parent, bilingual and/or bicultural families, high-risk students, and the gifted and talented are critical.

2. Designing a comprehensive, developmental counseling program based on the needs assessment.

The counseling program should be developed in concert with representative students, parents, faculty, and administrators.

Guidance, coordination, and consultative services provided by counselors must be linked to the developmental and special needs of the student body and simultaneously address the unique requirements of individuals who differ substantially from their classmates.

3. Assessing the individual learning styles of students, counselors, and teachers.

Counseling students to help them develop and understand their own learning-style preferences as well as recognize the implications of their preferences for learning.

Providing inservice education and consultative services for teachers, counselors, and administrators to help them identify their own learning styles and understand how their teaching and counseling styles affect students.

4. Planning and implementing teaching and counseling interventions compatible with the learning-style needs of students.

Matching specific teaching and counseling techniques, approaches, and interventions with selected student or group requirements.

Using a variety of techniques and interventions to accommodate individual traits.

5. Evaluating teaching and counseling outcomes to determine the extent to which program and counseling objectives have been achieved.

Identifying outcome measures such as (a) improvement in achievement, attendance, retention, self-concept and self-efficacy, and students' attitudes and (b) reduction in the number of disciplinary referrals and suspensions. Each measures student change.

Using evaluative data to continually refine the counseling program.

MATCHING INDIVIDUAL LEARNING STYLES WITH APPROPRIATE COUNSELING INTERVENTIONS AT THE SECONDARY SCHOOL LEVEL

An examination of how learning-style characteristics change as students advance from grade to grade was conducted by Price (1980). A total of 3,972 students in grades 3 through 12 completed the Dunn, Dunn, & Price (1979) Learning Style Inventory (LSI) during the 1979–80 school year. Some of the statistically significant findings revealed were as follows:

• The higher the grade level, the more sound, light, and intake preferred. Increased sound and intake needs may respond to the hormonal changes adolescents experience, but longitudinal reports have shown that the older students become, the more light they need as a group; however, individuals differ.

• The higher the grade level, the less preference for a formal design. Previous researchers reported a correlational relationship between global versus analytic processing styles and sound, light, design, intake, and persistence. As Chapter 2 revealed, global processors tend to prefer sound, soft lighting, informal seating, intake, and frequent breaks while learning; analytic processors prefer the opposite—quiet, bright light, formal seating, and intake only after their tasks have been completed. Once they have begun working, analytics tend to prefer to stay on task until they are done. Extrapolating from a combination of the Price (1980), Dunn, Cavanaugh, Eberle, and Zenhausern (1982), and Dunn, Bruno, Sklar, and Beaudry (1990) findings, it may be that either the older the students or the longer they remain in school, the more analytic their processing style becomes.

• Self-motivation decreased during grades 7 and 8, but a gradual increase was evidenced thereafter among many students. However, the higher the grade level, the less teacher motivated and the less motivated in general the students. The largest shift occurred between grades 7 and 8, when some students changed from being peer motivated to being self-motivated and others became unmotivated, with grade 11 revealing the highest peak for being unmotivated.

Although Price (1980) did not differentiate between high and low academic achievers in his analysis of how learning style changes over time, many researchers have revealed significant differences between the learning styles of high- versus low-achieving adolescents (Cody, 1983; Gadwa & Griggs, 1985; Kroon, 1985; Milgram, Dunn, & Price, 1993a; Murray, 1980; Nations-Miller, 1993; Pederson, 1984; Ricca, 1983; Snider, 1985; Tappenden, 1983; Vignia, 1983; Williams, 1989; Yong & McIntyre, 1992; Zak, 1989). It is therefore likely that individual achievement affects adolescent motivation and causes increases among some adolescents and diminution among others.

An overall decrease in the need for structure was evidenced as students moved from grade to grade. These findings parallel those of David Hunt (1979), who also found that the older the student, the less the need for external structure. Students' needs for varying amounts of structure can be accommodated by grouping students according to their preferences. For example, in group counseling with adolescents who require a high degree of structure, the following procedures are desirable:

1. Clearly delineate counseling objectives and goals during the initial stages of counseling. Arrive at goals by mutual effort and agreement between the counselor and counselees.

2. Use the highly structured counseling approaches emphasized in behavioral and cognitive models. These employ a problem-solving methodology.

3. Use individual learning-styles homework prescriptions and time-management strategies to help students apply what they are learning to their daily activities. There is available a software program that analyzes individual learning styles and describes how the individual should study based on his or her traits (Dunn & Klavas, 1992).

4. Use a thematic approach when counseling global students who need structure. Identify areas of common concern such as stressful incidents in the student's life, personal relationships with family, friends, or lovers, conflict resolution, or self-efficacy as one way to focus discussion and activities. In consultation with teachers and parents, emphasize the need for accommodating students' high-structure preferences by stressing the importance of (a) using highly structured classroom techniques, including advanced organizers, multisensory instructional packages (MIPs), programmed learning sequences (PLSs), and computer-assisted instruction and (b) giving specific, well-organized homework assignments with guidelines on how to proceed with each task.

   Conversely, students who prefer low structure often resent many guidelines. Instead, they welcome choices, options, and learning with creative, divergent approaches. In group counseling, for example, client-centered and existential approaches are desirable because they encourage students to identify areas of concern, explore these concerns in a variety of ways, and arrive at change through insight and understanding. In consultation with teachers and parents, emphasize the need for accommodating students who prefer low structure by providing (a) classroom instructional strategies that permit many opportunities for individual choices, such as contract activity packages (CAPs) or independent study; (b) options for how they may complete homework assignments; (c) opportunities for creative writing, brainstorming and brainwriting, open discussions, and designing their own curriculum at times to allow for the pursuit of mastering objectives through a variety of methods.

5. Allow some open-ended homework and individual projects that permit students to reinforce classroom learning through a variety of strategies. This practice responds to the needs of nonconformists and those who prefer variety rather than routines and patterns.

Although the secondary school years are generally perceived to be a period of strong peer influence, the need to learn and study alone in grades 9 through 12 is greater than during any other interval. The highest preference for learning with peers occurred during grades 6 through 8; the lowest preference occurred in grade 12, followed by grade 9, with a slight increase in grades 10 and 11.

Again, Price (1980) did not examine the variable of high achievement versus low achievement in his analysis of how learning style changes over time. As other researchers have revealed, highly achieving and gifted students prefer learning alone (Perrin, 1984; Milgram, Dunn, & Price, 1993a). Other students prefer learning in pairs, with peers, with either an authoritative or collegial teacher, or in various groupings. In addition,

Price's data may have reflected another era. Between 1967 and 1972 when the first learning-styles experimentation began, students did not become peer motivated much before seventh or eight grade. During the ensuing decades peer motivation was evidenced earlier and earlier as students moved from first grade to seventh grade. Price may be reflecting patterns that existed circa 1979–80, which may no longer be accurate. Sociological preference is a learning-style variable that changes over time for most students. However, every study of gifted students' learning style reveals the need for learning alone unless tasks cannot be mastered successfully. At that point primary gifted children preferred learning with their *gifted* classmates exclusively, and adolescent gifted students in nine nations preferred an authoritative adult.

The younger the students, the more tactual and/or kinesthetic they were. Those modalities among primary and early elementary students were followed by the development of visual preferences and, beginning with grades 5 and 6, the development of auditory preferences.

THE DEVELOPMENTAL STAGE OF ADOLESCENCE

Adolescence normally encompasses students between 13 and 18 years of age usually enrolled in grades 7 through 12. Today's adolescents are faced with adapting to an increasingly complex society in which changes occur at a very rapid rate. This stage of maturation is challenging and potentially hazardous for many young people, who are required to cope with (1) internal development that produces physiological, maturational, and cognitive changes characterized by formal operational thought and (2) moral development marked by values clarifications that often conflict with the external demands of adolescents' social world.

Although most adolescents master these challenges successfully, others encounter special problems such as depression and suicidal ideation; the risk of acquiring a sexually transmitted disease; pregnancy with the likelihood of single-parenthood, poverty, and the need to assume adult responsibilities without the benefit of a support system; ostracism from what had been a familiar lifestyle; substance abuse; underachievement and dropping out of high school; eating disorders; cults; violence and assault; and a variety of handicapping conditions. Collectively, adolescents must confront the tasks of becoming increasingly more autonomous and independent, disengaging from parents and assuming more responsibility, developing effective peer relationships, testing and clarifying personal values, and engaging in educational and vocational decision making. Because of increases in the number of single-parent families, working mothers, and divorce, many youth have minimal support in resolving these issues. Because parents and other significant adults are less available to youth, new demands have been placed on our schools. Unless society is willing to see each future generation of adolescents become increasingly alienated and self-destructive, teachers and counselors must provide nurturing and assistance to teenagers in order to fill this vacuum.

Identity

According to Erikson (1968), the search for identity is the primary task and crisis of adolescence, in which the young person struggles to establish self as a separate, unique individual while simultaneously maintaining some connection with the meaningful elements of the past. In the process of "finding themselves," adolescents attempt to develop a sexual, moral, political, and religious identity that is relatively stable and consistent. The ultimate goal, termed identity achievement, occurs when adolescents attain their new identity through selective repudiation and mutual assimilation of childhood identifications (Erikson, 1968).

Identity achievement is a complex process mastered in bits and pieces over an extended period of time. It is problematic for some adolescents, who might resolve this issue in a variety of different and ineffective ways:

1. *Identity foreclosure* or premature identity results when adolescents accept earlier roles and parental values without reservation, introspection, or consideration of options and personal choices.
2. *Negative identity status* refers to adopting roles and values diametrically opposed to expectations and parental values, such as when an adolescent raised as a devout Lutheran embraces atheism as a way of negating parental influence.
3. *Identity diffusion status* addresses adolescents' inability to commit to anything in terms of values, goals, or lifestyle, resulting in erratic or apathetic behavior.
4. *Moratorium status* allows adolescents time out, during which experimentation in alternative identities and lifestyles takes place.

If identity achievement is a challenging process for the culturally mainstreamed adolescent, it is doubly complex for adolescents who belong to an ethnic minority. As minority youth move into adolescence and enter schools with a heterogeneous population, they become increasingly aware of their own ethnic-minority status.

Identity for Minority Adolescents

Identity achievement for adolescents in general is complex, difficult, and onerous. However, for ethnic minorities, the process may be particularly complicated and painful. Key variables that affect how effectively individuals of minority status negotiate this mandate are identified as follows:

1. The extent of acculturation within the family is of critical importance and can range from families characterized by enclave living with parents totally immersed in the minority culture to those who deny or deemphasize their cultural roots and embrace the mainstream culture.

2. The extent to which the values, beliefs, and practices of the minority culture differ from those of the mainstream—ranging from superficial to profound differences.

3. The extent to which minority adolescents experience discrimination, prejudices, and stereotyping varies from profound rejection to the honoring of diversity and validation of the minority culture.

4. The socioeconomic status of the minority adolescent, which suggests that experiences differ for impoverished, inner-city African-Americans in comparison with their middle-class, suburban counterparts, just as experiences differ for newly arrived Vietnamese youth versus third-generation Filipino adolescents.

5. The economic and political climate of the times, which can range from recession, unemployment, and restrictive immigration policies to a thriving economic climate, extensive employment opportunities, and a relatively open immigration stance.

Adolescents from minority backgrounds may cope with these challenges in a variety of different ways. Adopting a negative identity involves rejecting the values of both the ethnic minority and the dominant culture. Adolescents with a negative identity may engage in antisocial and criminal behaviors in defiance of the expectations of both groups. Other adolescents pursue identity foreclosure, which involves prematurely choosing the values of one culture exclusively. Streitmatter (1988) found that African-American, Native American, Mexican-American, and Asian-American adolescents were more likely to foreclose on identity issues than those of European-American heritage. The minority adolescents had stopped searching for their own selfhood, perhaps because the process was too painful.

Some minority groups prize family closeness, respect for elders, and a deemphasis of self-interest for the sake of the family. Harrison, Wilson, Pine, Chan, and Bureil (1990) found that this clash of parental directives and cultural expectations of independence and self-determination can present dilemmas some adolescents find irreconcilable. Counselors at a high school in New York City attribute the suicides of three adolescent girls to the clash between their parents of the Sikh religion, who had arranged marriages for their daughters shortly after their birth, and the values of the mainstream that emphasized individual choice in the selection of a marital partner.

Stages in Minority Identity

Atkinson, Morten, and Sue (1993) conceived the minority identity development model, which describes five stages of development as follows:

1. *Conformity* reflects a preference for the values of the dominant culture over those of the minority culture; at this stage adolescents affiliate with a peer group that is predominantly mainstream and behave in ways that devalue or deny minority affiliation.
2. *Dissonance* is characterized by confusion and conflict toward both the dominant culture and the minority culture; this stage is usually provoked by a critical incident that involves experiencing either prejudice or ethnic pride.
3. *Resistance and immersion* denote the stage of active rejection of the dominant group and acceptance of one's own cultural subgroup in which the adolescent affiliates exclusively with the minority group and may perceive bias and injustice as widespread.
4. *Introspection* includes an indepth examination of the values of both the minority and dominant cultures.
5. *Synergetic articulation and awareness* delineate developing an identity that selects elements from both the dominant and minority group values; at this stage the adolescent becomes biculturally successful.

Summary

Ethnic identity develops over time, with individuals usually vacillating between extremes of assimilation and separation before achieving a mature self-affirmation. Ideally, each adolescent should find his or her own historical roots, gender role, vocational aspirations, and political values, all influenced by community, culture, and unique individuality. To facilitate this process in adolescents, teachers and counselors must be acutely aware of their own stage of multicultural development.

Chapter 4

Multiculturalism and the Learning-Style Characteristics of Major Cultural Groups in the United States

An astute observation was made several generations ago that every person is like *all* persons, like *some* persons, and like *no other* person (Kluckholn & Murray, 1953). Expanding on this basic principle, Cox (1982) conceptualized a tripartite world-view model in which human universality, cultural specificity, and individual uniqueness interact to influence the development of each individual. Application of Cox's model to the construct of learning styles has been corroborated by meta analytic evidence: Accommodating individual learning styles through compatible teaching and counseling interventions results in increased academic achievement universally (Sullivan, 1993).

This chapter reveals that each cultural group tends to have some learning-style elements that distinguish it from other cultural groups. However, a consistent finding among researchers is that each individual within a family, classroom, or culture has unique learning-style preferences that differ from those of their siblings, parents, peers, and cultural group. Thus, teachers and counselors need to be aware of three critical factors:

1. Universal principles of learning do exist.
2. Culture influences both the learning process and its outcomes.
3. Each adolescent has unique learning-style preferences that affect his or her potential for achievement.

The growth of the minority population in the United States, which has always been a multicultural society, is projected to increase rapidly during the next decade. In 1990 minorities constituted 25 percent of our total population, but the percentage of minority school-age youth exceeded 30 percent. Just seven years ago school enrollments in 23 of the nation's largest cities were comprised mostly of minority students. By the year 2000 the *current minority will have become the majority* in the 53 most-populated U.S. cities (Rodriguez, 1988).

These extreme population changes have generated a new consciousness of our nation's diversity and an increased interest in addressing the educational needs of youth from different cultures. Despite the many positive past attributes of American education, there is mounting evidence that our schools are addressing neither the uniqueness nor the cultural diversity of minority youth, as evidenced by their exorbitantly high school dropout rates and widespread academic underachievement (Asher, 1987).

Cultural values influence the socialization practices of all ethnic groups, which, in turn, affect how adolescents prefer to learn. Baptiste (1988) asserted that schools need to promote educational equity by treating diverse cultural groups as equally legitimate and by teaching positively about various cultures. He advocated that educational institutions adopt the premises of multicultural education by integrating information about contributions and perspectives of different cultural groups into the entire curriculum and by using teaching strategies that build on different learning styles.

It is important to recognize that culture is critical when defining an individual. The Office of Pastoral Research of the Archdiocese of New York (1982) observed that the

loss of one's culture is a painful experience; it is the loss of oneself. For the most part, people struggle to retain their culture. It is the basis of their sense of identity, the source of their psycho-sociological strength. Behavior which brings a person honor in his own culture may bring ridicule or condemnation in the new.... Caught in the upheaval of meaning, the newcomer is confused, upset, frustrated and may easily become aggressive, hostile, or emotionally upset. (p. 67)

Extensive diversity has been evidenced among the five cultures examined in this chapter. Native Americans include 517 separate groups located in Alaska and the lower 48 states. Vast cultural differences have been reflected among the Navajo, Eskimo, and Cherokee and among European Americans from English, Scandinavian, Lithuanian, or Greek backgrounds. Although Hispanics include people from Mexican, Puerto Rican, Cuban, and Central and South American backgrounds, each cluster reflects unique cultural attributes. Similarly, comparisons between African Americans from West Africa and Caribbean populations reveal different cultural characteristics; the same findings have been reported concerning

Asian Americans from China, India, Japan, the Philippines, and the Pacific Islands.

Language differences present the greatest challenge to immigrant populations and first-generation Americans. Standard English is the language of the mainstream, and groups that speak either nonstandard English, which may either be African-influenced or Appalachian-influenced or have limited English proficiency, such as Latinos and Asians, have additional challenges when coping in their newly adopted country.

Cultural anthropologist Asa Hilliard (1988) made some interesting observations about learning. He stated that the brain is to computer hardware what learning style is to computer software and that impressive evidence exists that individuals' educational experiences can expand the "software" they use. Dunn, Griggs, Olson, Gorman, and Beasley's (in press) meta analytic report on a decade of quality experimental studies based on the Dunn and Dunn learning-style model appear to have provided Hilliard with support for his hypothesis. The 3,181 culturally diverse participants in the 36 studies represented broad ranges of ages, grade levels, geographic locations, and socioeconomic levels. Meta analysis determined the effects of accommodating learning-style preferences on academic achievement. Many practitioners had reported significantly higher achievement among previously at-risk and underachieving students after their learning-style preferences had been accommodated by style-responsive instructional strategies. Those achievement gains were reported for (1) elementary students (Andrews, 1990; Klavas, 1993; Lemmon, 1985; Stone, 1992; Turner, 1993), (2) secondary students (Brunner & Majewski, 1990; Elliot, 1991; Gadwa & Griggs, 1985; Harp & Orsak, 1990; Orsak, 1990a, 1990b), and (3) college students (Clark-Thayer, 1987; Mickler & Zippert, 1987; Nelson, Dunn, Griggs, Primavera, Fitzpatrick, Bacilious, & Miller, 1993; Lenehan, Dunn, Ingham, Signer, and Murray, 1994). In addition, a U.S. Office of Education four-year investigation that included on-site visits, interviews, observations, and examination of national test data concluded that learning-styles-based instruction was one of the few strategies that positively affected the achievement of classified special education students (Alberg, Cook, Fiore, Friend, Sano, et al., 1992). Similar gains were found by Stone (1992) with learning-disabled elementary students, by Brunner and Majewski (1990) with mildly handicapped high school students, and by the Buffalo City Schools with learning-disabled and emotionally handicapped K–8 students (Quinn, 1994). However, despite the statistically higher gains made with all these special populations in disparate geographical areas, Sullivan (1993) found that college and adult learners showed greater gains than elementary school or secondary school students; that middle-class students were more responsive to learning-style accommodations than either lower-middle-, upper-middle-, or lower-class students; and that average academic achievers were more responsive to learning-style interventions than high, low, or mixed achievement groups.

Neither geographic area nor ethnicity was a significant moderating variable; that is, students of different ethnic backgrounds did not perform significantly differently from one another following the experimental interventions. An important finding was that the accommodation of learning style through complementary teaching or counseling interventions resulted in significantly improved academic achievement and attitudes toward learning for all cultural groups (Sullivan, 1993).

To summarize, culture can be a major variable that affects adolescents' educational experiences, but even culture affects individuals differently. Other important variables that affect how adolescents perform in school and react to schooling include age, educational level, gender, learning style and the teaching style(s) to which individuals are exposed, leisure-time interests, maturity, parental occupations, opportunity, religious beliefs, and special talents and gifts. These variables combine to affect individuals differently. However, when multicultural and learning-style diversity are respected and accommodated instructionally and socially, adolescents—indeed human beings of all developmental levels—perform better academically than when those variables are not respected and not accommodated.

CORNERSTONES OF EFFECTIVE MULTICULTURAL COUNSELING

The following tenets are cornerstones for counseling multicultural adolescents:

1. Human behavior, its concomitant outcomes, and the process of counseling occur within a social and cultural context.

2. For a counselor to view an individual's concerns or problems as separate from their cultural and social context is to misunderstand them.

3. It is essential that counselors become aware of their own cultural biases and increase their sensitivity to the realities and needs of the culturally diverse populations they serve. The culturally sensitive counselor is aware of what is universal as well as distinct to each individual.

4. Differences between the counselor's and counselee's beliefs, attitudes, values, and perceptions will affect the effectiveness of the various counseling techniques and strategies used. Although the counselor and the counselee may not necessarily agree on all these variables, the extent to which they both respect and are willing to accommodate each other's beliefs, attitudes, values, and/or perceptions will determine the quality of their interactions and relationship.

5. The goal of becoming culturally sensitive is that increased awareness and appreciation of various cultures will enable the counselor to work creatively and flexibly with a variety of students and thus counsel more adolescents more effectively than ever before.

NATIVE AMERICANS

It is estimated that Native Americans arrived in North America approximately 12,000 years ago. According to the U.S. Census data, in 1990 this group comprised less than 1 percent of our total population, or approximately 2 million people. As in all cultures, extensive diversity exists within this group too. For example, 517 federally recognized native groups and 365 state-recognized "Indian tribes" live in Alaska and the lower 48 states, and each maintains unique customs, traditions, and social organizations (U.S. Senate Select Committee on Indian Affairs, 1985). Approximately 38 percent of the Native Americans in the United States live within 275 reservations located primarily in the West.

Life on the reservation has been characterized by high unemployment, large numbers of people living below the poverty line, and low educational attainment. Traditionally, reservation residents have been employed in farming, raising livestock, hunting, fishing, mining, timber production, and craft industries. More recently, Native Americans have recognized the economic potential of the approximately 50 million acres of property they own and have founded regional industries to engage in building, operating, and maintaining airports, hydroelectric plants, casinos, resort hotels, and sawmills.

Historically, the U.S. government's policies toward Native Americans have vacillated, commencing with the displacement of eastern tribes to the land west of the Mississippi River, allocation of land to individual tribal members, and establishment of reservations with tribal ownership; more recently, the government has assisted in moving Native Americans into urban areas through job training, education, and housing. Government policy has fluctuated between attempting to integrate and assimilate Native Americans into the mainstream culture to encouraging Native Americans to maintain their cultural uniqueness. Gradually, through defeat, demoralization, and displacement, the Native American culture and its populace's means of earning a living have been eroded (Axelson, 1993).

Values

Important differences exist in the values of the many Native American groups, including the regional variations that affect their world views, the differences between urban and rural reservation tribal life, and beliefs, languages, customs, and intergenerational perceptions. Despite these differences, many deeply entrenched and ongoing identical values have remained central to the Native American culture in general for thousands of years: These common beliefs include the Native American concept of God, self, others, and the world (Axelson, 1993).

The Native American spiritual God is viewed as positive, benevolent, and an integral part of daily living. God is the creator of all things, and living in harmony with God's plan involves respecting all of nature as part of daily existence. The self is perceived as part of, and congruent with, the universe. Admired personality traits include bravery, patience, honesty, respect for others, controlled emotions, and self-respect. Interpersonal relationships, group living, sharing, and helping others are fundamental values. On a reservation every person knows his or her genealogy and has a strong sense of community and tribal identity. The world is viewed as interconnected with living and nonliving things having a function and place in the universe. Time is measured according to natural phenomena such as the phases of the moon, the changing seasons, the rise and fall of tides, and the movements of the sun.

Learning-Styles Research

Cognitive Processing

A number of researchers (Kaufman & Kaufman, 1983; Keefe & Monk, 1986; Krywaniuk, 1974; More, 1987) compared Native American and Caucasian students and found that the Native Americans scored higher on simultaneous processing measures and lower on sequential processing measures than Caucasian students. Simultaneous processing involves synthesizing separate elements into a whole. Sometimes called global conceptualization, simultaneous processing requires perceiving an entire concept or idea initially before examining or mastering the facts (Dunn, Beaudry, & Klavas, 1989). After the concept has been understood, the details can gradually be absorbed. Conversely, sequential processing refers to learning information in a serial, analytic, step-by-step ordered manner. For example, when learning to read, sight-word vocabulary tasks require simultaneous processing, whereas phonics tasks require sequential processing. More (1987) hypothesized that research concerning simultaneous and sequential data reveal a serious mismatch between the learning styles of Native American students and traditional strategies used to teach children to read. He maintained that beginning reading programs still emphasize sequential processing through a heavily phonetic approach and that this may account for the extensive reading problems of many Native American students—problems that persist into adolescence and adulthood. Dunn, Dunn, and Perrin (1994) criticized sequential reading approaches for most young children, who tend to be simultaneous (global) rather than sequential (analytic) processors (pp. 353–361).

The construct of field dependence versus field independence is classified as a component of cognitive style. Field independence is measured by the degree to which individuals can separate a figure from its background, a part from the whole, or themselves from the environment. Field-independent persons are analytic, dislike rigid systematization and routines, and engage in active, participant approaches to learning. Conversely, field-dependent persons are less able to separate each part from the whole, engage in spectator approaches to learning, are intuitive and attentive to social cues, and often are described as emotionally receptive.

Anastasi (1988) cited evidence that this cognitive style exhibits considerable stability through childhood and early adulthood. Weitz (1971) found that Algonquin and Athapaskan Indians scored high on field independence; females, adolescents, and traditional groups scored higher than males, children, and urban populations. However, contradictory findings were revealed by Keefe and Monk (1986) on the analytic skill subscale of the Learning Style Profile (LSP). This subscale correlates significantly with the construct of field independence. Analysis of variance results revealed highly significant differences among five ethnic groups, with Asian Americans scoring highest on the analytic skill subscale and Native Americans scoring lowest.

Visual Imagery

The use of imagery as a tool for understanding complex concepts has been widely reported as being an important part of learning among traditional Native American cultures. Many researchers reported that Native Americans use imagery coding whereas non–Native Americans use verbal coding (Bryant, 1986; Karlebach, 1986; More, 1987). Although popular, that conclusion would be disputed by Dunn, Dunn, and Perrin (1994), who ascribed imagery coding to simultaneous processors, who, they report, tend to comprise the majority of K–2 children they have tested in the United States. Longitudinal data suggest that the longer students remain in school, the more sequential and analytic their processing becomes. However, even among adolescents, large numbers of students remain holistic (global-right) processors. Among the gifted and talented students in nine diverse nations, 18.5 percent were sequential-analytics, 26 percent were simultaneous-globals, and 55.5 percent were integrated, that is, able to master new and difficult material in either processing style *if* they were interested in the subject matter (Milgram, Dunn, & Price, 1993a).

On the basis of a literature review they had conducted, Swisher and Deyhle (1987) concluded that Native American youth have strong visual perception and learn most effectively through observation, watching, and modeling. Kaulbach (1984) reviewed studies on the performance of Native American students on visual, auditory, and kinesthetic perceptual tasks. He concluded that Native American youth are most successful at processing visual information and have the most difficulty with auditory perception. It should be noted, however, that Kaulbach did not include tactual tasks in the repertoire to which the Native Americans had been exposed and that hands-on, manipulative learning is the approach most preferred by many underachievers (Carbo, 1980; Garrett, 1991; Kroon, 1985; Martini, 1986; Quinn, 1994; Stone, 1992; Weinberg, 1983; Wheeler, 1980, 1983).

Normative data on the LSP (Keefe & Monk, 1986) revealed highly significant differences among five racial groups on the spatial rotational skill and spatial pattern recognition subscales. In contrast with the widely reported conclusions in the literature, Native Americans scored lowest among the five groups on these essentially visual LSP subscales. It is difficult to reconcile these contradictory findings, except to note that (1) there is great diversity within Native Americans, and frequently the sample selected for study is representative of a single tribe rather than the population at large; (2) previous researchers may have extrapolated that Native Americans are highly visual because they rarely score well on verbal and auditory skills, in comparison performing better on visual tasks; and (3) few researchers have compared populations on the four most frequently used learning modalities: auditory, visual, tactual, and kinesthetic; most research testing includes auditory and visual subscales only.

Reflective Versus Impulsive Processing Styles

More (1987) suggested that the ways in which Native American and non–Native American students react during classroom question-and-answer sessions can be ascribed to the cultural differences between them. He reported that Native American students tend to be reflective learners who respond in a slower and more accurate manner than their non–Native American counterparts, who tend to be impulsive learners who use trial-and-error approaches to learning. This type of across-the-board assertion conflicts with the data of many learning-style researchers who found that no single style exists within any culture; each culture encompasses multiple styles (Dunn & Griggs, 1990; Dunn, Griggs, & Price, 1993a; Ingham & Price, 1993; Milgram, Dunn, & Price, 1993a; Milgram & Price, 1993; Sinatra, de Mendez, & Price, 1993; Suh & Price, 1993).

Sociological Style

In relation to sociological preferences, Swisher and Deyhle (1987) reported that Native American youth are more apt to participate in group or team projects and in situations where they have control in volunteering participation as opposed to teacher-dominated recitations. Furthermore, because Native American cultural values stress cooperation and interdependence among people, they extrapolated that Native American youth tend to feel uncomfortable in competitively structured situations.

Hadfield, Martin, and Wooden (1992) conducted a study of 358 Navajo middle school youth. In their study they used both the LSP (Keefe & Monk, 1986) and the Mathematics Anxiety Rating Scale for Adolescents (Suinn, 1982). Findings revealed that spatial, categorical, and sequential skills were the best predictors of mathematics achievement in this population. Another interesting finding was that the mean anxiety of Navajo youth was significantly higher than the mean predicated on national normative data. Recommendations for working with this population included using hands-on (tactual) activities, focusing attention on the relevance of mathematics to the students' daily life situations, introducing each lesson with an overview and then following up with related details and facts, using relaxation techniques, and doing group work.

The entire population at Baboquivari High School in Sells, Arizona, consisting of 237 Tohono O'Odham students in grades 7 through 12, was tested with the Learning Style Inventory (LSI) (Dunn, Dunn, & Price, 1979). The learning-style elements identified as of considerable importance to this group overall were learning in a cool environment, being of low persistence, not requiring mobility, and being unmotivated by adults. Those elements identified as important were formal design, learning with peers, rejection of auditory learning, no need for intake, low motivation, and afternoon learning as the least preferred time of day. Thus, these Tohono O'Odham students in grades 7 through 12 preferred learning formally in peer groups, did not require intake while learning, expressed only minimal desire to achieve in school, and reported afternoon as their worst time during the day for concentrating on new and difficult material (Vaughan, Underwood, House, Schroth, Weaver, Bienversie, & Dotson, 1992).

It should be noted that different groups were described as having different traits dependent on the instrument used to identify their style. Experience with style strongly negates the possibility that an entire group of people in the same culture reveal identical styles. It is far more reasonable that researchers report as *group* characteristics those traits found in the most individuals in that population. However, even if many individuals do have the same trait, multiple learning-style traits exist and it is unlikely that individuals have more than a few traits in common. In addition, many studies revealed that the people in each group who did share the same learning-style trait often did not constitute a majority; they merely represented the larger or largest cluster of people with that trait. Finally, even when a large cluster of people with the same trait was found in a given culture, there were often similar-sized clusters in other groups. It may be convenient to report characteristics that represent the largest number of group members, but it is inaccurate to ascribe to all members of the same culture the traits of many in that culture.

Summary of Research

There appear to be patterns that distinguish the Native American group overall from other cultural groups, although these patterns or trends vary according to the learning-style element studied and the assessment tools used. These patterns provide a framework for working with *some* Native-American adolescents, but they cannot be applied indiscriminately. In the environmental stimulus area, there seems to be a preference for cool temperature and a formal design; in the emotional domain there is evidence of low persistence or a tendency to take many breaks while learning before completing a task; in the sociological domain there is a preference for peer and team learning but a tendency not to be adult motivated; in the physiological stimulus, according to many reports there is a preference for visual learning and a rejection of auditory learning, but whether the participants were tested for tactual or kinesthetic preferences is not clear; in addition, two studies did not show that Native American students learned more with visually based instruction (Kleinfeld & Nelson, 1991); there is also a need for low mobility and a rejection of learning in the afternoon; and in the psychological domain there is a preference for simultaneous processing, field independence, and reflective learning.

Counseling and Teaching Implications

Native American adolescents confront their identity crises in a more complex manner than mainstream adolescents. Lee and Richardson (1991) stressed the importance of counselors' being aware of three distinct family patterns among Native Americans, including the *traditional* family, which attempts to follow culturally defined lifestyles; the *nontraditional* family, which prefers to live within the mainstream culture and retains minimal elements of historical Native American family life; and the *pantraditional* family, which seeks to live within the ancestral culture of nomadism and isolation from non–Native Americans. As in all cultures, adolescents may either accept parental lifestyles as reflected in these three different orientations or pursue a lifestyle different from that of their parents and family influences. Sue and Sue (1990) hypothesized that the stress caused by being caught between the expectations of parents to maintain traditional values and the pressure to adapt to the mainstream culture may account for the high rates of truancy, school failure, drug abuse, pregnancy, and suicide among Native-American adolescents.

Adolescents who adhere to the values of the traditional or nontraditional family may each confront numerous issues that affect learning and education (Sue & Sue 1990). The cultural emphasis on nonverbal communication may cause individuals to develop less English proficiency than would otherwise be expected. Basic academic learning skills may be underdeveloped and the value of education may be perceived as minimally important, understandably leading to lesser academic motivation. In addition, adolescents may experience the normal concerns about failure and its impact on the family and tribe. As occurs in many cultures, adolescents may also experience difficulty in establishing long-term goals. In a culture that values repression of emotions, young people may find it difficult to engage in other than reflective behaviors. Further, paternalism by government agencies has been accused of inadvertently increasing dependency, and adolescents may be unaware of the world of work in the mainstream culture (Sue & Sue, 1990).

In addition to addressing values issues, counselors need to be aware of the special problems of the Native American population, including widespread abuse of alcohol and drugs, low career aspirations and a lack of positive role models, separation from the family of origin and subsequent placement in non–Native American foster homes for significantly high numbers of adolescents to provide them with high school education opportunities that may be lacking in their own geographical areas, and the highest school dropout rate (35.5 percent) and the lowest percentage (16 percent) of college graduates among the various ethnic groups.

The learning-style differences within the Native American population are greater than the mean differences between Native Americans and other ethnic groups. Thus, when counseling and teaching Native American adolescents, it is important to understand the group cultural heritage and values. However, although it is important to keep the characteristics associated with each group in mind, in reality it is not possible to respond to the learning-style preferences of an overall group, for the members within each group often differ significantly from each other—which is precisely why we have highlighted the discrepancies that exist among research reports. Therefore when counseling and teaching Native American adolescents, it is equally important to identify and respond to the *individual's* learning-style preferences.

Thus, educators might expect greater than average numbers of Native American adolescents to exhibit the following characteristics:

- a preference for cool temperature and formal design in the learning environment;
- a need for varied instructional strategies and grouping patterns while learning and a tendency to focus on a number of diverse learning activities simultaneously;

- an interest in peer learning and group counseling, characterized by an egalitarian orientation when permitted to choose the approach with which individuals care to become involved; and

- a visual/perceptual/spatial mode rather than a verbal mode as per one body of literature but testing to determine whether a tactual or kinesthetic mode might be more effective for individual students—particularly underachievers—as per another body of literature.

Given these characteristics, Native American students should be approached through a variety of counseling and teaching strategies. Strategies that would tend to be effective with this population include

- using imagery, symbolism, meditation, and relaxation: however, experiment with other strategies where the need for diversity is indicated;

- allowing time for reflective learning, pausing longer for student responses, and not singling out quieter individuals in a group setting;

- responding to the needs of the simultaneous processor by providing an overview of counseling content initially, using advanced organizers, making connections between the relevance of counseling content (career education, study skills enhancement, psychological education, problem solving, etc.) and real-life problems and concerns, permitting reasonable leisure intervals (breaks) during the concentration efforts, and remembering the correlational studies that reported that simultaneous global processors often require sound, soft illumination, and intake while learning;

- consulting with teachers and providing inservice activities concerning the importance of creating a cooperative environment and deemphasizing competition within the classroom; and

- consulting with parents to learn more about their cultural orientation, value system, and their aspirations for the adolescent;

- identifying *each* adolescent's strong learning-style preferences and counseling the youngster through his or her individual strengths.

HISPANICS

The term *Hispanic* is a U.S. government designation for people of Latin American descent living in the United States; many people from Central and South America are more responsive to the term *Latino* (Arrendondo, 1991). According to the U.S. Census of 1990, Hispanics numbered 22.4 million persons, or 9 percent of the population. These statistics represent a 53 percent increase over the 1980 census data, which makes this group the fastest-growing minority within the nation.

Hispanics generally reside in the urban areas of California, New York, and Texas and are united by customs, language, religion, and values. There is, however, extensive diversity within this group that originates mainly from the Caribbean, Central America, Mexico, South America, and Europe. The physical appearance of Hispanics varies greatly, including a resemblance to North American Indians, African-Americans, Latins, and Europeans (Sue & Sue, 1990).

Black, Paz, and De Blassie (1991) reported that Hispanics receive less education, employment, income, health care, and other social services than other minorities. The majority are employed in semiskilled or unskilled occupations that provide a limited range of career role models for adolescents. In addition, Hispanic adolescents are frequently undocumented persons in constant fear of being apprehended and deported. Some of these youth were victims of war and political strife and left El Salvador, Guatemala, or Nicaragua seeking a stable lifestyle.

First-generation adolescent Hispanics generally have very limited English proficiency; their native language is Spanish, and they may have had minimal formal education prior to their entry into the United States. In 1974, in a landmark decision, the U.S. Supreme Court unanimously ruled that the San Francisco Unified School District's failure to provide English language instruction for non-English-speaking children denied them a meaningful opportunity to participate in the public educational program (*Lau vs. Nichols*). The Lau decision recognized the special educational needs of minority students and legitimatized the right to quality bilingual and bicultural programs for non-English-speaking youth.

Values

Family commitment is of paramount importance in most Hispanic cultures. That commitment includes a loyalty to the family, a strong family support system, the sense that adolescent behavior reflects on the honor of the family, hierarchial order among siblings, and a duty to care for members who are disabled, infirm, or aged. This strong sense of other-directedness conflicts with the U.S. mainstream emphasis on individualism (Vasquez, 1990). Indeed, their culture's emphasis on cooperation in the attainment of goals can result in Hispanic adolescents' discomfort with this nation's conventional classroom competition.

Hispanic adolescents are more inclined than Anglos to adopt their parents' commitment to religious and political beliefs, occupational preferences, and philosophical lifestyle (Black, Paz, & De Blassie, 1991). Spirituality, the dignity of each individual, and respect for authority figures are valued throughout the Hispanic culture. The majority of Hispanics are Roman Catholics committed to the Church's teachings of respect for all forms of life, procreation, human dignity, service to others, and morality.

Stereotyped sex roles tend to exist among Latinos; the male is perceived as being the dominant, strong provider, whereas the female is perceived as being nurturing, submissive, and self-sacrificing. Although the term *machismo* has been equated with male chauvinism, in Latino cultures it is most closely aligned with the concept of chivalry, which includes being gallant, courteous, charitable, and courageous (Baron, 1991). Hispanic male adolescents have more and earlier independence than the male adolescents of the general population in the United States, but Black, Paz, and De Blassie (1991) found that Chicano secondary school students evidence lower levels of self-esteem than their Anglo (European-American) counterparts.

Hispanics are educationally behind every other minority group. Nearly half of Hispanic students leave before completing high school—more than double the rate for African-Americans and three times higher than the rate for Anglo students (Sue & Sue, 1990). Among the various Hispanic cultural groups, Puerto Ricans have the highest dropout rate, over 70 percent. These statistics negatively affect the Hispanic's occupational choices and contribute to the lack of Hispanic role models in such professions as engineering, physics, computer technology, and higher education, all of which require an education.

Learning-Styles Research

Research on the learning styles of Hispanic-Americans is limited. Much more research is available on Native Americans, perhaps because a great deal was conducted in schools located on reservations. Within the Latino groups, the majority of studies have been focused on the learning styles of Mexican-Americans.

Five investigations compared various ethnic groups of students in elementary school through college level using the LSI (Dunn, Dunn, & Price, 1979). These included the following:

1. Jalali (1988) compared rural fourth-, fifth-, and sixth-grade Mexican-American students with African-American, Chinese-American, and Greek-American youth.

2. Dunn, Griggs, and Price (1993a) compared fourth-, fifth-, and sixth-grade Mexican-American students with a comparable group of Caucasians.

3. Vazquez (1985) studied high-risk, urban Puerto Rican college students.

4. Yong and Ewing (1992) compared the learning-style preferences among gifted African-American, Mexican-American, and Chinese-American sixth-, seventh-, and eighth-grade students.

5. Sims (1988) compared Mexican-American, African-American, and European-American third- and fourth-grade students.

Learning-style elements within the environmental stimulus include sound, temperature, design, and light. A cool temperature and formal design were identified as important elements for Mexican-American, elementary and middle school students (Dunn, Griggs, & Price, 1993a, Jalali, 1988; Yong & Ewing, 1992) and Puerto Rican elementary and middle school students (Vazquez, 1985), and Vazquez (1985) found that adult Puerto Ricans needed a quiet environment and bright light while learning.

The emotional stimulus includes responsibility, structure, persistence, and motivation. Sims (1988)) reported that third- and fourth-grade Mexican-Americans were the least conforming of the three ethnic groups compared, but Yong and Ewing (1992) found that Mexican-American middle school adolescents were conforming. These disparate data may have been the result of age and lifestyle differences; students in the Yong and Ewing study were older and from urban Chicago whereas students in Sims' study were younger and from rural Oregon. Vazquez (1985) described Puerto Rican college women as nonconforming but highly persistent and motivated. Both Yong and Ewing (1992) and Sims (1988) reported that Mexican-Americans required a high degree of structure as compared with other groups.

The sociological elements are concerned with whom and how each student learns easily—alone versus with peers, with an authoritative teacher versus with a collegial teacher, being teacher or parent motivated, and/or through routines versus through a variety of social interactions. The groups that most preferred learning alone were Caucasians as compared with Mexican-Americans (Dunn, Griggs, & Price, 1993a), and Mexican-Americans as compared with African-Americans (Sims, 1988). The most peer-oriented students were the Chinese-American and Mexican-American fourth, fifth, and sixth graders in Jalali's (1988) study, Caucasians when compared with the Mexican-American third and fourth graders in Sims' (1988) investigation, and Mexican-American fourth, fifth, and sixth graders when compared with Caucasians in the Dunn, Griggs, and Price study (1993a). Thus, although Mexican-American students in Texas were peer oriented in comparison with same-age African American and Caucasian students in New York, they were less peer oriented when compared with Caucasian students in Oregon. Both geographical and socioeconomic differences in these populations could account for the variations in findings. It should be noted, however, that the data were not inconsistent; students merely differed in their degree of peer orientation.

Mexican Americans required significantly more sociological variety than either African Americans or Caucasians (Dunn, Griggs, & Price 1993a; Jalali, 1988). Mexican-American males were authority oriented, and Mexican-American females were strongly peer oriented (Dunn, Griggs, & Price, 1993a).

Time of day, intake, perceptual strengths, and mobility make up the physiological stimulus. Puerto Rican college students were strongly evening, late morning, and afternoon preferenced rather than early morning preferenced. In two studies Mexican Americans most preferred learning in the afternoon (Dunn, Griggs, & Price, 1993a; Jalali, 1988). Sims's (1988) population of Mexican Americans in Oregon disliked learning in the afternoon. Sims (1988) also found that Caucasians preferred intake (eating, snacking, drinking while learning) significantly more than Mexican-Americans.

Latinos' strongest perceptual strength was reported as kinesthetic by Yong and Ewing (1992) and Vazquez (1985). Sims (1988) also found that Mexican-American students were kinesthetically strong, but he reported that African Americans had significantly higher LSI kinesthetic scores than did Mexican Americans. Both Caucasians and African Americans were significantly more auditory and visual than Mexican Americans (Dunn, Griggs, & Price, 1993a; Sims, 1988). Interestingly, Sims (1988) revealed Caucasians' high need for mobility in comparison with Mexican Americans, and Dunn, Griggs, and Price (1993a) reported that Mexican-American females had a significantly higher need for mobility than their male counterparts—a disparate finding compared with the U.S. population in general in which males usually evidence higher mobility needs than females.

When attention is paid to group characteristics, Native American and Hispanic students have similar learning-style preferences for cool temperature, formal design, and peer learning. They differ in that in general Native Americans tend to be visual but not auditory, reveal low levels of persistence, are neither adult motivated nor afternoon learners, and display a relatively low need for mobility, whereas Latinos prefer learning kinesthetically, need bright light and a quiet environment, and require structure.

The construct of field dependence versus field independence is a component of cognitive style. Research reported by Ramirez and Casteneda (1974), Kagan and Buriel (1977), and others indicated that overall, Mexican Americans, African Americans, and some other minority students are more field dependent than mainstream students. They described field-dependent or field-sensitive individuals as more group oriented, sensitive to the social environment, cooperative, and positively responsive to adult modeling; these individuals are less competitive, more comfortable in trial-and-error situations, and less interested in the fine details of concepts, materials, or tasks than are nonsocial persons.

Kagan (1981) found that Mexican-American youth in rural environments were more field-dependent than Mexican-American youth in urban settings, and that the latter displayed more field-independent styles. Hudgens (1993) examined a sample of Anglo, African-American, and Hispanic middle and secondary school students in a midwestern, urban setting. The Group Embedded Figures Test (Witkin, Oltman, Raskin, & Karp, 1971), the Nowicki-Strickland Locus of Control Scale (Nowicki & Duke, 1983), and the California Achievement Test were used to measure cognitive style, locus of control, and academic achievement respectively. Results indicated that (1) field-independence and internal locus of control were correlated with high academic achievement; (2) minorities were more field-dependent than Anglos; (3) females outperformed males on language skills, math computations, and study skills; and (4) greater internal locus of control was present in African-American males and Hispanic females compared with greater external locus of control in African-American females and Hispanic males. In conclusion, research during the past several decades indicates that Hispanics tend to have a greater tendency toward a field-dependent cognitive style in comparison with mainstream students.

Normative data used for the LSP (Keefe & Monk, 1986) were a culturally diverse, representative group of secondary school students throughout the United States, including 82 (1.8 percent) Hispanics. Among the eight scales of the LSP that measure cognitive processing, analysis of variance revealed that four of the scales showed highly significant differences among the five culturally diverse groups.

The analytic skill subtest, which involves identifying simple figures hidden in a complex field and using the critical element of a problem in a different way, is highly correlated with field independence. The group results, ranging from most field-independent to least field-independent were Asian Americans, Hispanics, Caucasians, African Americans, and Native Americans. This finding seems to contradict the findings of previous researchers (Hudgens, 1993; Kagan, 1981; Kagan & Buriel, 1977; Ramirez & Casteneda, 1974), who found that Hispanics tend to be field dependent. Although the LSP manual neither differentiated among nor classified as such the Hispanics who participated in its norming procedures, the differences in findings may have been due to its nationally representative sample; other studies tended to involve Mexican American students only. In addition, the LSP norming procedures were restricted to adolescents, whereas other studies focused on either elementary, adult, or mixed-age populations. Finally, that learning style changes over time may also have contributed to the disparity among data.

On the LSP sequential processing skill subscale, which involves learning information sequentially or verbally and readily deriving meaning from presentations in a step-by-step, linear fashion, the group results from highest to lowest were Caucasians, Hispanics, Asian Americans, Native Americans, and African Americans. Since high-level verbal skills are required in this subtest, it is logical that Caucasians, who tend to be monolingual and more proficient in English than bilingual adolescents, would score highest on this subscale. However, this does not explain why bilingual groups (Hispanics and Asian Americans) scored higher than African Americans, who tend to be monolingual as well.

Spatial rotational skill and spatial pattern recognition involve identifying geometric shapes, recognizing and constructing in mental space, and rotating objects in the imagination. Results on these subscales from highest to lowest were Asian Americans, Caucasians, Hispanics, African Americans, and Native Americans.

Counseling and Teaching Implications

Hispanic Americans are a highly diverse group and include very distinct subcultures that differ significantly as to customs, values, and educational orientation. Sue and Sue (1990) assert that it is difficult to generalize with regard to Hispanics because important differences exist among them concerning their levels of acculturation, family solidarity, ethnic identification, orientation, and sex roles.

First-generation Hispanic adolescents and their parents can usually communicate more freely in Spanish, which implies the need for Spanish-speaking teachers, counselors, and educational assistants in our schools and, particularly, in large urban areas where Hispanics are sizable in number. Amodeo and Brown (1986) analyzed the differences between Mexican and American schools and pointed out that in Mexico students' interactions with their teachers tend to be formal. Students in Mexico are expected to be punctual and are required to respect authority. They are graded on manners as well as on academic performance, and students must be acknowledged before they are permitted to speak. Further, the lecture method is widely used.

Identity formation and individuation are challenging and sometimes problematic for immigrant Latino adolescents, originating from strong family values of loyalty and allegiance. These values conflict with the behavioral styles of mainstream adolescents, who strive for self-expression and individuality. Group counseling with peers who are experiencing similar conflicts can lead to ventilation, insight, and resolution of these dilemmas. Traditionally taught to unquestioningly obey the expectations of parents, adolescents often lack the verbal communication and decision-making skills crucial to solving their intrapersonal issues (Black, Paz, & De Blassie 1991). Referral for pastoral counseling may be indicated if the youth is Roman Catholic, since Hispanics usually trust and respect priests.

Martinez and Dukes (1987) studied Anglo-American, Mexican-American, and African-American secondary school students and found that Mexican Americans had lower levels of self-esteem in the public domain than did their Anglo counterparts when intelligence was controlled for in the inquiry. However, the Mexican-American students scored higher than their Anglo counterparts in terms of self-satisfaction. The authors concluded that racism influences self-image across all social classes by promoting minority students' rejection of their own ethnicity and encouraging conformity to the Anglo cultural norm. When teaching and counseling Hispanic adolescents, educators need to be sensitive to these conflicts and plan interventions that acknowledge and celebrate cultural diversity.

Based on this learning-styles research, teachers and counselors should expect greater-than-average numbers of Hispanic adolescents to exhibit preferences for a cool environment, formal design, conformity (especially for first-generation adolescents), peer-oriented learning (dependent upon socioeconomic status and geographic region), kinesthetic instructional resources, and a high degree of structure. Examples of structured, kinesthetic strategies that might be effective with this population include role playing of interpersonal conflicts, covert and overt modeling of desired behaviors, psychodrama to better understand the motivations of others, and game therapy to develop problem-solving and coping skills.

For responsive teaching strategies, look not for cultural-group characteristics. Instead, emphasize the learning-style strengths of each individual and teach students how to match instructional resources and methods to their own processing, perceptual, environmental, sociological, and other preferences (see Chapters 6–10).

AFRICAN AMERICANS

African Americans are the largest minority in the United States, numbering approximately 30 million, or 12.1 percent of the population according to the 1990 census data. Commencing in 1619 a total of 500,000 slaves were brought to the United States and Canada, and although the country outlawed international trade in slaves in 1808, some smuggling of people from West African nations occurred after that time (Axelson, 1993).

The aftermath of slavery is reflected in the suppression, prejudice, and discriminatory practices that characterized life for African Americans in the twentieth century. As a result, a matriarchal pattern and instability within the African-American family developed and is reflected in the high rate of female household heads (43.5 percent) and divorce rates (28.2 percent) today. The plight of this minority is exacerbated by several conditions: Black ghettos remain prevalent in our large urban areas; one-third of America's African-American population lives below the poverty level, with almost 50 percent of black children raised in poverty; more than 60 percent of all black births are to single women; and 12 percent of the unemployed are black males (Wilkins, 1994). This economic and social devastation has contributed to community disintegration—to crime, violence, a high rate of incarceration, and murder as the leading cause of death among African-American males ages 15 to 24. As an outgrowth, emotional despair and anger are prevalent among many African-

American adolescents, and these feelings are often accompanied by low self-concept and insecurity.

Although the high school graduation rate for this group has increased to 72 percent of African-American males and 77 percent of African-American females, this ratio still lags behind the 81 percent and 85 percent rates for Caucasians (Williams, 1994). Forty years after the U.S. Supreme Court ruled that segregated schools were inherently unequal (*Brown vs. the Topeka, Kansas Board of Education*), two of every three African-American children continue to attend schools predominantly comprised of minority students. This is partially due to socioeconomic disparities and related residency restrictions. Wilkins (1994) observed: "Blacks arrived on the North American continent in 1619. For almost 250 of the ensuing 375 years we had slavery or something very close to it. And for a century after that we had Constitutionally-sanctioned racial subordination. We have had something other than slavery or legal racial subordination for almost 29 years" (p. 33).

Values

Black cultural patterns have their roots in West Africa and are based on a strong religious orientation and an emphasis on feelings and interpersonal relationships (Hale, 1981). Although African Americans are predominantly Protestant, often having merged tribal African religion with Christianity, the black nationalist movement currently includes a half million people who practice a form of Islam. Although not a religion, Kwanzaa is a movement that seeks to celebrate aspects of African-American cultural identity (Axelson, 1993). The church in the African-American community is a source of indigenous social support, and frequently its clergy are recognized as the major leaders within the community (Richardson, 1991).

African-American culture is marked by a distinct pattern of thinking, feeling, and acting that has developed as one way of adapting to color discrimination (Shade, 1982). Children learn to judge and adjust to the moods of persons in authority, for example. Other socialization patterns include the African-American kinship network, which acts as a multigenerational social network for relatives, friends, and neighbors that serves as a support system for collective responsibility, and sociocentricism among African-American youth, who often prefer an oral learning modality and using spontaneous, empathetic, and highly sensitive body language to verbal cues (Atbar, 1975).

Hilliard (1976) maintained that African Americans process information from the environment differently from other groups in that they view things in their entirety and not as isolated parts; prefer to employ inferential reasoning; approximate space, time, and numbers; demonstrate proficiency in verbal and nonverbal communication; use intuition; and focus on people and not objects—all traits described as global or deductive by Dunn and Dunn (1992, 1993) and referred to as field-dependent by others (Jalali, 1988; Sinatra, 1982; Tanenbaum, 1982; Trautman, 1979). Frequently these cultural characteristics are undervalued in schools that emphasize (1) analytic styles rather than global or attributional styles, (2) written language, (3) inductive reasoning as opposed to deductive reasoning paradigms, and (4) content and factual information.

As noted previously, variables such as geographic region, gender, religion, and social class create intragroup variations within ethnic groups. Some authors argue that the importance of race in the United States has declined and that social class has created crucial differences among African Americans (Gordon, 1964; Wilson, 1978). However, in a review of research Banks (1988) concluded:

Studies indicate that ethnicity continues to have a significant influence on the learning behavior and styles of Afro-Americans students, even when these students are middle class. In other words, the research reviewed indicates that while ethnicity is to some extent class sensitive, its effects persist across social-class segments within an ethnic group. (p. 462)

Banks maintained that social scientists need to examine generational middle-class status as a variable because there are important behavioral and attitudinal differences between the African American who grew up poor and became middle class as an adult and the African American as a fourth-generation, middle-class member (Banks, 1988).

Learning-Styles Research

The learning-style cognitive element that has been the major focus of research is field dependence versus field independence. The findings among African Americans on this construct are consistent—except for differences within the group as to gender, level of academic achievement, and social class. Research indicates that African-American students tend to be significantly more field-dependent than Caucasians (Dunn, Gemake, Jalali, Zenhausern, Quinn, & Spiridakis, 1990; Hale, 1981; Hudgens, 1993; Shade, 1982). Perney (1976) reported significant differences in field dependence between African-American and Caucasian students and concluded that most of the difference was due to the high field-dependent scores of African-American girls. However, this study was based upon a very small sample of ten African-American females in sixth grade, and it would be unscientific to generalize these findings to different age groups and samples. When comparing European-American and African-American students, Shade (1983) found that differences in achievement level were more important than ethnicity in that high achievers from both ethnic groups tended to be more field-independent whereas low achievers tended to be field-dependent. Ritzinger (1971) studied African-American and European-American youth and reported that ethnic differences in field dependence and field independence tended to disappear when socioeconomic class was controlled.

Cohen (1969) conceptualized cognitive style as either analytic or relational. The analytic style is similar to Witkin's field independence, whereas the relational style is akin to field dependence. She found that these styles of thinking were related to the types of families and groups into which students are socialized. African Americans, who are members of groups that emphasize "shared function," tend to have relational or field-dependent styles, whereas Caucasians experience formal styles of group organization that are associated with analytic or field-independent styles.

When comparing the cognitive styles of five ethnic groups, Keefe and Monk (1986) found that African-American high school students ranked lowest on sequential processing, which is highly correlated with field independence. On the LSP subscales of analytic and spatial-rotational pattern recognition, African-American students ranked fourth, with only the Native American group ranking lower.

Five studies used the LSI (Dunn, Dunn, & Price, 1979) with African-American students. Jalali (1988) compared the learning styles of African-American, Chinese-American, Mexican-American, and Greek-American students in grades 4 through 6. Sims (1988) examined fourth- and fifth-grade African-American, Mexican-American, and Caucasian students. Roberts (1984) studied the learning styles of Jamaicans and Bahamian high school students of African descent. Jacobs (1987) differentiated between African-American and European-American middle school students who were high, middle, or low achievers. And Yong and Ewing (1992) assessed the learning styles of gifted African-American, Mexican-American, and Chinese-American middle school adolescents.

Within the environmental stimulus of learning style, data indicated that African Americans and Bahamians preferred more quiet while studying than did Chinese Americans (Jalali, 1988), Caucasians (Sims, 1988), or Jamaicans (Roberts, 1984). African Americans and Jamaicans were warm-temperature preferents in comparison with Mexican Americans (Jalali, 1988; Sims, 1988), Chinese Americans, Greek Americans (Jalali, 1988), Caucasians (Sims, 1988), and Bahamians (Roberts, 1984). Soft illumination was preferred to bright lighting by African Americans and Bahamians when compared with European Americans (Jacobs, 1987) and Jamaicans (Roberts, 1984). Jalali (1988) also found that African Americans required an informal design in contrast with Chinese Americans and Mexican Americans, who preferred formal seating while learning.

Within the sociological domain considerable congruence was revealed in terms of African Americans' requiring an authoritative figure present while learning (Jalali, 1988) and being highly parent and teacher motivated in comparison with Chinese Americans (Jalali, 1988) and European Americans (Jacobs, 1987). Jalali (1988) further reported that elementary school African-American students were more peer-oriented than their Chinese-American and Mexican-American counterparts and preferred the same, rather than a varied, grouping pattern while learning.

Findings concerning the emotional stimulus were contradictory in several areas. Jalali (1988) identified African Americans in New York as nonconformists in comparison with Chinese Americans and Greek Americans, but Sims (1988) found that African Americans in California were significantly more conforming than Mexican Americans. In addition, Sims (1988) reported that the African Americans in Los Angeles required low structure when compared with Caucasian students, but Jalali (1988) found that the African Americans in suburban New York required significantly more structure than Greek Americans in New York City. Although the grade levels of students in these studies were similar, the samples of African-American students were different. Jalali (1988) studied suburban, middle-class African Americans, whereas Sims's (1988) sample was comprised of urban, lower-class students. The disparity between the data among these African-American fourth, fifth, and sixth graders clearly demonstrates learning-style differences within the same subculture based on geographical diversity and/or socioeconomic status.

Roberts (1984) and Jacobs (1987) found that Bahamian and African-American underachievers were highly persistent learners in comparison with Jamaicans and European-American underachievers, and Yong and Ewing (1992) reported that the African-American adolescents they studied were persistent and responsible.

Yong and McIntyre (1992) examined the similarities and differences between 64 tenth-, eleventh-, and twelfth-grade gifted students and 53 learning-disabled African-American, Mexican-American, and American-born Chinese middle-grade students. The students with learning disabilities tended to prefer conventional seating (environmental) and were less motivated, persistent, and responsible (conforming) than their peers who were gifted. They were also late-morning preferents (physiological). These findings were a partial corroboration of previous research revealing that students with learning disabilities and underachievers tended to be less motivated and persistent than their nondisabled peers (Carruthers & Young, 1980; Cavanaugh, 1981; Dunn, 1981; Wheeler, 1983; Wild, 1979; Williams, 1989).

Within the physiological domain of learning style, the findings tend to be congruent. African-American students tend *not* to be auditory learners when compared to Greek-American students (Jalali, 1988), Bahamians (Roberts, 1984), and European Americans (Jacobs, 1987). However, they have strong visual and kinesthetic perceptual strengths in comparison with Mexican Americans, Caucasians (Sims, 1988) and Greek Americans (Jalali, 1988). Indeed, Yong and Ewing (1992) reported that African-American adolescents in Illinois were solely kinesthetically preferenced. Comparative findings concerning cultural subgroups are interesting, but they belie the fact that most elementary and secondary students primarily prefer learning through an experiential (kinesthetic) or hands-on (tactual) approach (Dunn, 1989b; Price & Milgram, 1993).

African-American students tended to prefer intake and high mobility while learning in comparison with Chinese Americans (Jalali, 1989; Sims, 1988). They also identified afternoon and evening as their peak learning times in comparison with Chinese college students (Lam-Phoon, 1986), who may have been the only subcultural group to prefer early - and late-morning learning. Morning was not the preferred time of day for either Korean or Filipino adolescents, who clearly indicated chronobiological preferences that increased incrementally from late morning to evening (Price & Milgram, 1993).

Counseling and Teaching Implications

African Americans have developed a sense of *collective identity* that has its roots in a strong religious orientation and an emphasis on feelings and interpersonal relationships. Fordham and Ogbu (1986) maintained that African Americans who try to behave like Caucasians, cross cultural boundaries, and "act white" experience opposition from their peers and community. These individuals undergo internal stress; they feel they are betraying their group and its culture. School is perceived as learning the white American cultural frame of reference.

African-American high school students in Washington, D.C., identified the following behaviors as unacceptable because they constituted conversion to a white culture: (1) speaking standard English; (2) spending time studying in the library; (3) going to the Smithsonian; (4) being on time; and (5) reading and writing poetry (Fordham & Ogbu, 1986). Excelling in school is frequently frowned upon by peers because it represents assimilating and embracing the Anglo culture. To counter these attitudes, schools need to develop counseling programs to help students learn how to divorce academic pursuit from the idea of "acting white" and to reinforce black identity in a manner that is compatible with academic pursuits (Fordham & Ogbu, 1986).

Because of African Americans' strong sense of family and kinship, teachers and counselors need to reach out to parents or significant family members to involve them in the educational process. Joseph (1984) suggested that when working with African-American parents, educators should inform adults about their rights and responsibilities as parents, teach parenting skills so that mothers and fathers can be more effective, and suggest that parents return to school so that they can become role models and promote their own vocational development. She further advised that it is important to reassure Haitian parents that school staff will not submit reports to the Immigration and Naturalization Services. When working with African-American families, counselors often have to assume multiple roles as educator, advocate, problem solver, and role model (Sue & Sue, 1990). Institutions that provide a network for indigenous social support should be incorporated into the counseling process (Lee & Richardson, 1991).

Counseling of adolescents and their families is frequently mandated by the schools, courts, and public agencies. Jordan (1991) pointed out that low-socioeconomic, African-American female adolescents tended to assume adult responsibilities of caring for the house and younger siblings at an early age. She recommended that bibliotherapy drawn from the rich literature of such authors as Alice Walker (*The Color Purple*; *The Temple of My Familiar*), Toni Morrison (*The Bluest Eye*), and Gloria Naylor (*The Women of Brewster Place*) be used with this population.

To summarize the learning-styles research: Educators can expect to find greater-than-average numbers of African-American adolescents with the following patterns: (1) field-dependent, rather than field-independent, processing styles, except for middle-class achievers; (2) a tendency to rank low in the cognitive skill areas of analytic, sequential processing and spatial-rotational pattern recognition in comparison with other ethnic groups, with the exception of Native Americans; (3) preferences for bright light, quiet, warm temperatures, and informal design while learning; (4) peer learners who reject variety but are highly parent and teacher motivated and require collegial authority figures present while learning; (5) afternoon and evening peak times, with occasional morning preferences; (6) a preference for intake and mobility; and (7) visual-kinesthetic learners who reject the auditory modality but may prefer some tactual resources.

ASIAN AMERICANS

According to the 1990 U.S. Census, there are 7.3 million Asian Americans who comprise 2.9 percent of the population and represent a 108 percent increase during this decade. The majority of Chinese, Filipino, Japanese, and Korean immigrants have settled in urban areas with the highest concentration of these Asian Americans located in California, New York, and Hawaii.

Earlier Asian immigrants arrived in large numbers during the last century: the Chinese from 1850 to 1882 and the Japanese from 1890 to 1908. When these groups migrated to this nation, they worked on the transcontinental railroad and provided inexpensive agricultural labor. The middle half of the twentieth century saw anti-Asian sentiment reflected in severe restrictions on immigration and citizenship (Axelson, 1993). However, the largest migration of Asians to the United States occurred after congressional passage of the Immigration and Naturalization Act in 1965.

Great diversity in history, culture, religion, language, and value systems exists among the Asian populations, which consist of three distinct groups: (1) South Asia, comprised in the main of Bangladesh, India, and Pakistan; (2) Southeast Asia, including Indochina (Laos, Thailand, and Vietnam) and the Philippines; and (3) East Asia, consisting of China, Hong Kong, Japan, Korea, and Taiwan. Regardless of this diversity, in contrast to other minority groups, Asian Americans are perceived by mainstream America as a highly successful group. Chinese Americans and Japanese Americans exceed both the national median income and educational attainment level. Overall, Asian Americans are well adjusted, function effectively in society, and have lower rates of juvenile delinquency, divorce, and psychiatric contact than other minority groups. However, Sue and Sue (1990) point out that this image of the Asian American as the "model minority" can be misleading in that there is a discrepancy between education and income, English language deficits are pronounced for large numbers, Asian-American ghettos in urban areas are overcrowded and crime-ridden, and mental health services are underutilized because Asian-Americans attach a stigma to seeking help for emotional problems.

Values

Asian Americans represent a very heterogeneous population whose members practice a broad range of religious and philosophical orientations. Those from South Asia, including India, Pakistan, and Bangladesh, are committed to either Hinduism or Islam. The Hindu religion of India still adheres to a caste system in some regions. There is a belief in reincarnation, a respect for all living things, and the worship of many gods. Pakistanis are committed to Islam and followers of Mohammed, who believe in one God and strive to live in accord with the five pillars of their religion, including daily confessions of faith, praying five times daily, charity to those less fortunate, fasting during the ninth month of the year, and a pilgrimage to Mecca at least once during each person's lifetime.

The majority from Southeast Asia, which consists of Cambodia, Indonesia, Laos, Thailand, and Vietnam, practice Buddhism, which preaches peace, harmony, strong family commitment, nonmaterialism, and the avoidance of extremes. Filipinos, in contrast, are predominantly Roman Catholics, believing in one God, following the teachings of Jesus Christ, and emphasizing brotherly love, justice, and charity. People from East Asia, which includes China, Hong Kong, Japan, Korea, and Taiwan, practice either Confucianism or Shintoism, which are predominantly a set of ethical standards that include obedience to authority, honesty, kindness, and respect for elders.

In spite of these religious variations, Asian Americans share many commonalities, including deference to authority; emotional restraint; specified roles defined in paternalism, with men and elders enjoying greater status than women and youngsters; a hierarchical, extended-family orientation; interdependence; harmony with nature; and commitment to learning and academic achievement.

Learning-Styles Research

Six research studies used the LSI (Dunn, Dunn, & Price, 1979) with Asian or Asian-American populations. Suh and Price (1993) compared 92 gifted Korean eleventh and twelfth graders with Caucasian students in the United States. Chiu (1993) studied 278 Taiwanese-American students in grades 7 through 12 and Anglo students in the same suburban high school. Lam-Phoon (1986) compared Asian college students in Singapore with Caucasian undergraduates in the United States. Yong and Ewing (1992) researched gifted African-American, Chinese-American, and Mexican-American middle school students. Jalali (1988) studied African-American, Chinese-American, Mexican-American, and Greek-American students in grades 4 through 6. And Ingham and Price (1993) compared 1,750 gifted Filipino adolescent males with gifted male students in the United States.

Within the environmental stimulus, Yong and Ewing (1992) found that middle school Chinese-Americans preferred significantly more quiet while learning than their African- and Mexican-American classmates, a trait corroborated by Ewing and Yong (1992) for gifted Chinese-American adolescents and by Lam-Phoon (1986), who compared college students in Singapore and in the United States. Conversely, Jalali (1988) reported that elementary school Chinese-American students preferred significantly more sound than their African-American counterparts. However, it should be noted that the American-born Chinese in Jalali's (1988) study and the Chinese Americans described by Yong and Ewing (1992) were populations that differed in age, grade level, and geographic residence; also, that Price (1980) documented that learning styles change as individuals grow older.

There were consistent findings in relation to other environmental elements. For example: Chinese Americans and Filipinos preferred bright light (Chiu, 1993; Ingham & Price, 1993; Yong & Ewing, 1992), whereas Korean adolescents preferred low light (Suh & Price, 1993); Filipinos,

Chinese Americans, and Koreans required a formal design (Ingham & Price, 1993; Jalali, 1988; Suh & Price, 1993); and Chinese-American and gifted Korean adolescents preferred warm temperatures (Jalali, 1988; Suh & Price, 1993), although Asians in Singapore (Lam-Phoon, 1986) and gifted adolescents in the Philippines preferred cool temperatures (Ingham & Price, 1993).

Emotional preferences included high motivation and persistence and a need for high structure among gifted Filipino adolescents (Ingham & Price, 1993) and Chinese-American students in the fourth, fifth, and sixth grades in comparison with same-grade African Americans and Greek Americans (Jalali, 1988). Lam-Phoon (1986) reported that Asian college students in Singapore were less conforming than American college students in Michigan, but Yong and Ewing (1992) and Jalali (1988) found that Chinese-American elementary and middle school youth were more conforming than other ethnic groups. Again, these populations were very different in age, educational level, and geographic region; they also represented varied cultural groups.

Sociologically, Chinese Americans (Jalali, 1988) and gifted adolescents from Korea (Suh & Price, 1993) were more peer oriented than other ethnic groups. Gifted Filipino adolescents (Ingham & Price, 1993) and Chinese-American elementary students (Jalali, 1988) preferred more varied sociological patterns than did Greek Americans and African Americans respectively. Young Chinese Americans, in comparison with young African-Americans, rejected having teacher and parent authority figures present while they learned (Jalali, 1988), but in comparison with American students Filipino adolescents favored the presence of authority figures when they were learning (Ingham & Price, 1993). In addition, gifted Filipino adolescents were significantly more parent motivated than gifted students in eight other cultures, namely, Brazil, Canada, Egypt, Greece, Guatemala (Guatemalan and Mayan), Korea, Israel, and the United States (Milgram, Dunn, & Price, 1993a).

When comparing the auditory, visual, tactual, and kinesthetic preferences of gifted adolescents from nine different cultures, Milgram, Dunn, and Price (1993a) found that auditory preference was strongest among Mayans and Guatemalans in Guatemala (Sinatra, de Mendez, & Price, 1993) and Canadians (Brodhead & Price, 1993), but least preferred by Israelis (Milgram & Price, 1993), Filipinos (Ingham & Price, 1993), and Koreans (Suh & Price, 1993).

Among Asian groups with comparatively strong visual preferences were the Filipinos (Ingham & Price, 1993), Koreans (Suh & Price, 1993), Chinese Americans (Yong & Ewing, 1992), and Chinese college students in Singapore (Lam-Phoon, 1986). However, Lam-Phoon (1986) reported that many Asians were also auditory. Ingham and Price (1993) found that

Filipinos, and Suh and Price (1993) found that Koreans, were more kinesthetic than tactual, auditory, or visual.

Indeed, more individuals across cultures have kinesthetic and tactual, rather than visual and auditory, strengths (Dunn & Dunn, 1992, 1993; Dunn, Dunn, & Perrin, 1994; Milgram, Dunn, & Price, 1993a). For example, in an international study of gifted versus nongifted adolescents, the populations of every culture examined—Brazil (Wechsler, 1993), Canada (Brodhead & Price, 1993), Israel (Milgram & Price, 1993), Greece (Spiridakis, 1993), Guatemala (Sinatra, de Mendez, & Price, 1993), Korea (Suh & Price, 1993), Mayan (Sinatra, de Mendez, & Price 1993), the Philippines (Ingham & Price, 1993), and the United States (Dunn, Griggs, & Price, 1993b)—all preferred learning kinesthetically (through experience) and then tactually (through a hands-on approach) as their secondary modality strength. These gifted students were all more kinesthetic than tactual, more tactual than auditory, and more auditory than visual (Price & Milgram, 1993), although some Filipinos (Ingham & Price, 1993) and Koreans (Suh & Price, 1993) rejected learning auditorially. Among different achievement groups, however, a visual preference often is stronger than an auditory preference. On the other hand, it is crucial that teachers and counselors examine individual differences rather than cultural-group differences, for apparently no more than 30 percent of any population prefers the same modality (Milgram, Dunn, & Price, 1993a, p. 232).

Jalali (1988) and Yong and Ewing (1992) reported that Chinese Americans required neither mobility nor intake while learning, and Suh and Price (1993) reported identical data for Koreans. Conversely, U.S. students preferred both intake and mobility (Dunn, Griggs, & Price, 1993b), and Canadians also preferred intake while learning.

Yong and Ewing (1992) reported that the optimal time of day for Chinese Americans to study was late morning. Theirs was not an unusual finding, for among gifted adolescents internationally, few preferred learning in the morning. Rather, the later the day, the stronger the group's chronobiological preference. Thus, most preferred evening to afternoon, afternoon to late morning, and late morning to early morning (Milgram, Dunn, & Price, 1993a, p. 232). These data were identical for students in Brazil (Wechsler, 1993), Canada (Brodhead & Price, 1993), Israel (Milgram & Price, 1993), Greece (Spiridakis, 1993), Guatemala (Sinatra, de Mendez, & Price, 1993), Korea (Suh & Price, 1993), Mayan culture (Sinatra, de Mendez, & Price, 1993), the Philippines (Ingham & Price, 1993), and the United States (Dunn, Griggs, & Price, 1993b). They were also accurate for Chinese middle school students (Yong & Ewing 1992) and Chinese elementary school students (Jalali, 1988).

Within the cognitive domain of the LSP, 78 Asian Americans—or 1.7 percent of those tested—showed significant differences in relation to the other four ethnic groups tested. On three of the subscales, the Asian Americans ranked highest: (1) analytic skill, which is highly correlated with field independence and which measures abstract analytic thinking, a rational approach to problem solving, and a tendency to process information relatively free from environmental cues; (2) spatial-rotational skill, which involves the ability to rotate objects in the imagination; and (3) spatial pattern recognition, which measures the ability to identify and construct geometric shapes mentally. The fourth subscale, sequential processing skill, involves processing information sequentially and deriving meaning from information presented in a step-by-step, linear fashion. Asian Americans ranked in the middle on this subscale, behind Caucasians and Hispanics but ahead of Native Americans and African Americans. These findings are partially supported by Nudd and Gruenfeld's (1976) data, which revealed that of six ethnic subcultures tested in Trinidad, Chinese were the most field-independent. Also, these cognitive-style strengths tend to validate the finding that Asian-American students perform better than other cultural minorities on standardized examinations (Coleman, 1966; Slade, 1982).

Counseling and Teaching Implications

Sue and Sue (1990) observed that mental health and psychotherapy are foreign concepts in most Asian cultures. They suggested that counselors respect the privacy accorded family issues by not probing. However, school counselors might find that young students who have fled war and repression in Cambodia, Laos, and Vietnam, for example, have frequently experienced interrogation, family separation, harassment, and violence. Coburn (1992) ventured that many of these youth suffer posttraumatic stress disorder, including nightmares, flashbacks, withdrawal, insomnia, and physiological problems. Many of the psychological symptoms of trauma, including problems with concentration, anxiety, and depression, interfere with a student's ability to learn. Therefore it is imperative that educators are sensitized to these special problems with selected Asian-American groups and intervene with sensitivity and empathetic understanding.

As with every minority group, the degree of acculturation is a critical variable in teaching and counseling the Asian-American student. Chen and Yang (1986) found that Chinese-American adolescents' attitudes toward dating and sex correlated with their degree of acculturation; that is, those highly acculturated had views similar to those of Caucasian adolescents, although Confucian values of loyalty, conformity, and respect for elders remained.

In the area of learning style, educators can expect greater-than-average numbers of Asian-American students to report the following preferences: (1) environmental preferences for formal design; (2) emotional requirements for a high degree of structure; (3) no clear sociological patterns; (4) some physiological requirements for morning or late morning learning but an increasing preference for concentrating on academics as the day waxes on toward afternoon and evening (some will be strongly visual, but the majority of adolescents across cultures appear to be preferentially kinesthetic and tactual when they have been assessed for four modalities); and (5) an analytic, field-independent cognitive style. In addition, because analytic, field-independent versus global, field-dependent styles tend to vary with achievement levels, educators can anticipate identifying more of the latter when students are not performing well in school. When global, field-dependent adolescents who do not achieve well are identified, counselors may suggest that teachers alter their instructional presentations to respond to these students' styles *or* they may place the individuals' LSI data onto the Homework Disk and provide the students with a prescription for studying and doing their homework through their learning-style strengths (Dunn & Klavas, 1992).

Bibliotherapy is a powerful counseling tool that involves recommending selective readings to address counselee concerns and centering the counseling intervention around an in-depth discussion of these readings. Hong (1993) edited a book based on the work of 33 Asian-American authors who described their adolescent experiences. The accounts are centered around such themes as vulnerability, adolescent rebellion, and feelings of misunderstanding. This type of counseling intervention is compatible with the visual strengths of many Asian Americans. Additional strategies such as role playing and dramatization, excursions, visits, and trips, and actively engaged experiences such as producing a newspaper, escorting the aged who require assistance, providing two-hour babysitting for single parents, or other community services, added to the intervention, will be compatible with the kinesthetic strengths evidenced in many adolescents internationally (Milgram, Dunn, & Price, 1993a).

EUROPEAN-AMERICANS

Following Native Americans, European Americans were the next ethnic group to emigrate to what is now the United States. After Christopher Columbus found New World in 1492, the first permanent settlement was established in 1596 by the Spanish at St. Augustine, Florida. The English founded Jamestown, Virginia, in 1607 and Plymouth, Massachusetts, in 1620. In 1623 the Dutch established New Amsterdam (New York), which was subsequently sequestered by the English in 1664. Gradually the English established 13 colonies along the eastern seaboard, but the colonists successfully converted them into an autonomous nation as a result of the American Revolutionary War, 1776.

Prior to 1880, 85 percent of the immigrants who settled in the United States were from northern or western Europe. Products of the Anglo-Saxon culture, these "old immigrants" established the base that was to become the mainstream culture of the nation. Between 1880 and 1920 the majority of immigrants came from southern and eastern Europe. These people became the cornerstone of our population of Italian, Polish, and Jewish Americans.

According to the 1990 census, approximately 200 million Caucasians comprised 80 percent of the total U.S. population. The graduation rate for this group was high: eighty one percent of the males and 85 percent of the females obtained high school diplomas.

Values

Axelson (1993) stated that the mainstream culture of the United States is based in the Christian, Anglo-Saxon tradition, which includes the following values: individual direction, determination, independence, and autonomy, along with equality among individuals; self-fulfillment and self-worth combined with a strong sense of family loyalty and the striving for gains through hard work and achievement; the extension of assistance to others when needed for their own development and self-fulfillment; mastery over nature and the environment; and dedication to God and moral living according to Biblical teachings.

The dominant-group thinking on cultural assimilation has changed over time. The melting pot theory of the nineteenth century held that all ethnic groups would eventually meld into a new community of people. However, bias was geared toward an acceptance of the Anglo-Saxon culture and a rejection of nonwhite cultural traditions. Recent years have seen a thrust toward cultural pluralism and the celebration of diversity. The goal is inclusion based on the belief that the dominant culture will benefit from coexistence and interaction with the cultures of minority groups (Axelson, 1993).

There is a wide divergence of opinion concerning the teaching of values in U.S. secondary schools today. At one end of a long continuum the former secretary of education, William Bennett, held that fundamental Judeo–Christian values of patriotism, self-discipline, thrift, honesty, and respect for elders must be taught. At the opposite end of that same continuum, Richard Cohen of the *Washington Post* postulated that life is a series of problems unresponsive to "antiquated" appeals to values; rather, those problems can be resolved only with appropriate technical tools. Lewis (1990) observed that even a "value-free" position represents another set of values, and he pointed to the absurdity of interpreting the First Amendment to the Constitution to mean that all references to Christianity or God must be stricken from public school textbooks. For example, he ridiculed discussing the early Pilgrims without mentioning their religion or passing over the role of the churches in abolishing slavery.

In a multicultural society the issue of how to teach values is a critical one and no less important nor controversial than it was several centuries ago. Different educational goals appear to be based upon conflicting value systems within diverse cultures. That was cogently expressed in 1774 by Native Americans when members of the Council of Five Nations politely declined scholarships to William and Mary College offered by the American colonists:

You who are wise must know, that different nations have different conceptions about things; and you will therefore not take it amiss if our ideas of this kind of education happen not to be the same with yours. We have had some experience of it; several of our young people were formerly brought up at the college of the northern provinces; they were instructed in all your sciences; but when they came back to us . . . they were ignorant of every means of living in the woods . . . neither fit for hunters, warriors, or counselors; they were totally good for nothing. We are, however, not the less obliged by your kind offer . . . and to show our grateful sense of it, if the gentlemen of Virginia will send us a dozen of their sons, we will take great care of their education, instruct them in all we know, and make *men* of them. (Drake, cited in Berger & Thompson, 1994)

Santrock (1992) summarized the values of mainstream adolescents today by indicating that they have shown a two-decade increase in concern for their own personal well-being, with a concomitant decrease in concern for the well-being of others, particularly for the well-being of the disadvantaged. Adolescents today reveal a commitment to self-fulfillment and self-expression, yet they have evidenced a small increase in involvement in community action programs. It appears they have a strong interest in spirituality, with more than 90 percent believing in God or a universal spirit. Further, they are less experienced sexually, less permissive toward sex, and value religion more if they attend church frequently than when they have only a minimal or no commitment to formal religion.

It is likely that most people, regardless of ethnicity, would agree that behavior should be guided by universal ethical principles such as valuing the dignity and worth of each individual. Kohlberg (1976) identified three levels of moral development (preconventional, conventional, and postconventional reasoning) and six sequential stages. His research identified most adolescents as being at the conventional reasoning level and at either the interpersonal norms stage, in which a person values trust, caring, and loyalty to others as the basis for moral judgments, or the social morality stage, in which moral judgments are based on understanding the social order, law, justice, and duty. Kohlberg perceived a strong correlation between cognitive development and moral development, and he observed that the moral development of adolescents could be affected positively if they received instruction in rational decision making, problem solving, and inductive and deductive reasoning.

Learning-Styles Research

Within the cognitive domain of learning styles, research comparing ethnic groups indicates that European Americans tend to be more field-independent than African Americans and Hispanic Americans, who demonstrate greater field-dependence (Hudgens, 1993; Perney, 1976; Ramirez & Price-Williams, 1974). However, as pointed out previously, these ethnic differences tend to decrease when socioeconomic status (Ritzinger, 1971) and achievement levels (Shade, 1983) are considered, with greater field independence among middle-class achieving students and greater field dependence among lower-class underachieving youth. The field-independent student is described as able to visually structure or select and use relevant information embedded in a larger interrelated context.

A number of researchers (Kaufman & Kaufman, 1983; Krywaniuk, 1974; Moore, 1984) compared Caucasians with Native Americans and found Caucasians higher on sequential processing skill and lower on simultaneous processing. These findings were supported by Keefe and Monk (1986), who used the LSP to test 3,866 Caucasian secondary-school students. In comparison with students in the four other ethnic groups described in this chapter, Caucasians ranked highest in sequential processing skill, a skill that correlates significantly with field independence. Other LSP cognitive subscale findings that significantly differentiated among the ethnic groups, as reported by Keefe and Monk (1986), were that Caucasians ranked third behind Asian Americans and Hispanic Americans on the analytic subscale and Caucasians ranked second behind Asian-Americans on the spatial-rotational pattern recognition skill subscale.

Cattey (1980) compared Anglo Americans to Chinese Americans and Navajo Indians and found that Anglos were more left-hemisphere dominant and thus tended to employ rational, inductive reasoning and sequential processing styles to a greater extent than did the other two ethnic groups.

To summarize the research on the cognitive-style strengths of European Americans: Overall they tend to be more field independent, sequential processors, and left-hemisphere dominant. As a group they also have considerable skill in spatial pattern recognition in comparison with other ethnic groups.

Six correlational studies compared the learning-style characteristics of Caucasians with other ethnic groups. Chiu (1993) contrasted secondary school Taiwanese Americans and Anglos. Jalali (1988) studied fourth through sixth-grade African, Chinese, Mexican, and Greek Americans. Sims (1988) examined the styles of third- and fourth-grade Caucasians, African, and Mexican Americans. Jacobs (1987) assessed middle school high-, middle-, and low-achieving African-American and European-American students. Lam-Phoon (1986) compared the learning styles of Asian Americans, Caucasians, and Asians in Singapore who were enrolled in college. And Dunn, Griggs, and Price (1993a) compared fourth- and fifth-grade Mexican-American and European-American students.

Within the environmental stimulus, a number of researchers reported that Caucasians preferred warmer temperatures while studying than Taiwanese Americans (Chiu, 1993), Mexican Americans (Dunn, Griggs, & Price, 1993a), and Asian Americans (Lam-Phoon, 1986). European Americans specified a need for informal design while studying in contrast with Chinese Americans and Mexican Americans, who desired formality (Dunn, Griggs, & Price, 1993a; Jalali, 1988). Additional findings were that European Americans preferred sound and bright light while concentrating, whereas African Americans preferred quiet (Sims, 1988) and dim lighting (Jacobs, 1987).

The element within the emotional domain that was identified as significant most frequently was responsibility or conformity. Caucasians were more conforming than Taiwanese Americans (Chiu, 1993), African Americans (Jalali, 1988), and Asian Americans (Lam-Phoon, 1986). Jacobs (1987) found that European American underachievers were less persistent than African American underachievers, who were significantly more nonconforming. There was a discrepancy in the degree of structure preferred as reported by Sims (1988), who cited high structure needs for Caucasians in comparison with African Americans; whereas Jalali (1988) reported that Greek Americans preferred considerably less structure than Mexican, Chinese, and African Americans. Although the students in both studies were comparable in age, geographic and ethnic subgroup differences could account for the disparate findings.

The sociological stimulus revealed congruent findings, with Caucasians preferring to study independently and needing less variety, whereas Chinese Americans (Chiu, 1993) and Mexican Americans (Dunn, Griggs, & Price, 1993a; Jalali, 1988) were peer oriented and needed a variety of sociological groupings. Gender differences were reported on the need for variety; both Caucasian and Mexican-American females needed more variety than the males of those ethnic groups (Dunn, Griggs, & Price, 1993a). Caucasians were more teacher and parent motivated than were Taiwanese Americans (Chiu, 1993), but less so than African Americans (Jacobs, 1987).

The most significant perceptual difference among the various ethnic groups was auditory. Caucasians had stronger auditory perception than

Taiwanese-Americans (Chiu, 1993), African Americans (Jacobs, 1987, Jalali, 1988), and Mexican Americans (Dunn, Griggs, & Price, 1993a), but less strong auditory perception than Asians in Singapore (Sims, 1988). Caucasians were less visual than African Americans and Asians (Lam-Phoon, 1986; Sims, 1988) and less kinesthetic than African Americans (Jalali, 1988). Caucasians needed more mobility and intake while learning than did Chinese Americans (Chiu, 1993; Jalali, 1988) and Mexican Americans (Sims, 1988). The peak energy time for Caucasians was evening, as opposed to morning for Mexican Americans and Chinese Americans (Jalali, 1988; Sims, 1988) and afternoon for Taiwanese Americans, who reported low energy levels in the evening (Chiu, 1993).

Counseling and Teaching Implications

Educational and counseling theoretical frameworks and applications to practice are based on western European foundations and cultural values. These models assume that the student or counselee is highly motivated to examine personal concerns and problems; is analytic, verbal, and able to identify emotional issues; and remains open to disclosing experiences that might be labeled personal and private by individuals of some ethnic groups.

Sue and Sue (1990) observed that many counseling goals are based on European-American values. One value is the importance of "insight" in understanding and resolving personal and interpersonal concerns or issues—an attitude that certain socioeconomic groups and ethnic minorities do not particularly value. Another value is the use of self-disclosure to facilitate the counseling process, a perception that conflicts with values of privacy and hesitancy to show emotions among some minorities. Also important in European-American culture is the definition of sound mental health in terms of competence, autonomy, resistance to stress, and self-actualization, all of which conflict with some minority values that prize collective interpersonal effort above individualism. The definition of abnormal behavior is based on the extent to which behavior deviates from white middle-class norms. European Americans place emphasis on the development of long-range goals as opposed to interest in immediate concrete, short-range goals—the focus of some minority group members. In addition, European Americans place emphasis upon rational, analytic, linear, and verbal interventions that stress the discovery of cause-effect relationships; these contrast with some ethnic approaches that are intuitive, holistic, and nonverbal.

Caucasians are more likely than other groups to seek and pursue counseling. A number of studies revealed that Caucasians are more likely to utilize counseling services and persist in counseling in comparison with minority group members, who are more likely to terminate a relationship after one session (Ivey & Authier, 1978; Sue, 1977; Sue, McKinney, Allen, & Hall, 1974).

Chapter 3 addressed the importance of identity formation during adolescence. Rowe, Bennett, and Atkinson (1994) viewed white racial consciousness as part of identity development, asserting that individuals may or may not have achieved white racial consciousness. Individuals with an unachieved racial consciousness often represent one of three possible types: (1) the avoidant type, who demonstrates a lack of consideration of his or her own white identity as well as an avoidance of concern for ethnic minority issues; (2) the dependent type, whose views are conditioned by those of dominant family members; and (3) the dissonant type, who is confused about a sense of white racial consciousness and ethnic minority issues. Conversely, individuals who have achieved racial consciousness may represent one of three possible types: (1) the dominant type, characterized by a strong ethnocentric perspective that justifies the dominance of ethnic minority persons by the majority culture; (2) the conflictive type, who is opposed to obvious discriminatory practices but is usually opposed to any program or procedure designed to reduce or eliminate discrimination; and (3) the reactive type, who is aware of discrimination as a significant feature in U.S. society and vigilant in identifying inequitable acts (Rowe, Bennett, & Atkinson, 1994). Within typical secondary schools are European-American adolescents who adhere to these six differing levels of racial consciousness. Ethics and morality require that educators and counselors help adolescents develop a sense of racial consciousness congruent with democratic principles.

In comparison with other ethnic groups, European-Americans are more likely to respond to traditional counseling interventions that use an analytic, rational, and inductive reasoning approach. Strategies, such as rational-emotive therapy, which involve an A-B-C approach in which A is the activating event, B is the belief system (which is generally negative, self-defeating, and amenable to change), and C is the resulting feeling or emotion, are more likely to be embraced by mainstream adolescents (Ellis, 1962). The role of the counselor in using this model is to help adolescents describe the activating event, crisis, or experience; identify the belief system that causes negative emotions; assist in identifying alternative, more self-enhancing beliefs; select an alternative belief and engage in self-talk to reinforce that belief; and practice the resulting new behaviors in a social situation.

Summary

The background, values, learning-styles research, and implications for counseling and teaching the five major culturally diverse groups in the United States have been discussed in this chapter. Multicultural education is concerned with applying educational theory and practice to the particular cultural needs, expectations, and values of various ethnic groups to enhance learning and development.

Each individual is unique and must be viewed as influenced by personal experiences, specific cultural climates, and common human interactions (Axelson, 1993). The danger of assuming that all members of the same cultural group think, learn, feel, or behave in the same manner is cogently stated by Lee and Richardson (1991):

In discussing the concept of multicultural counseling (and teaching), there is the danger of assuming that all people from a specific group are the same and that one methodological approach is universally applicable in any counseling (or teaching) intervention with them. Indeed, when reviewing much of the psychological and counseling literature related to multicultural issues, one might be left with the impression that there is an all-encompassing reality for a particular cultural group and that all people from that group act, feel, and think in a homogeneous fashion. Such an impression often leads to a monolithic perspective on the experiences of a specific group of people as well as to stereotypical thinking in which individuals are considered indistinguishable from one another in terms of attitudes, behavior, and values. Counseling (educational) professionals with such a perspective run the risk of approaching clients not as distinct human beings with individual experiences, but rather merely as cultural stereotypes.(p. 6)

Research on the learning styles of various ethnic groups is limited because of several factors:

1. Demographic variables other than ethnicity that affect learning style often are not isolated; factors such as gender, socioeconomic class, geographic region, primary language, religious affiliation, and number of generations in the United States are frequently not considered because the sample sizes are too small to introduce multiple variables.

2. There is great diversity within ethnic groups. For example, there are markedly different cultural backgrounds among adolescents from Columbia who may be illegal aliens; teenagers from Puerto Rico, who may spend five months in the New York City public schools and the remainder of the academic year in the San Juan schools; and third-generation Cuban youth whose grandparents arrived shortly after the revolution in 1959 and were employed as professors in the California university system. Although these three groups of adolescents may be Hispanic, their individual, family, and cultural attitudes may be equally as diverse. Frequently research is focused on only one of these cultural subgroups, such as the Puerto Rican adolescents in New York City, and the findings cannot be generalized validly to include all Hispanics.

3. The instruments used to assess learning styles vary greatly as to reliability, validity, and definition, and they range from unidimensional instruments that measure the extent of field dependence or independ-

ence to multidimensional, carefully constructed instruments such as the LSI or LSP. Using unidimensional instruments results in limited findings with minimal implications for the teaching and counseling practice.

4. The learning-styles research presented in this chapter is limited to correlational studies that focus on the significant differences among various culturally diverse groups. When assessing culturally different adolescents on the 22 elements that constitute learning styles, one may find significant differences among Hispanic Americans, Asian Americans, and African Americans on the element of structure; nonetheless, all three groups may cluster more toward the high side of this continuum than the low. Thus it is risky to conclude, for example, that Asian Americans have a low need for structure in comparison with other groups when, in fact, they may require a relatively high degree of structure, though much less than many members of other groups. Although there are quality experimental research studies that measure the impact of accommodating different learning-style preferences through complementary teaching and counseling interventions, most of these studies do not isolate the variable of cultural difference.

5. On any 1 of the 22 elements of learning style, the within-cultural-group differences are greater than the between-cultural-group differences. For example, although African Americans and European Americans differ significantly as a group on the construct of field dependence versus field independence, with African Americans being more field-dependent, the differences within both groups are broad, ranging from individuals who are highly field-dependent to those who are strongly field-independent.

Keeping these limitations in mind, the correlational research that revealed significant differences among the various ethnic groups is summarized in Figure 4.1. These findings suggest that, for example, within the African-American group overall one would expect to find more adolescents with a stronger kinesthetic perception than among a comparable group of Caucasians. However, one would also expect to find many Caucasians with strong kinesthetic perception, as well as many African Americans who reject kinesthetic approaches to learning. Therefore counseling and teaching of adolescents cannot be approached with a "cultural-group mindset." Instead, the learning-style strengths of each student must be assessed, and interventions must be designed that are compatible with these preferences. Given this prescription, the instructional interventions described in the following chapters, including tactual and kinesthetic resources, programmed learning sequences, contract activity packages, and multisensory instructional packages, are designed to accommodate adolescents from diverse cultural groups with a wide variety of learning-style preferences.

Figure 4.1
Correlational Research Findings on the Learning Styles of the Major Cultural Groups in the United States*

Stimulus Area	Relatively Low			Relatively High →	
Cognitive Style:					
1. Field Dependence vs. Independence	African-American	Hispanic-American	Native-American		European-American
2. Analytic Skill	Native-American	African-American	European-American	Hispanic-American	Asian American
3. Sequential Processing Skill	African-American	Native-American	Asian-American	Hispanic-American	European-American
4. Simultaneous Processing	European-American				Native-American
5. Spatial Pattern Recognition	Native-American	African-American	Hispanic-American	European-American	Asian-American

76

Environmental:

1. Noise Level (Quiet vs. sound)	African-American	Hispanic-American	Asian-American		European-American
2. Light-(Dim vs. Bright)	African-American			Hispanic-American	European-American
3. Temperature-(Cool vs. Warm)	Native-American	Hispanic-American	Asian-American	European-American	African-American
4. Design (Informal vs. Formal)	European-American	African-American	Native-American	Hispanic-American	Asian-American

Emotional

1. Motivation	Native-American				Asian-American
2. Persistence	Native-American				Asian-American
3. Responsible	African-American	Asian-American	Hispanic-American	European-American	
4. Structure	African-American	European-American	Hispanic-American	Asian American	

Sociological Stimulus

Alone vs. Peers	European-American	Asian-American	Hispanic-American	African-American	Native-American
Authority Figures	Asian-American		European American	African-American	
Varied	European-American	African-American	Asian-American	Hispanic-American	Native-American

Figure 4.1 (continued)

Stimulus Area	Relatively Low			Relatively High	
Physiological Stimulus					
Auditory	Native-American	African-American	Hispanic-American	Asian-American	European-American
Visual	Hispanic-American	European-American	Asian-American	African-American	Native-American
Tactile	no significant differences among groups				
Kinesthetic	European-American	Native-American	Hispanic-American	African-American	
Intake	Asian-American	Native-American	Hispanic-American	European-American	African-American
Morning vs. Evening	Asian-American	Hispanic-American	European-American	African-American	
Afternoon	Native-American	Asian-American	African-American		
Late Morning	no significant differences among groups				
Mobility	Asian-American	Native-American	Hispanic-American	African-American	European-American

Note: Figure 4.1 merely shows relative standing on a continuum and may be used only in concert with the text in Chapter 4.

Chapter 5

Identifying Adolescents' Individual Learning-Style Strengths

WHY USE AN IDENTIFICATION INSTRUMENT?

Learning style encompasses at least 21 different variables, including each person's environmental, emotional, sociological, physiological, and cognitive processing preferences. Thus, a comprehensive instrument that measures all or most variables has a distinct advantage over more limited instruments, such as those that assess only one or two variables on a bipolar continuum (Griggs, Griggs, Dunn, & Ingham, 1994). The single variable that a narrowly focused instrument fails to examine may be the one most crucial to a student's achievement. It is necessary therefore to consider all characteristics of style likely to affect how each student learns.

Even experienced teachers cannot identify through observation all the variables of a student's learning style. Some variables of style are not observable, and certain behaviors associated with other variables often are misinterpreted (Beaty, 1986; Dunn, Dunn, & Price, 1977; Marcus, 1977). For example, frequently adolescents who do not sit quietly are perceived as hyperactive, immature, emotionally disturbed, or troublesome. Teachers rarely consider that such young people may have an unusually high energy level, require an informal seating design, be kinesthetic learners who learn best when actively involved, and need mobility, concentrating best when moving from one section of the room to another while learning. Any of these characteristics can be accommodated once the student's style is certain. Dependent on the trait and the teacher's willingness to experiment, the student might be permitted to move from one center in the classroom to another as long as tasks are completed and provided the movement does not distract any-one with a different learning style; the student might, alternatively, be allowed to sit on a pillow, bean bag, or carpet square while concentrating or he or she might learn with a kinesthetic floor game in a quiet corner of the room.

It is important to identify learning style with a comprehensive instrument and crucial to use one that is reliable and valid, for an unreliable or invalid instrument will provide incorrect information. Experimental research verifies that students can describe their learning-style preferences accurately, but style should be clearly explained to students before they are tested.

PREPARING STUDENTS FOR LEARNING-STYLES ASSESSMENT

We know that many adolescents cannot remember three-quarters of what they either hear or read, and many of these young people do not read well. Such learners cannot feel good about themselves in an auditory/visual-dominant school. Therefore it is important to identify students' learning styles to determine the perceptual strength(s) they do have and to teach students to capitalize on their strengths for studying.

Step 1: Explain Style

Begin by explaining the differences in learning styles that exist among all classes, families, and cultures. Tell the students that their mothers' styles are likely to be different from their fathers', and their style is probably different from each classmate's.

Step 2: Give Global Examples of Different Styles

With grades 5–8, after some discussion read either *Two-of-a-Kind Learning Styles* (Pena, 1989) about Global Myrna and Analytic Victor, two middle schoolers who enjoy their leisure activities together but who must study separately because their learning styles are so different. For older students you could use *A Guide to Explaining Learning Styles to High School Students* (Bouwman, 1991) to develop an understanding of the concept of learning styles. As you read the story with your middle school or junior high school class, tape-record it and explain that you are preparing them for a learning-styles assessment. Break the small tab at the top of the tape to prevent accidental erasure of the contents. Glue the plastic box in which the tape comes to the back of the story-book. Tell the students that any time individuals wish to hear the story read again, they can use the tape attached to the back of the book and replay it as often as they wish. Record the tape so the reader hears when to turn the page. A few students will choose to hear the tape repeatedly.

Step 3: Encourage Thinking about Style

Encourage students to guess the styles of members of their own family and then to write why they believe those are their relatives' styles. After they have obtained information by interviewing family members, they can graph the styles and compare them with the styles of their classmates' families. They can guess and illustrate their own learning styles and perhaps write poems about how they *feel* knowing about their style.

Step 4: Explain That Everyone Has Learning-Style Strengths

Explain how important it is for each person to understand his or her style strengths. Accentuate that everyone has learning-style strengths, but each person's strengths are different. Introduce learning about one's strengths through a series of questions—which each person must answer truthfully—to learn how each should be taught, do homework, or study efficiently. Tell students in advance that one day in the near future you are going to give them an assessment that asks many questions about how they each prefer to learn new and difficult information. When the results are returned from that assessment, you will be able to tell each student exactly how to study to remember difficult information.

Step 5: Administer the Learning Style Inventory

The Learning Style Inventory (LSI) (Dunn, Dunn, & Price, 1989) assesses individuals' learning styles in grades 5–12. Tell students this instrument is an important and useful first step toward identifying the conditions under which each person is most likely to concentrate on, learn, and remember new and difficult academic information.

Careful analysis of each student's LSI printout reveals those elements critical to the individual's learning style. Further, the LSI aids in prescribing the type of environment, instructional resources, social groupings, and motivating factors that maximize personal achievement. Tell students that learning style is based on complex reactions to many different things in their lives (stimuli, feelings, and established patterns). As a result, patterns tend to develop and repeat themselves whenever each person concentrates on new and/or difficult material.

The words *think, learn, read, write,* and *concentrate* are used interchangeably throughout the LSI; tell students it is not necessary for them to differentiate among their meanings. Comparisons of answers to questions that include these words, and to others that seem to ask the same thing in varied ways, contribute to determining the accuracy of the student's overall profile.

ASSESSING STUDENTS THROUGH THE LEARNING STYLE INVENTORY

The LSI does not measure underlying psychological factors, value systems, or the quality of attitudes. Rather, it yields information concerned with the patterns through which learning occurs. It summarizes the environmental, emotional, sociological, and physiological preferences a student has for learning, not *why* they exist. In addition, by examining the cluster of preferences related to sound, light, design, persistence, and intake, the LSI often provides insight into the processing style of strongly global and strongly analytic respondents. Finally, the LSI evidences how students prefer to learn, not the skills they use to do so (Dunn, Dunn, & Price, 1989, pp. 5–6).

The LSI uses dichotomous items and can be completed in approximately 30–40 minutes. It reports a Consistency Key to reveal the accuracy with which each respondent has answered the questions. The Ohio State University's National Center for Research in Vocational Education published the results of its two-year study of instruments that diagnose learning styles and reported that the LSI had established impressive reliability and face and construct validity (Kirby, 1979). Since examination by that center almost two decades ago, the LSI has evidenced remarkable predictive validity (Dunn, Bruno, Sklar, & Beaudry 1990; Dunn, Della Valle, Dunn, Geisert, Sinatra, & Zenhausern, 1986; Dunn, Dunn, Primavera, Sinatra, & Virostko, 1987; Dunn, Giannitti, Murray, Geisert, Rossi, & Quinn, 1990; Dunn, Krimsky, Murray, & Quinn, 1985; Lenehan, Dunn, Ingham, Signer & Murray, 1994).

In a comparative analysis of the style conceptualization and psychometric standards of nine different instruments that measure learning-style instructional preference, the Dunn, Dunn, and Price LSI was the only one rated as having good or very good reliability and validity (Curry, 1987). Of the 18 instruments reviewed in the document, including an additional 9 concerned with information processing, the LSI was one of only 3 with good or very good reliability and validity. The LSI is an assessment that is easy to both administer and interpret. Perhaps because of that, Keefe (1982) revealed that it "is the most widely used in elementary and secondary schools" (p. 52).

INFORMATION PROVIDED BY THE LEARNING STYLE INVENTORY

The LSI assesses individual preferences in the following areas: (1) immediate environment (sound, light, temperature, and seating design); (2) emotionality (motivation, persistence, responsibility/conformity; and need for internal or external structure); (3) sociological style (learning

Figure 5.1
Dunn and Dunn Learning Styles Model

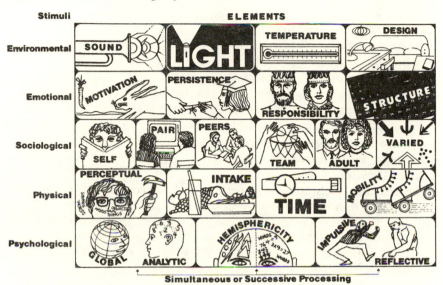

alone, in a pair, as part of a small group or team, with peers, with an authoritative or collegial adult, and/or either in a variety of ways or in a consistent pattern); (4) physiological set (auditory, visual, tactual, and/or kinesthetic perceptual preferences; food or liquid intake, early morning, late morning, afternoon, or evening, time-of-day energy levels, and mobility needs; and through correlation with sound, light, design, persistence, peer orientation, and intake scores (Dunn, Bruno, Sklar, & Beaudry, 1990; Dunn, Cavanaugh, Eberle, & Zenhausern 1982), indications of global (right) or analytic (left) cognitive/psychological processing inclinations (see Figure 5.1).

The LSI

- permits students to identify how they prefer to learn and also indicates the degree to which their responses are consistent;
- provides a computerized summary of each student's preferred learning style; that summary is called an Individual Profile (see Figure 5.2);
- suggests a basis for redesigning the classroom environment to complement many students' multiple styles;
- describes with whom each student is likely to achieve most effectively, for example, alone, in a pair, with two or more classmates, with a teacher, or dependent on the task, with students with similar interests or talents; it also describes whether all or none of these combinations are acceptable.

- explains for whom to provide options and alternatives and for whom direction or structure is appropriate;

- sequences the perceptual strengths through which individuals should begin studying and then reinforce new and difficult information and explains how each student should study and/or do homework (Dunn & Klavas, 1992);

- indicates the methods through which individuals are likely to achieve well, for example, contract activity packages (CAPs), programmed learning sequences (PLSs), multisensory instructional packages (MIPs), tactual manipulatives, and/ or kinesthetic games, or any combination thereof;

- extrapolates information concerning which children are nonconforming and determines how to work with those who are;

- pinpoints when is the best time of day for each adolescent to be scheduled for difficult core subjects, thus permitting grouping students for instruction based on their learning style energy highs;

- itemizes for whom snacks are an integral part of the learning process (Mac-Murren, 1985);

- notes for whom movement while learning may accelerate the learning process; and

- suggests for whom analytic or global approaches are likely to be important.

Figure 5.2
Learning Style of Carina George

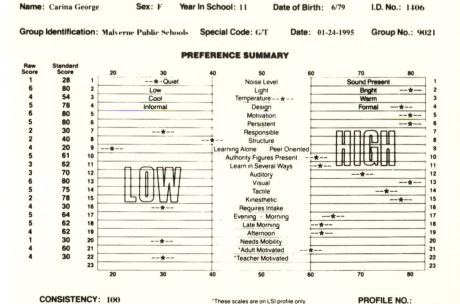

Name: Carina George   **Sex:** F   **Year In School:** 11   **Date of Birth:** 6/79   **I.D. No.:** 1406

Group Identification: Malverne Public Schools   **Special Code:** G/T   **Date:** 01-24-1995   **Group No.:** 9021

PREFERENCE SUMMARY

Raw Score	Standard Score		Scale	
1	28	1	--★-Quiet / Noise Level / Sound Present	1
6	80	2	Low / Light / Bright --★--	2
4	54	3	Cool / Temperature --★-- / Warm	3
5	78	4	Informal / Design / Formal --★--	4
6	80	5	Motivation --★--	5
5	80	6	Persistent --★--	6
2	30	7	--★-- Responsible	7
2	40	8	--★-- Structure	8
4	20	9	--★-- Learning Alone Peer Oriented	9
5	61	10	Authority Figures Present --★--	10
3	62	11	Learn in Several Ways --★--	11
3	70	12	Auditory --★--	12
6	80	13	Visual --★--	13
5	75	14	Tactile --★--	14
2	78	15	Kinesthetic --★--	15
4	30	16	--★-- Requires Intake	16
5	64	17	Evening - Morning --★--	17
5	62	18	Late Morning --★--	18
4	62	19	Afternoon --★--	19
1	30	20	--★-- Needs Mobility	20
4	60	21	*Adult Motivated --★--	21
4	30	22	--★-- *Teacher Motivated	22
		23		23

CONSISTENCY: 100   *These scales are on LSI profile only.   **PROFILE NO.:**

The Individual Profile

The Individual Profile for the LSI includes the student's name or number, gender, date LSI was administered, school, teacher, grade, and class number. A Consistency Score, which indicates how accurate the responses are for this particular student, is provided in the lower left-hand corner of each Individual Profile (see Figure 5.3). To interpret an individual's profile, use the Preference Summary.

Note that the rectangle which constitutes the Preference Summary for each student has numbers beginning with 20 at the upper-left-hand side through to 80 at the upper right-hand side. Take the following steps.

1. Bracket the upper section of the Preference Summary to include everything between 70 and 80. Label this section "strong preference." Any learning style element that falls within 70–80 on an Individual Profile is extremely important. That person will always learn new and difficult information more easily, and retain it better, when that particular element is responded to. Thus, in Figure 5.2, Carina George will always learn better in bright than in low lighting; at a conventional desk and seat than on an easy chair; when given a variety of resources or methods than with patterns or routines.

Figure 5.3
Learning Style of Shabob Ahman

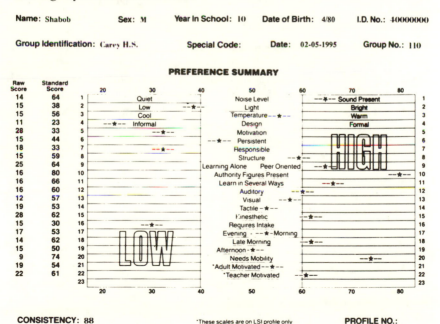

2. Bracket the upper section to include everything between 60 and 69. Label this section "preference." A preference is almost as important as a strong preference, but the person with a preference has some limited options. That learner will usually or often learn new and difficult information more easily, and retain it better, when that particular element is addressed. The learner, however, can occasionally learn well despite the preference. It is important to remember that more than three-fifths of learning style appears to be biologically imposed (Restak, 1979; Thies, 1979). Thus, it is not easy for students to compensate for their preferences, and it is very difficult indeed to overcome a strong preference.

3. Bracket the upper section to include everything between 20 and 29. Label this section "opposite strong preference." An opposite strong preference is just as important as a strong preference, but it responds to the opposite of the element printed in the center of the Preference Summary. Thus, Carina George (Figure 5.2), who scored 28 on sound, will always work better in a quiet, rather than in a noisy, environment. She is not an adolescent who can work well with music or any kind of sound while she is concentrating on new and/or difficult academic material.

4. Bracket the upper section to include everything between 30 and 39. Label that section "opposite preference." An opposite preference is just as important as a preference, and almost as important as an opposite strong preference, but the individual can occasionally overcome an opposite preference, though not too frequently.

5. Bracket the entire middle-upper section of the Preference Summary from 41 to 59. Label this section "not important" or "it depends." Elements that fall within this middle section suggest ways that the individual may learn, but these means will be used only when the student is interested in the topic.

Thus, the LSI Individual Profile for each student represents how he or she responded to the series of questions for each subscale. That information describes how the student should be taught, with whom, in which environment, at what time of day, and with which methods or approaches (i.e., through CAPs, PLSs, MIPs, or tactual and/or kinesthetic resources). See, for example, Figure 5.2, Carina's Individual Profile. Figure 5.4, an LSI Group Profile, will also be of interest.

INTERPRETING CARINA GEORGE'S INDIVIDUAL PROFILE: WHAT IS HER LEARNING STYLE AND HOW SHOULD SHE BE TAUGHT?

When "reading" a profile, first scan the student's demographic information to learn age, gender, and Consistency Score—that is, how accurate this information is for that individual. Carina is a seventeen-year-old girl in the eleventh grade. Her Consistency Score (lower left corner) is 100 percent. You may use any data with a Consistency Score of 70 or above; do not use information on an Individual Profile with below 70 percent consistency. If that occurs, and you have read *Two-of-a-Kind*

Figure 5.4

**LSI Group Profile Indicating Percentage of Students Who Require Each
Learning-Style Element**

Price Systems, Inc., Box 1818, Lawrence, Ks. 66044-1818

RESPONSES BY SUBSCALE - standard score >=50   7-23-1995

GROUP IDENTIFICATION: LRNG. STYLES NET NUMBER   GROUP NO.: 781

LSI AREAS	SUBSCALE	RESPONSES	PERCENTAGE
NOISE	1	10	50.00
LIGHT	2	1	5.00
TEMPERATURE	3	3	15.00
DESIGN	4	2	10.00
MOTIVATION	5	3	15.00
PERSISTENT	6	1	5.00
RESPONSIBLE	7	4	20.00
STRUCTURE	8	8	40.00
LEARNING ALONE/PEER ORIENTED	9	8	40.00
AUTHORITY FIGURES	10	5	25.00
LEARN IN SEVERAL WAYS	11	2	10.00
AUDITORY	12	1	5.00
VISUAL	13	3	15.00
TACTILE	14	7	35.00
KINESTHETIC	15	5	25.00
REQUIRES INTAKE	16	9	45.00
EVENING-MORNING	17	7	35.00
LATE-MORNING	18	0	0.00
AFTERNOON	19	6	30.00
NEEDS MOBILITY	20	4	20.00

NUMBER OF STUDENTS 20   TOTAL RESPONSES 89

Learning Styles or *A Guide Explaining Learning Styles to High School Students*, retest and send the new answer sheet to Price Systems; it will be reprocessed without cost.

Environmental Information

Scan the first four elements of the environmental stimulus and determine each student's preferences for a classroom that is either quiet (40 or below) or sound-filled (60 or above), well illuminated (60 or above) or softly illuminated (40 or below), cool (40 or below) or warm (60 or above), and formal (60 or above) or informal (40 or below). Carina prefers quiet, and because her LSI score is below 30, her preference is strong. She also strongly prefers bright light and seating at a conventional desk. Scored in the 41–59 range, temperature is not important to her. When interested in what she is learning or doing, Carina is unaware of temperature, except when it is in the extreme; when bored, Carina will become aware of temperature discomfort.

Emotional Information

Carina is highly motivated and persistent (scores in the strong preference range of 70 or above) and does not require external structure, sometimes preferring to provide her own structure. Her low responsibility score means that she is low on responsibility to other people's beliefs; she is a nonconformist and likes to do things her way. When working with nonconforming adolescents like Carina, experiment with doing the following three things.

1. Explain why what the youngster is to do is important to you.
2. Speak collegially; do not address the nonconforming student in an authoritative or directive tone. Instead, make believe you are talking with the teacher next door (assuming you respect the teacher next door!).
3. Give the student outcome choices, so that he or she can decide how to show you that what you requested has been completed.

For example, you might say, "Carina, it is important to me that you translate this chapter into a contract activity package you can use. I know you can progress faster than most students and I do not want you to be bored. However, if you do not find the material interesting, speak with the librarian, Mrs. Jiminez; perhaps she can help you find multimedia related to this topic. You might see whether our local museum can add information that we do not have in the school library. And if you prefer, you can translate the material into a videotape—or another media form— that might make the topic more interesting. Which of these alternatives makes sense to you?" Once a nonconformist commits to a choice, he or she will usually follow through.

Teachers often believe that having motivated, persistent students in their classes makes teaching easy. All the elements of Carina's Learning Style Profile show us that she is a student who remembers easily by listening, seeing, or reading; by taking notes; or through using manipulatives. She also learns well experientially. Because she is motivated, she enjoys learning; because she is persistent, once she begins an assignment or project, she continues until it has been completed. Thus, she works attentively and finishes tasks before most of her classmates. Because she is a motivated nonconformist, she will not hesitate to tell her teacher that she had done the assignment and requires it to be corrected (she scores high on Authority Figure Present and thus wants feedback from her teacher.) If told to wait for others to complete their work, she will say she is ready to continue.

Carina needs little external social approval for the things she wants to do. Thus, an adolescent like Carina who has completed her assignment and is motivated to learn, who is highly persistent and nonconformist, will ask for individual attention. If her teacher is whole-class oriented or does not understand that this adolescent's learning style dictates her need for constant feedback from the authorities in her life, tension is likely to develop. Many gifted students experience such frustration, and many teachers do not understand why they do not perform well in school or become angry with schooling in general.

Sociological Information

Carina is a strong learning-alone student (scoring only 20 on the LSI Individual Profile); thus, she is not peer oriented. Carina may be offered the choice of working with peers when she wishes, but she should be permitted to do difficult assignments on her own. Carina is not a good candidate for cooperative learning or small-group techniques unless she opts for those strategies when permitted to choose.

Despite her high nonconformity score (Responsibility, LSI score below 31), Carina wants feedback from the authority or authorities in her life (LSI score of 61). She also likes variety (LSI score of 62 on Learning in Several Ways) and so becomes bored quickly when required to engage in patterns and routines. Given this information about Carina, her teacher would be wise to permit her to choose alternative ways of learning.

Perceptual Strengths

Most people have just a single perceptual strength, as indicated by LSI scores of 60 or higher. Scores of between 41 and 59 indicate that a person *can* remember what is learned through that modality, but only if interested in what is being studied. Carina's scores are all above 70, indicating that she remembers easily what she hears, what she sees or reads, what she writes or manipulates, and what she experiences. Thus, she has multisensory perceptual strengths. Unlike most students, Carina does not need to sequence her perceptual exposures when introduced to new and difficult material. She can learn through all senses. That gift contributes substantially to high school achievement and makes it easy to conjecture that Carina performs very well academically, particularly because her high perceptual strengths are combined with high motivation and high persistence.

Other Physiological Information

Carina's low intake score (below 31) indicates no need for snacking while learning. Her chronobiological scores (60 or above on every segment of Time of Day) suggest a consistently high energy level. Whereas most people have only a single energy high each day, Carina has three. Such students may be deemed hyperactive by teachers who do not understand why they never sit still. Such students have so much energy, they cannot contain it.

Visualize a student with high energy levels who is motivated and persistent, who completes work quickly because of strong perceptual strengths and a need for variety, and it is easy to understand why that student is always "on the go." Because few people experience such energy drive, that youngster appears hyperactive. Consider, too, Tingley-Michaelis's (1983) admonition that youngsters labeled hyperactive in school were many times fidgety because their teachers wanted them "to think about something" when, instead, the children needed "to do something" (p. 26). Tingley-Michaelis also chastised teachers for believing that activities prevented rather than enhanced learning. Indeed, when previously restless youngsters were reassigned to classes that did not require passivity, their behaviors were rarely noticed (Fadley & Hosler, 1979; Koester & Farley, 1977).

Observe Carina's low mobility score (30 on the LSI); she does not need to be in constant motion. Instead, she needs to learn experientially, through doing. This type of adolescent should be permitted to choose from among approved alternative projects and should be enabled to complete them through any perceptual strength. Thus, Carina might demonstrate her learning by creating a building or miniature setting, painting or drawing, dramatizing or role playing, graphing or charting, and so forth. Those activities should respond to her need for variety, multiple perceptual strengths, preference for learning alone, and need to complete many tasks at her own fast pace.

Adult Motivation Scores

Although Carina wants to please some adult in her life, that adult is probably a parent or an-other-than-teacher figure. Her low teacher motivation score (30 on the LSI) suggests she is not in need of pleasing her teacher, although she does want feedback (high on Authority Figure Present).

Analysis of LSI Data from Individual Profile

Let's consider what a teacher might do to improve instruction for Carina, given her LSI Individual Profile. In terms of the classroom environment, Carina might be seated near a window or under a direct light. Because of her need for quiet, her desk should be away from the center of activity, perhaps even in a corner of the room. If no carpeting is on the floor, a small rug placed beneath Carina's desk and seat will help to absorb sound.

CAPs would be an excellent instructional method for Carina. They provide the choices nonconformists require and suggest multisensory materials a good student like Carina could use easily and well. The teacher should set aside some time to review Carina's work periodically, add comments to her grade to provide the feedback she needs, and permit her a range of means to demonstrate mastery of the objectives. Because Carina is capable of becoming an independent learner, she should be able to design her own activity, reporting, and resource alternatives after just a few experiences using the CAP system. Eventually she would develop the ability to read textbook information and convert it into a CAP through which she could teach herself anything either required by teachers or of interest to her.

Determining Global or Analytic Processing Inclinations

Previous studies revealed correlations between individual learning-style characteristics and global and analytic processing styles (Cody, 1983; Dunn, Bruno, Sklar, & Beaudry, 1990; Dunn, Cavanaugh, Eberle, & Zenhausern 1982). Global learners tend to prefer learning with what conventional teachers perceive as distractions—sound (music, tapping, or conversation), soft illumination (covering one's eyes or wearing sunglasses indoors), an informal design (lounging comfortably), being peer oriented (wanting to work with a friend), and needing intake (snacks) while studying. Furthermore, globals tend not to be persistent; they begin working with a burst of energy that lasts for a relatively short period, and then they want a break. Globals return to their task and work again for another short interval, and then want another break. Globals also dislike working on one thing at a time; they often become engaged in multiple tasks simultaneously and concentrate on several in varying sequences. Thus globals may begin an assignment in the middle or at the end.

Analytics, on the other hand, tend to prefer learning in silence, with bright lighting, and a formal design—a conventional classroom. They rarely eat, chew, drink, or smoke while learning; instead, they eat afterward. Analytics tend to be persistent; they may not always start an assignment immediately, but once they do begin, they have a strong emotional urge to continue until the task is done or until they come to a place where they feel they can stop.

These five elements—sound, light, design, persistence, and intake—correlate significantly ($p \leq .01$) with processing style. Many global learners also prefer to learn with peers and have strong tactual perceptual preferences. This is true of many fewer analytics at the high school level.

It is not necessary to have all five elements to be either a global or an analytic processor; having three elements of the same group indicates tendencies in that direction. Thus, Carina prefers quiet, bright light, a traditional desk and chair, and no intake; also, she is persistent. Thus, looking again at the Individual Profile of Carina, we see that she has five analytic qualities, and thus so the teacher would be safe to assume that Carina learns best through step-by-step sequential lessons that begin with the data or details and gradually build up to an understanding.

Implications for Counseling Carina

The use of self-management strategies in counseling Carina is indicated because she is (1) highly motivated and persistent, (2) independent, (3) strong perceptually, and (4) highly analytic. Through the use of a self-management program Carina can direct her own behavioral change, presuming the counselor has explained the steps involved and will meet with her periodically to offer support. Such self-management can be used to decrease or eliminate self-defeating behaviors such as smoking, obesity, procrastination, insomnia, depression, alcohol abuse, perfectionism, or test anxiety. Similarly, this intervention can be used to increase self-enhancing behaviors such as exercising, increasing academic achievement in science, volunteering in the community, or finding part-time summer employment.

Cormier and Cormier (1991) outline a comprehensive, ten-step self-management program. Assuming that Carina is motivated to work on her problem with obesity, the counselor might work with her in the following ways:

Step 1: Standard Setting and Self-Evaluation

Carina identifies and records her eating behavior. She gathers and records baseline data on (1) when she eats (e.g., time of day); (2) what she eats, consisting of a listing of foods eaten, quantity, and caloric count if known; (3) antecedents to eating, such as what triggers her eating (e.g., watching television, studying, or going to McDonald's with friends after a movie); and (4) consequences, such as feeling bloated, having an upset stomach, or thinking negatively.

Step 2: Goal Setting

The counselor works with Carina to set a behavioral goal that is desirable, measurable, attainable, and observable. For example, Carina's goal might be to lose 15 pounds within two months—a goal that meets all the criteria specified.

Step 3: Counselor Explains Self-Management Strategies

The counselor explains to Carina how to develop a chart that will record her eating behavior, which has been problematic, together with the antecedents and consequences. The chart is a daily log in which time of day and foods eaten are recorded. Also, Carina's body weight is recorded daily. Carina will learn to recognize the triggers that stimulate eating behavior and begin to eliminate, for example, looking at the food advertisements on television by going to the next room and doing floor exercises for two or three minutes. The counselor explains the importance of self-reward following a desired response and explores rewards meaningful to Carina, possibly things like buying a new blouse with the money she has saved by not eating a hamburger and french fries when with friends.

Step 4: Carina Selects One or More Self-Management Strategies

Carina decides to use at least one of the following strategies: (1) self-monitoring and recording her eating behavior, (2) gradually eliminating the antecedents or "triggers" that precede her eating binges, or (3) rewarding herself for refraining from overeating and/or losing four or more pounds within a two-week period.

Step 5: Carina Makes A Verbal Commitment

During a counseling session, it is important to gain a verbal commitment from Carina asserting that she will follow the program outlined in Steps 2 through 4.

Step 6: Carina Seeks Social Support

It is usually helpful to tell family and friends about your goal in order to elicit social support during the period of change. The counselor might role play a meeting with Carina's mother in which Carina states: "Mom, I want to lose weight because I feel unattractive and upset. I've set a goal to lose 15 pounds during the next two months. You could really help me with this if you buy more vegetables and fruits for me to snack on and eliminate purchasing nuts, candy, and potato chips."

Step 7: Counselor Instructs Carina on Selected Strategies

The counselor continues to explain to Carina how to implement the self-management strategies explained in Step 3 and selected in Step 4. For example, the counselor shows Carina how to record her eating behaviors on a chart and designs the chart with Carina to reflect a daily log recording (1) time of day of eating; (2) specific foods eaten and caloric content, based upon a caloric listing that the counselor provides; (3) antecedent events that precede eating; (4) consequences experienced after eating; (5) body weight; and (6) positive social support received.

Step 8: Carina Keeps a Record of Strategies Used

Carina begins daily record keeping and periodically rewards herself on the achievement of subgoals. For example, her overall goal is to lose 15 pounds within a two-month period. A weekly subgoal would be to lose two of those pounds.

Step 9: Counselor Meets with Carina to Review Data

Weekly counseling sessions should be scheduled with Carina to determine whether the self-management program strategies are effective and her subgoal is being achieved. If unforeseen antecedent events, such as personal illness, have interfered with the implementation of the program, they are noted. In addition, the counselor and student consider which rewards are particularly effective.

Step 10: Self-Evaluation and Self-Reinforcement

After approximately six counseling sessions, Carina and her counselor decide whether Carina should continue with the existing program, using self-evaluation and self-reinforcement, or whether the original goal needs to be revised.

The effectiveness of any counseling intervention depends upon whether or not it results in counselee change in a desired and positive direction, and although an analysis of Carina's learning-style strengths indicates that a self-management program is congruent with her expressed preferences, her counselor may have to consider other interventions if the program proves ineffective.

INTERPRETING A SECOND LSI INDIVIDUAL PRINTOUT

Examine Figure 5.3 (p. 85), Shabob's Individual Profile. Shabob is a twelve-year-old seventh grader attending Carey Middle School. His Consistency Score is 88, which is acceptable.

Environmental Information

Scan the first four elements of the environmental stimulus and determine which learning-style elements are important to Shabob. In contrast to Carina George, who requires quiet, Shabob prefers sound—music or conversation in the background while learning. He also prefers soft lighting and an informal design; conventional seating makes Shabob physically uncomfortable and unable to concentrate on new and difficult information for any length of time. However, when permitted to study on a floor, carpet, beanbag, or pillow, Shabob's attention span increases and his power of concentration is enhanced. Temperature is not important to Shabob.

Emotional Information

Shabob is unmotivated (LSI score of 33) and has a low responsibility score (33), suggesting that he is a nonconformist (Dunn, White, & Zenhausern, 1982). When interested in what he is learning, he can be persistent and function with an average amount of structure. However, when either not interested in or unable to master the material, he has a short attention span and does not follow directions.

Sociological Information

Shabob is strongly peer oriented (LSI score of 64), wants feedback from an authority (LSI score of 80), and prefers a great deal of instructional variety rather than patterns or routines (LSI score of 66). Unlike Carina George, he does not enjoy learning alone but, rather, will perform better when permitted to learn with peers.

Perceptual Strengths

Shabob has good perceptual strengths. He remembers both the information he hears (LSI score of 60) and the information he gathers through experiences (LSI score of 62 on kinesthetic). In addition, his visual and tactual scores (57 and 53 respectively) are good when he is interested in what he is learning.

Other Physiological Information

Shabob's best time of day for difficult learning is in the late morning (LSI score of 62), but if interested, he is capable of learning at any time of day. He needs frequent mobility (LSI score of 74) and cannot sit passively for lengthy periods of time.

Adult Motivation Scores

The LSI scores that range between 41 and 59 indicate that Shabob functions best, concerning those elements, when interested in what he is learning. He does want to please an adult but will make the effort only when what he is learning holds his attention.

Shabob is strongly teacher motivated. When a student's score on Teacher Motivated is 60 or above, also examine the LSI score on Authority Figure Present. If both are 60 or above, that youngster may need an authoritative teacher—someone firm. However, if the LSI Teacher Motivated score is 60 or above and the Authority Figure Present score is 40 or below, experiment with a collegial, rather than authoritative, approach, which would appear to be a better match of teaching and learning style.

Analysis of LSI Data from Individual Printout

Shabob's low motivation may be reversed if his teacher responds to his learning-style characteristics. The conventional classroom is unmotivating to students like Shabob, who thrive in the midst of varied activities and peer interaction and who are permitted choices. Our first suggestion is to redesign a section of the classroom to permit Shabob and others like him casual, informal seating. Obviously, rules need to be established; for example, students may do their work anywhere they wish as long as they are responsive to the teacher's directions, consider others and do not distract anyone, complete their assignments, and give evidence of better grades than they earned before they were permitted to choose their working places.

Shabob needs soft lighting. Undoubtedly he will choose a section of the classroom away from the lights and windows and, perhaps, even underneath or behind furniture items. Noise not only does not disturb Shabob but probably blocks out extraneous sounds such as classmates' breathing or moving in their seats, sounds of which many of us are unaware. You might be willing to experiment with earplugs, earmuffs, clean cotton, or earphones for classmates who need quiet.

Another strategy that may motivate Shabob is to permit him to study, learn, and complete assignments with classmates, rather than alone. Many young people function poorly cognitively when required to concentrate on difficult tasks by themselves; they give up easily. Conversely, they are stimulated by interaction with others. Experiment with permitting Shabob to work with others provided that the pair or group completes the task, functions in an orderly, quiet manner, and performs as well or better than previously.

In addition to permitting Shabob to complete tasks with classmates, give him the feedback he needs. He should understand that you are trying to help him achieve better and are there to assist, question, monitor, and guide (because he needs an authoritative presence).

Shabob's perceptual strengths are varied: He is auditory (LSI score of 60) and kinesthetic (LSI score of 62), and his visual and tactual scores are all in the middle third of the Individual Profile. That midrange indicates that when interested, he is capable of remembering what he sees or reads and what he writes, draws, or expresses manipulatively. Shabob's problems are the low motivation score, his inability to adjust to traditional classroom settings, and his preference for working with others rather than alone. He also wants a variety of instructional experiences and becomes bored with patterns and routines.

He does not require intake and if interested can concentrate at any time of day, but his best, most alert period is in the late morning. Thus, he should be scheduled for his most important subject between 10:00 A.M. and 12:00 A.M.—with some variation to respond to his need for variety.

When choosing an instructional method appropriate for Shabob, keep in mind that he has good perceptual memory, wants to learn with peers, likes variety, and is a nonconformist—meaning that he requires choices and some flexibility. Ordinarily CAPs are not recommended for unmotivated learners because to succeed with them students must be independent learners, a quality not usually associated with unmotivated adolescents. However, Shabob is capable of learning with a CAP because learning comes easily to him when he is interested (no perceptual strengths below 40) and most of his problems appear to stem from the mismatch between his learning style and the traditional school environment. A CAP would let Shabob work anywhere in the classroom where he feels comfortable, with a peer or two, and would provide variety (choices of objectives, resources, and activity and reporting alternatives). However, Shabob could also work well with PLSs, which provide more structure than he necessarily needs but would permit another alternative to respond to his need for variety while learning. A MIP is unnecessary for someone with a variety of learning-style strengths, and he could use tactual/kinesthetic materials by choice if he found them attractive. However, Shabob could create those resources as part of the activity alternatives of a CAP.

Determining Global or Analytic Processing Inclinations

Here is Shabob's real problem. You may recall that while learning global people often prefer sound, soft illumination, an informal design, and intake. Also, globals are not persistent learners; they rarely stay on task for an extended period when engaged in difficult academic studies.

No wonder Shabob is unmotivated! He has five global characteristics; in addition he prefers working with peers and requires a great deal of movement rather than passivity. Traditional classrooms respond better to analytics than to globals, and Shabob's additional needs for mobility and peer interaction are more than enough to reduce his motivation to learn. Awareness of Shabob's learning style should encourage the teacher to begin new units with an anecdote (short story related to the topic and demonstrating why this subject matter is relevant and interesting), humor, illustrations, and/or symbols to gain the concentration and attention of global learners.

The second half of this book describes how to develop different delivery systems so that the same curriculum content can be taught in ways that respond to diverse students' learning-style strengths.

Implications for Counseling Shabob

The use of action-oriented group counseling strategies, such as role playing and art therapy, is indicated for Shabob because he is peer oriented, a nonconformist, unmotivated, auditory as well as kinesthetic perceptually, and global or right-dominant. Through a thematic approach in group counseling, Shabob can learn to deal more effectively with interpersonal problems by developing techniques for anger control, conflict resolution, decision making, or sharing with friends and siblings.

As Shabob's counselor, you learn he has difficulty with controlling his anger because you have received numerous referrals from his classroom teachers, the lunchroom aide, and the dean of discipline regarding his name calling, arguing with teachers, and fighting with peers. You decide to conduct group counseling sessions with seventh-grade boys and focus on interpersonal issues. You select between eight and ten boys for the group, including (1) several boys who are functioning exceptionally well interpersonally and can serve as role models for Shabob and others; (2) mostly average-functioning boys from different ethnic and cultural backgrounds; and (3) Shabob and perhaps one other boy who is immature and experiencing interpersonal problems. You interview each boy individually to explain the purpose of the group and to ascertain whether each prospective member will commit to the group and meet for approximately ten sessions at a specified time.

During the working stage of the group, in this case from three to eight sessions, introduce themes relevant to the issues and concerns members expressed during the initial group counseling stage. In the case of Shabob, the theme is anger control. Introduce anger control to accommodate Shabob's global learning style by beginning with a newspaper article such as the following:

Yesterday a thirteen-year-old was seriously wounded by a knife attack that missed hitting his heart by less than an inch. The victim is in the Intensive Care Unit at Chilton Memorial Hospital and is listed in critical condition.

Police have arrested a classmate who had been good friends with the victim until the dispute broke out; it started over a girlfriend. Sergeant Wilson quoted the assailant as saying that he "just lost his temper" and that he doesn't remember drawing or using the knife. School officials have suspended the assailant, and the case will be heard in Family Court.

Elicit group members' thoughts about to the newspaper story and pose the following questions for discussion:

- How do you think the assailant feels about this incident in retrospect?
- Are there ever incidents that justify the use of violent force?
- What other options did the assailant have for expressing his anger to the victim besides attacking him with a knife?
- Have you ever experienced "a fit of rage" in which you were out of control?

Typically, group members will express a wide range of opinions concerning how to deal with anger, ranging from irresponsible, violent acts to resolve issues to those identifying a variety of viable, effective alternatives. Counselors need to emphasize that every action has consequences, in this case school suspension and possible referral to a juvenile detention facility for the assailant. Additionally, counselors need to reinforce the positive thoughts and feelings of group members who identify responsible alternatives to resolving the issue and serve as role models for other group members.

The objectives of the group session on anger include

1. exploring the origins of anger and pointing out that anger is experienced by everyone and is neither good nor bad;
2. distinguishing between appropriate, responsible, and effective versus inappropriate, irresponsible, and ineffective responses to anger;
3. encouraging students to take personal responsibility for their own thoughts, feelings, and behaviors; and
4. participating in experiential activities during the session in order to gain insight into anger control.

Counselors can use the technique of brainstorming to help group members identify effective ways to express anger (see Chapter 6 for guidelines for brainstorming). Examples of how to channel anger through brainstorming might include the following:

- List all the ways you might channel your energy into productive work or recreational activities, such as painting, building a model plane, jogging, or playing softball to help control your anger.
- Identify all the acceptable items you may punch to "let off steam."
- Count to ten very slowly, taking a deep breath as you do so, and slowly exhale to the count of ten. Repeat this deep breathing exercise several times to help you relax.
- Pick up the phone, call a good friend, and talk out what is upsetting you.
- Close your eyes and listen to music, concentrating on the lyrics to take your mind off the situation.
- Write exactly how you feel about the situation, expressing your thoughts and feelings fully.
- Remind yourself that even though you feel angry, you are still in control of your own behavior.
- Separate yourself from the scene of conflict for a brief period of time until you can begin to think more rationally.
- Use self-talk to calm yourself.

For group members who are tactual and visual, it is helpful to engage in a series of exercises focused on the topic of "My Personal Experiences with Anger." Involve group members in the following exercises:

- What makes you angry? Draw a picture about it. Write down something to explain the picture.
- Think about words that trigger your anger. Write down as many of these words as you can think of.
- When someone makes you angry, what can you do? Make a list of all your ideas.
- Visualize someone with whom you are presently in conflict. Write down all the feelings that this person provokes in you.

An exercise congruent with the kinesthetic learner's need for experiential activities involves role playing vignettes that describe situations that usually provoke anger (guidelines for role playing are described in Chapter 7). Consider the following vignettes for role playing with middle and junior high school students:

- Your younger brother just scribbled all over your math homework and you will need to start over again. What can you do?
- You're in the playground with a friend and practicing basketball throws. The class bully comes up, grabs the ball from you, and starts dribbling it down the field. How do you feel? What can you do?

- The boys next to you in the lunchroom are throwing food. The lunchroom aide comes up to you, speaks harshly, and orders you to clean up the mess. How do you feel? What can you do?

- Your older sister has promised to help you with your general science homework after dinner. You want to begin work but she's watching television and says, "This is a really good program and I've changed my mind about helping you. Do your homework alone!" How do you feel? What do you do?

- You have looked forward to going to the high school football game all week. On Saturday morning, your Dad says to you, "Sorry, Son, you've got to help me with chores around the house today." How do you feel? What do you do?

Role playing these vignettes provides a forum for helping adolescents identify incidents in their lives that provoke anger. It also identifies solutions that are responsible and self-enhancing. Each vignette should be discussed and evaluated immediately. It might be desirable to repeat the scenario using different group members or switching roles.

In conclusion, the use of brainstorming, drawing and writing exercises, and role playing are theoretically sound counseling techniques for Shabob's expressed learning-style preferences. However, as in the case of Carina, these interventions need to be evaluated in relation to Shabob's behavioral changes. For example, do you receive fewer disciplinary referrals from his teachers after the group counseling sessions? Do his parents observe and report fewer episodes of fighting and hostility with siblings and peers?

SUMMARY

This chapter described how the *Learning Style Inventory* printouts permit teachers and counselors to better understand the diverse adolescents with whom they need to interact. As each individual's learning-style data are analyzed by the St. John's University Homework Disk (Dunn & Klavas, 1992), the disk automatically provides printed directions for how that student should study and do homework through his or her personal preferences. Turner (1992) reported dramatic success when gifted elementary students were issued such prescriptions and others reported statistically higher grades, grade point averages, and retention for college freshmen who used the adult version of this program (Lenehan, Dunn, Ingham, Murray, & Signer, 1994; Nelson, Dunn, Griggs, Primavera, Fitzpatrick, Bacilious, & Miller, 1993).

Chapter 6

Managing the Implementation of a Learning-Styles Program

Beginning a new instructional program can be either energizing and self-actualizing or exhausting and frustrating. What determines the end result is the interest you and your students have in the innovation and your adoption of a practical, relatively easy to implement plan for gradually altering past practices.

Although Figure 6.1 graphically illustrates Klavas's (1991) stages in the implementation of a learning-styles program, except for the requirement of identifying students' learning styles as a basis for what you decide to implement, you can vary the plan to respond to your teaching style and risk-taking tolerance. It is not necessary to implement every stage in the plan, and it is certainly wise to proceed slowly so that you and your students are comfortable and successful with each stage you try. This plan is based on research that examined the factors that helped or hindered the development of successful learning-styles programs in different regions of the United States (Klavas, Dunn, Griggs, Gemake, Geisert, & Zenhausern, 1994).

STAGE 1: IDENTIFYING LEARNING STYLES

Begin by identifying your students' learning styles with the Dunn, Dunn, and Price (1979) Learning Style Inventory (LSI). Analyze each printout with the software package Homework Disk (Dunn & Klavas, 1992), which explains each student's traits and points out how that student can study and concentrate best by capitalizing on his or her individual strengths. You will want parents to be certain that their teenagers do homework according to their learning styles. Thus, before you send home students' home-

Figure 6.1
Klavas's Learning-Style Implementation Model

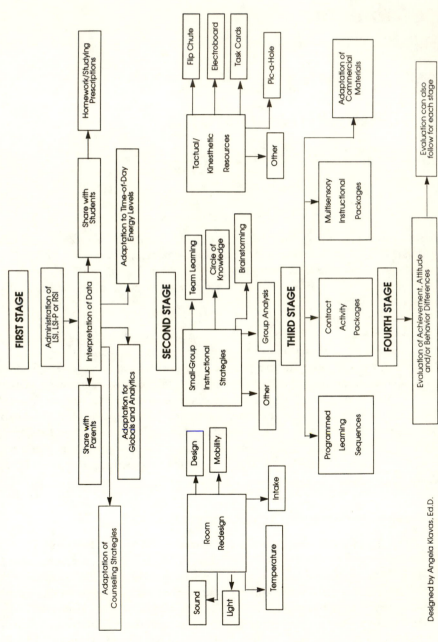

Designed by Angela Klavas, Ed.D.

work prescriptions, explain to the students and their parents what the Homework Disk's guidelines mean and how they should be used.

Next, choose any of the following steps to continue the process.

• Enlist the aid of available guidance and counseling professionals to encourage students to follow their learning-style homework prescriptions when studying. *Learning Styles Counseling* (Griggs, 1991a) is an excellent resource for specialists to read and follow.

• Provide core subject classes at varying times to complement different students' time-of-day preferences. For example, schedule students for their most difficult class or classes at their best time of day. Arrange for them to take formidable tests, such as the Standardized Achievement Test (SAT), during their energy highs rather than lows.

• Encourage students to study at their best time of day. Recognize their chronobiological highs and allow them to use those periods productively. Allow for some leisure activities during their lows.

• Experiment with introducing new topics globally followed by analytic reinforcement and then reversing the sequence the next day. Explain the difference between the two types of processing styles so that students become aware of their own style and how they are reacting to each lesson.

• After you feel comfortable about responding to at least some of the environmental elements of learning style that are important to your students (see Stage 2), share what you are doing with their parents. Appendix A lists resources that can assist you. The resources include a booklet specifically designed for parents to explain learning style. They also include a cartoonlike filmstrip and accompanying cassette to explain the concept. In addition, *Bringing out the Giftedness in Your Child: A Guide for Parents* (Dunn, Dunn, & Treffinger, 1992) describes how parents can use learning styles with their offspring at home to develop talent and ability. Once parents become aware of the various resources that teach students through their strengths, they may be willing to assist you in developing programmed learning sequences (PLSs) (see Chapter 8), contract activity packages (CAPs) (see Chapter 9), and/or multisensory instructional packages (MIPs) (see Chapter 10).

STAGE 2: REDESIGNING THE CONVENTIONAL CLASSROOM

Seating Preferences

Most schools provide wooden, steel, or plastic chairs and desks for every student. Branton (1966) found that when a person is seated in a hard chair, approximately 75 percent of the total body weight is supported on only four square inches of bone. The resulting stress on the lower back often causes fatigue, discomfort, and the need for movement—squirming, fidgeting, rocking, or getting out of the chair.

Research by Hodges (1985) and Shea (1983) and subsequent studies by Nganwa-Bagumah (1986) and Nganwa-Bagumah and Mwamwenda (1991) documented the significantly higher achievement that occurred when students were permitted to bring cushions from home to put on either their chairs or on the floor; complete assignments on carpeted floors, on bean bags, or in a designated informal section of the room; and/or learn on an easy chair, couch, or other casual furniture. Interestingly, the need to relax while concentrating is more crucial for adolescents than for either primary or elementary students, for whom it is important (Dunn & Griggs, 1988a).

Experimental Alternative for Seating Arrangement

Request that parents donate cushions, bean bags, carpet squares, rugs, summer lawn furniture, couches, rocking chairs, or easy chairs. Establish firm rules for their usage, such as the following:

- Only those students whose LSI printout confirms that an informal design is advantageous may use the alternative seating.
- No student's learning style should interfere with or distract anyone with a different style.
- Any student who abuses the privilege must forfeit it.
- The grades of each student permitted to sit informally must be at least as good or better than he or she received prior to this experiment, or the system is not working and there is no reason to continue.
- All assignments must be completed and on time. They may, however, be done anywhere in the classroom as long as these rules are respected, the teacher can actually see every student when desired and students sit politely, like ladies and gentlemen. Explain exactly how ladies and gentlemen sit, if necessary.

Illumination Preferences

Few educators fully comprehend the negative effects of florescent lighting on some students. Florescent bulbs emit rays that stimulate analytics, who find it difficult to concentrate on demanding academics in low light. However, the same illumination that stimulates analytic processors overstimulates global processors and often makes them hyperactive and restless. Reducing the amount and type of light in the environment for adolescents who strongly prefer soft lighting results in significantly increased test scores (Dunn, Krimsky, Murray, & Quinn, 1985; Krimsky, 1982).

Ott (1973) reported the positive and negative effects of natural versus artificial light on plants. The identical exposure was beneficial for some but detrimental for others.

Experimental Alternative for Illumination Preference

Try one or more of the following alternative lighting arrangements:

- Keep one bank of lights on and the other off. Permit students to sit wherever they feel most comfortable.

- Turn the lights off in a single corner of the room. Permit poor readers to sit in the darkened area. Observe differences in behavior and attention spans during the first six-week period; then look for achievement gains.

- Make colored acetate—for writing on overhead projectors—available to poor readers. Encourage individuals to select a color of their choice—green, blue, red, pink, lilac—and to place the acetate on top of each page as they read. Look for changes in attention span, focusing, and behavior. Improvement is likely to be observable in at least 5 to 10 percent of poor readers.

- Use colored, fire-proof Dennison paper, available in stationary stores, between the light bulb and the glass that covers it in one or more corners of the room to disperse illumination effects.

- Turn the lights off entirely in a classroom of underachievers and teach in natural daylight. Examine the effects over a six-week period. You may not appreciate the atmosphere but most of your students will!

- Permit students to wear visors, sunglasses, or caps with visors when they squint, appear uncomfortable, ask for that privilege, or their LSI printout indicates a score of 40 or below. Many students are uncomfortable in what appears to be normal lighting to adults, who require significantly more illumination than do adolescents.

- Cover large, bright white surfaces when not in use.

- Create a space with dark curtains where students who need soft illumination may work, or permit such students to shade their working area or den with transparent, dark-toned fabrics.

Sound Preferences

Individuals vary extensively in their ability to concentrate on difficult cognitive tasks in either quiet or noise (Pizzo, 1981; Pizzo, Dunn, & Dunn, 1990). In addition, strongly analytic processors require quiet, whereas strongly global processors think lucidly with sound—music, background talking, waves crashing, or birds singing. If you experiment with providing sound for students whose LSI printouts reveal scores of 60 or higher, do not permit any music with lyrics (DeGregoris, 1986). When the words of a song are known, the mind begins repeating them rather than concentrating on the assigned task.

Experimental Alternative for Sound Preferences

Schools report interesting results when providing one or more of the following treatments (Dunn & Griggs, 1988a).

• Place students who require quiet away from traffic and activity patterns.

• Use soft cotton or rubber ear plugs, jogger's earmuffs, or nonfunctioning listening sets during test or study conditions for those who need quiet. Permit baroque music for those who need sound.

• Cover a small area of the classroom floor with carpeting for students who are distracted by sound—approximately 10 to 12 percent of the school population dependent on age and achievement level.

• Separate the students who need quiet from the ones who need sound and from those for whom sound is unimportant. Provide self-contained spaces with a blocked-out view of class activities for those who are distracted by noise. (You will find that more girls require quiet than boys.) Place those who function best with sound near the hub of involvement.

Persistence Versus Short Attention Spans and Needing Breaks

Once certain students begin an assignment, they have a strong emotional need to stay on task until the work is done; they often concentrate in long, uninterrupted periods. Such youngsters, more often than not, are analytic. Many global processors, on the other hand, begin a task with a burst of energy, work for a short period of time, and then need a break; in addition, they dislike working on one thing at a time and, instead, prefer to engage in multiple tasks simultaneously.

Classrooms, thus, should permit analytics a quiet section in which to work on required assignments without noise, people, or activity distractions. On the other hand, classrooms should provide global processors with diversified activities, projects, and interactions. Instructional environments need to include both settings if all adolescents are to succeed academically. In addition, teachers can allow for these varying needs through the following:

• Placing desks and chairs in dens, alcoves, "offices," and private spaces where students' movements will not disturb their classmates.

• Finding varied sizes of desks and chairs suitable to adolescents' diversified height and girth.

• Allowing students to stand or lounge while they are concentrating. Do not require them to sit while they complete tasks. Sitting while concentrating is extremely difficult for those who require informal seating, mobility, and kinesthetic learning.

- Allowing kinesthetic students—those who rarely sit still for more than a few moments—to walk back and forth quietly in a specifically designated aisle or section of the room while they read, complete assignments, or think. They will not take advantage of your concern for their comfort and achievement.

- Structuring assignments to permit those who need variety, mobility, breaks, and peer interaction to (1) move about the room as they study, (2) go from one activity to another, or (3) migrate purposefully from one section to another.

- Arranging for designated walkways on the periphery of the room for strongly kinesthetic adolescents or those in need of frequent mobility; individual, paired, and small-group work areas; and sections for both formal and informal seating.

Experimental Alternative for Attention Requirements

Divide the room into subdivisions to permit students who require a few moments of relaxation between serious concentration periods to change their location and engage in short-term, instructionally oriented activities different from the main tasks in which they have been engaging. They will need space away from those who persist in distracting them. Provide varied instructional resources so that global adolescents may concentrate on more, relatively short exercises rather than on fewer, comparatively longer exercises. Thus, diversified areas are needed for global students to work on assignments, take breaks, be involved in something else for a short interval, and return to their major focus.

These same subdivisions of the room will permit analytics to continue to work without interruption. For they need to complete tasks before they relax and engage in alternative activities.

Sociological Preferences

With whom we study difficult material successfully is only tangentially related to whether we have global or analytic tendencies. Individual analytics and globals learn best in a variety of patterns: alone, in a pair, in a small group of peers, in a team, with a favored authoritative or collegial teacher, and/or in a variety of patterns (e.g., sometimes alone, sometimes in a cooperative group). Individual sociological patterns depend on age and achievement levels. Some people learn consistently in one way, others in two or more, yet others in varied patterns; and some have no preference at all. However, global adolescents are more people oriented than are analytic adolescents (Dunn, Cavanaugh, Eberle, & Zenhausern, 1982). People-oriented adolescents learn better with either a single friend or two friends, or in a small group—in contrast with the 13 percent who learn best alone and the 28 percent who consistently need a teacher.

Experimental Alternative for Sociological Needs

Permit students to complete all or most assignments, with the exception of tests, alone, in a pair, in a small group or with you. With this arrangement, class space needs to accommodate individuals, pairs, and small and large groups.

Temperature Preferences

In every family some members feel warm when everyone else is comfortable; others feel cool under identical conditions. Responses to temperature are unrelated to global or analytic processing, but as biological reactions they can be accommodated in the classroom. Such accommodations seriously affect achievement (Murrain, 1983).

Experimental Alternative for Temperature Preferences

Adolescents who seem devoid of energy or who are consistently withdrawn may be responding to temperature discomfort, among other possibilities. The teacher can try any of the following:

- Provide curtains that block out the sun during the warmest times.
- Provide a fan. Those who feel comfortable with its effects will choose to sit near it.
- Provide water and paper cups in the classroom for those who need a drink or to wet their faces or wrists. Again, establish well-understood rules and expect students to abide by them. Also place linoleum or plastic beneath the basin so that water on the floor does not become a problem.
- Allow students to keep sweaters in their desks or the closet for when they feel cool.
- Encourage students to wear layers of clothes that can be removed or maintained dependent upon the temperature and their individual reactions to its variations.
- Remember that the warmest part of most rooms is the center of the room, although being near a sunny window in warm weather may certainly be warmer.

Putting It All Together into a Learning-Style Environment

Remember that you must first administer the Dunn, Dunn, and Price LSI to identify the students' learning styles. Develop your own plan based on the number of students with each of the style characteristics described above; for example, if you have many students who require informal seating, begin your transition into style with seating arrangements. Should you have a large cluster of students who need quiet, subdivide your room into activity-oriented and quiet areas. Involve your

Figure 6.2
Redesigning the Educational Environment

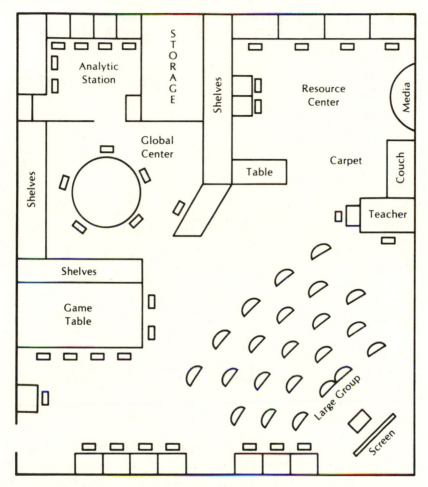

students in redesigning the classroom. In fact, once students' styles have been identified, discuss the differences that most certainly will exist in every class, make a list of things that can be done to respond to those differences, give students copies of Figures 6.2 and 6.3, and then permit students to redesign the classroom to respond to all their strong learning-style traits. Have individuals and groups share their pasteup models with the class and then conduct a secret ballot to determine the sections and ideas that receive the most votes. Locate dividers such as empty cardboard boxes from television sets, washing machines, or dryers. Use file cabinets, screens, tables, plants, bricks, plastic, empty telephone company wire spools, yarn, or bookcases that, when placed

Figure 6.3
Patterns of Classroom Items

Brunner's design of patterns of classroom items that students may cut out and piece together to develop varied samples of a redesigned classroom based on their learning style preferences.

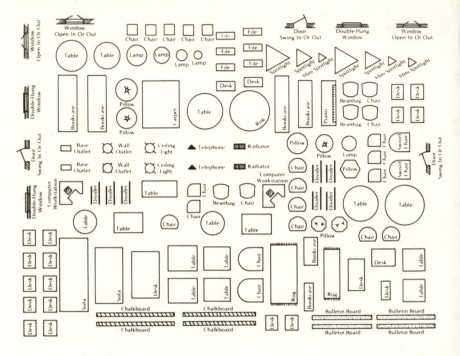

perpendicular to the wall or to each other, provide privacy through the formation of dens, alcoves, offices, nooks, stations, or other areas. Clear the floor area one section at a time, perhaps beginning with the far wall or one side (see Figure 6.3). Redesign one wall area after another until the room has at least one area that appeals to the style of each student. When all or most students are satisfied with their own place in the redesigned classroom, suggest retaining the floor plan for at least one week to permit a period of adjustment. Changes can be made after that time. Consider alternatives at a later date after the redesigned classroom has been field tested. Keep a record of the number of behavior problems, incidents, and incomplete assignments before and after the revised classroom. Compare grades before and after. Question students about the arrangement. See if they permit you to return to the conventional classroom environment without balking!

STAGE 2 ALTERNATIVE: TACTUAL AND KINESTHETIC RESOURCES

Students who do not perform well in school usually have tactual and/ or kinesthetic strengths. (See Chapter 7 for easy-to-follow guidelines for teaching such adolescents to teach either themselves or each other using pic-a-holes, flip chutes, electroboards, multipart task cards, and floor games.) Perhaps once or twice each week show students how one or more of these resources function and help them develop their own. We strongly advise that students be required to create their own materials so that they appreciate their value and thus take better care of them than they would had someone else made them, learn at least one method for teaching themselves, can rely on their ability to teach themselves when you are no longer their teacher, and have at least these methods for becoming successful academically.

Examine Your Priorities

Next, decide on which group of students you most wish to concentrate.

1. If you believe it wise to provide motivated students with a method for progressing academically at their own speed to avoid subjecting them to the repetition and interruptions that often occur during whole-class instruction or to help nonconforming students who do not focus successfully stay on track or perform well, then develop one or two CAPs on required curriculum topics or units. Another alternative is to adapt the available CAPs to professionals through St. John's University's Center for the Study of Learning and Teaching Styles (see Appendix A). Introduce the first CAP or two to the entire class. Motivated students—those with auditory or visual preferences and most nonconformists—who have experienced working with a CAP under supervision and with guidance usually function well independently with the third and subsequent CAPs.

3. However, if you are concerned with students who need structure and cannot function independently, begin by introducing a PLS to the entire class (see Chapter 8). After students have worked with one or two PLSs under supervision, those who need structure will function well independently with subsequent PLSs because the method itself is so structured.

4. If your major concern is with those adolescents who remember very little of what you teach, introduce the tactual and kinesthetic resources in Chapter 7 to the entire class; then review the content with a follow-up PLS. Be certain to teach all the students to make their own tactual materials, even if they are not tactual or kinesthetic; the pic-a-hole, flip chute, task cards, electroboard, or floor game are equally effective as a reinforcement strategy provided that each student is *introduced* to new and difficult material through his or her modality strength. Thus, students with tactual strengths will begin learning

with tactual resources but can reinforce the information through kinesthetic and/or visual or auditory resources, whereas students with kinesthetic preferences will begin learning kinesthetically (through a floor game or experiential participation, for example) but can reinforce the information through tactual, visual and/or auditory resources.

5. However, if your immediate concern is with the at-risk underachievers, and potential dropouts, begin with an MIP (see Chapter 10).

Although none of these approaches will be effective with all students, using them for the first time with the entire class enables individuals to determine which methods interest them most, allow them to understand difficult material most easily, and best respond to their style strengths. After their first experience with each method, assign students to the approach that is most likely to benefit them based on their learning-style traits or permit them to choose the method each prefers—*provided* that their grades and behaviors become better than ever before!

STAGE 2 ALTERNATIVE: SMALL-GROUP INSTRUCTION

Another beginning stage for capitalizing on students' learning styles is the use of small-group as opposed to large-group instruction. Approximately 28 percent of adolescents are peer oriented, although many can learn with classmates at least some of the time. Thus, as a transition from teacher-directed instruction, experiment with team learning to introduce difficult new information, circle of knowledge to reinforce it, brainstorming to develop problem-solving skills, and case studies for all these reasons and to provide variety and interest.

Team Learning

Identify the most difficult information in any unit or topic you intend to cover. Develop an explicit title for the team learning so students will know what they learn from completing the assignment. Later, when you use CAPs, you can include many team learning units. An example of the team learning title could be "Team Learning: Who Do You Think You Are? Genealogy—Digging for Family Roots."

After you name the technique, write the numbers (1) through (4), as shown below, and then next to each number place a line on which the team members will write their names. Add another line for the recorder's name.

Team Members:

1. _____   3. _____
2. _____   4. _____

Recorder: _____

Either take information directly from a textbook or write your own text to teach students what they need to know to successfully master the objectives. The material should be written concisely and succinctly and should be followed by a series of questions—at least one of each of the following three types.

1. Questions or objectives that require factual responses. For example: "Explain the meaning of *genealogy* and use the word in a sentence." Or "Explain *lineal descent* and why it is important in royal families."

The purpose of posing factual questions for students to answer at the end of the team learning is to be certain that each is learning the required body of knowledge in the curriculum.

2. Questions to which there are no "right" or "wrong" answers wherein to get the answer students must think, hypothesize, analyze, or otherwise engage in higher-level, critical-thinking skills. For example: "List at least five advantages and disadvantages of tracing a family's genealogical past."

The purpose of posing higher-level, critical-thinking questions is to develop the student's ability to think cognitively and to have many experiences doing so.

3. Questions that require the creative application of the information being learned. For example: "Write a humorous poem describing what might happen when people trace their genealogical past by exploring their 'family tree.' " Or "Develop an illustrated family tree based on your family's genealogical past."

The purpose of requiring creative applications of difficult material is to enable students to internalize the material through its application and to provide students with opportunities to be original,—particularly as members of a group developing abilities or talents and/or showing others how to be creative. (See Team Learning in the CAP *Heredity: The Genes We All Wear* in Chapter 9 for an example of this small-group technique.)

When the team learning text and questions are ready, assign students to groups of four or five to demonstrate the team learning strategy. After students become familiar with this strategy and show responsibility when working on a team, you may wish to permit them to select their own teams. Teams should be allowed to choose where they complete the team learning based on their members' preferences for design, mobility, light, and sociological grouping.

When comfortable, the team should elect, assign, or accept a volunteer recorder. It is the recorder who needs to write the team's answers to the questions you have posed. Short, succinct answers are required to keep the discussion and the process moving. Some of the team members may elect to write answers too, but they need not unless they believe writing will help them remember the material.

All members assist in determining the answers in the team learning material, but all their effort should be concentrated on *their* team—not another team. One way to promote quiet and order is to tell the class that any team member who hears the answers of another team has your permission to use the answers. At that point in the exercise, teams must work quietly to develop their answers.

Impose a time interval on the teams, for example, "Have your answers ready in 15 minutes." At the end of that time, regardless of whether all teams have completed the assignment, you announce that their development time is over and ask the first question that was posed. Call on any team's recorder for the answer. After one has been given ask, "Did any team have another, different answer?" Discuss the answers that differed from each other and guide the class toward an understanding of the topic by eliciting their responses and then adding information you want them to have. Team learning itself focuses on the major points; the after discussion can include everything you would normally emphasize for that topic or lesson.

While the teams are developing their answers, walk around and hear what is being said; observe who is contributing, who is uninvolved. Doing this will help you determine which students work well together and which belong in different groups. There is a chemistry that either does or does not develop among certain people, and as you observe the team learning process, you will become aware of which students "click" together and which do not. Indeed, if they are to do their best work and learn to the maximum of their potential, they need to "click." After two or three team learning exercises, some students will develop team relationships and begin to question and analyze the material with enthusiasm and animated-but-productive conversations. Be certain to share the teams' creative assignments. Anything not completed should be assigned as homework to be done alone or with others.

Circle of Knowledge

A Circle of Knowledge is used to reinforce the new and difficult material related to each objective the students need to master. The information from two difficult objectives may be combined into a single circle of knowledge. The title of the Circle of Knowledge should be explicit so that students know exactly which objectives can be met—or partially met—with this particular small-group strategy. Each CAP might include several Circles of Knowledge, one for each difficult objective. The Circle of Knowledge title should be identical to the team learning title except that this one will begin with "Circle of Knowledge," as in the following example: "Circle of Knowledge: List all the reasons you can to show how differences in customs and attitudes can be an asset in society."

As with the team learning, after you name the technique, write the numbers (1) through (4), as shown below, and then next to each number place a line on which the students who will be working together on this particular Circle of Knowledge will write their names. Add another line for the recorder's name.

Circle Members:

1. _____   3. _____

2. _____   4. _____

Recorder: _____

If individuals want to work on the Circle of Knowledge alone or in a pair, they may do so. Otherwise, they should place three or four chairs (no desks) into a tightly knit, small circle. You establish the criterion (or criteria) for selecting each circle's recorder for this one circle. For example, the person wearing the most color blue, or the tallest person in the circle, or the one with the most buttons. The person best matching that description becomes the recorder and is the only person in the circle permitted to write the answers.

On the chalkboard or an overhead projector, pose a single question or problem to which there are many answers or solutions and clearly indicate how much time you are allowing for the circle to develop its answers. Consider the following examples:

- Name all the ways in which people everywhere in the world are basically similar to each other. ($2\frac{1}{8}$ minutes)
- List as many occupations as you can. ($3\frac{2}{3}$ minutes)
- List all the ways of saying "Thank you" in as many foreign languages as you can. ($1\frac{9}{10}$ minutes)
- Develop as many examples as you can that are equivalent to 3/5. ($2\frac{5}{7}$ minutes)
- Name the origin of "American" foods that originally came from other countries. [Examples: sauerkraut, spaghetti, enchiladas, macaroni, tortilla, quiche, wontons, croissants, pizza, hot dogs, noodles, hamburgers]
- Name American foods that were unknown in Europe before they were used in the New World. [Examples: tomato, potato, chocolate] (Tiedt & Tiedt, 1990, p. 64)

Designate which member in each circle should give the first answer to the question; for example, "The first answer must be given by the person in the circle wearing the most buttons" or " . . . by the person who lives closest (or farthest) from the school." Beginning with that designated person who must give the first answer, going clockwise around the circle, each member in turn adds another answer to the list the recorder is writing. Each circle lists as many answers as its members can think of in the short amount of time allowed. Going in rotation, from left to right, each circle goes through as many rounds as possible.

Because Circle of Knowledge is a review, used after team learning, most students should be able to add an answer during the first or second round. When a player cannot think of an answer, the circle must stop, unless someone else in that same circle has an answer. In that case, the person with an answer may "give it away" to the classmate in that circle whose turn it is but who cannot think of an answer. However, the answer may not be communicated with words, written or verbal. The answer can be shared through pantomime, dramatics, illustration, drawing, or whatever, as long as no words in any format are used.

If the student has an answer, it pays to give that answer to the circle member who cannot think of a response. When no answer is forthcoming, the circle stops. Because part of winning is derived by having many answers, it is wiser to give one member's answer to the one whose turn it is so that the circle can add another answer to its list. Also, when it is the turn of the member who voluntarily gave up the answer to keep the circle going, others in the circle who have an answer may give up theirs to the next classmate who cannot remember under pressure.

Each circle quietly answers the same question simultaneously (in whispers). Only the members of the same circle should be able to hear the response their co-members give to the recorder. Although members other than the recorder may not write answers, they may illustrate or draw possible answers to help the teammate who is answering. No member may (1) skip a turn, (2) give an answer out of turn, or (3) provide a verbal or written answer. Any help given to the person who cannot think of an answer must be given only by acting or drawing, as indicated above.

Call time at the predetermined moment. All circles stop adding to their lists. Note the number of answers given, but give no credit for quantity.

The chalkboard or a transparency on an overhead projector is divided into columns, one for each circle in the room. Thus, if there are six circles of four students each and one pair working together, form seven columns. Number each column and assign that number to a circle. Thus, Circle 1's answers will eventually be written in the section labeled "Column 1"; Circle 2's answers will be written in the section labeled "Column 2," and so forth.

Call on each circle one at a time, asking for an answer to the question. Anyone in the circle called on may answer, but if someone from another circle calls out an answer out of turn, the circle you do call may take for its own the answer just called out—provided it has not already been recorded. After a circle has been called on and one of its members has called out an answer, you write what was called out onto that circle's column. Write whatever was called out, whether correct or not. At that point, every recorder for each circle—or someone else in the circle—should cross off that answer on that circle's list to prevent calling out the same answer a second time. Once an answer has been given, it may not be given again by another circle. If someone in any circle calls out an answer already called out and recorded in one of the columns, that answer is a duplicate. One point is deducted from the column of the circle each time a duplicate response is called out.

In turn, each circle calls out one answer when it is called on to do so. A round is ended when each circle has had two chances to provide an answer. When the first round is complete, examine the answers in all the columns. If an incorrect or duplicate answer has been recorded, cross it off the list and deduct one point. This process continues until a circle has no answers left, at which time you add up all the points for that circle. Give one point for each correct answer listed and deduct one point for each incorrect or duplicate answer. Record the total number of remaining answers in that column and circle that circle's total score. Although that circle may no longer contribute answers, it may challenge another circle's responses and gain one point for each successful challenge.

Any member of any circle may challenge an answer from another circle if the answer called out is believed either incorrect or a duplicate. The challenge may occur at any time, but the moment you hear "Challenge!" turn to the challenger and ask, "Why are you challenging?" The challenger need only respond, "That answer is wrong" or "That answer is already on the board [transparency]." If the challenger is correct, one additional "challenge point" is given to the challenger's circle. Thus extra points can be gained throughout the game for listening carefully and recognizing answers that were already given or are incorrect. The members of a circle may discuss whether to challenge before they actually do, but they need not. Anyone in the circle may challenge quickly to prevent another circle from challenging first. However, every circle loses one point for each incorrect challenge, so members need to be certain before they challenge publicly.

After every circle has used up all its answers and, thus, had its total score recorded and circled, the circle with the highest total score wins. However, everyone wins because circle of knowledge is an effective reinforcement strategy. It is multisensory and gamelike and therefore fun; it is competitive between groups but cooperative within groups; it is different from conventional reinforcement techniques; in short, it provides variety. The format for presenting a circle of knowledge is illustrated in Figure 6.4. For an example, see Circle of Knowledge in the CAP *Heredity: The Genes We All Wear* in Chapter 9.

Figure 6.4
Format for Circle of Knowledge Members' Names and Responses to Questions

Circle Members:

1. _____   3. _____

2. _____   4. _____

Recorder: _____

1._____	26._____
2._____	27._____
3._____	28._____
4._____	29._____
5._____	30._____
6._____	31._____
7._____	32._____
8._____	33._____
9._____	34._____
10 _____	35._____
11._____	36._____
12._____	37._____
13._____	38._____
14._____	39 _____
15._____	40._____
16._____	41._____
17._____	42._____
18._____	43._____
19._____	44._____
20._____	45._____
21._____	46._____
22._____	47._____
23._____	48._____
24._____	49._____
25._____	50._____

Role Playing

Adolescents who in any way differ from the mainstream often experience ostracism and ridicule by peers. The name calling, whispering behind the back, or laughter they endure hurts. Ask any victim. Minority adolescents are particularly vulnerable to such assaults on their dignity.

It is crucial that we help all students recognize the harmful effect of name calling. One way to do this is to:

invite students to develop a list of all the epithets they can think of, from *Fatty* to *Honky*. Be sure to include names you have heard them use, as well as racial or ethnic labels they may hear. . . . Putting these names on the board in "print" defuses some of their power to hurt. (Tiedt & Tiedt, 1990, p. 126)

Follow the listing with a sober discussion of how the students would feel were they called similar names. Discuss how each new group is considered odd by established groups and how in time all begin to feel part of one community. Discuss what might happen if another nation attacked the United States. Would we not pull together and act as a single unit—Americans? Were extraterrestrials to attack Earth, would we not ally ourselves against the common enemy?

Discuss the human need to belong, and that only insecure people "put down" others. Relate racial, religious, and cultural differences to learning styles—not the same but equally good. Make it clear that name calling reflects on the speaker and not on the person being offended. Use role playing to help students experience situations in which they need to find new ways of expressing their concerns. Use it to help them experiment with alternative ways of expressing anger, fear, discomfort, and embarrassment. Outline a sketchy scenario and use role playing to "lighten potential tensions in a heterogeneous classroom or when students begin to taunt a 'different' student" (Tiedt & Tiedt, 1990, p. 126). Establish the objective—for example, "new ways to show others that their behavior is not acceptable"—and invite your young actors and actresses to play parts. Let the students take it from there, but be ready to intercede if they fall into previously established negative patterns.

Role playing can make every subject come alive and is highly effective for sensitive issues where students need to develop an understanding of human frailty—their own as well as that of others.

Brainstorming

Brainstorming is a small-group technique that (1) develops multiple answers to a single question, (2) provides alternative solutions to either real-life or curriculum problems, (3) releases creativity, and (4) is used as a subset of decision making—a higher-level, critical-thinking skill (Knoll, 1994). Brainstorming is an associative process that encourages students to call out—one of the few times this behavior is permitted in school. Thus it responds to personal motivation and does not suppress natural spontaneity. In this regard it is responsive to impulsive learners but unresponsive to reflective learners. Brainstorming is:

- *stimulating*: It offers a unique, freewheeling, and rapid-fire strategy that builds enthusiasm in many participants.

- *positive*: Quiet and shy students often become active participants because they are not criticized; their contributions are masked by the group process. Conversely, those who usually dominate discussions are structured into offering succinct suggestions.

- *focused*: Diversions and distractions are eliminated. Stories and speeches irrelevant to the question are eliminated.

- *spontaneous and creative*: Students serve as a sounding board that generates new ideas. Creativity is released during the momentum of the process.

- *efficient and productive*: Dozens of suggestions, facts, ideas, or creative solutions are generated in a matter of minutes. Additional steps or plans of an activity can be brainstormed, as well as more specific answers for general responses. This is known as subset brainstorming.

- *involving and image building*: Self-image is enhanced for students who see their ideas accepted and then included in the list being generated. Group pride and cohesiveness increase as members begin to function as part of the larger unit creating the list of responses.

- *ongoing and problem solving*: The results are recorded and may be modified and used in new situations (Dunn & Dunn, 1992, 1993; Dunn, Dunn, & Perrin, 1994).

Procedures

The brainstorming leader serves as a recorder. His or her functions include recording all responses, asking for clarification or repetition, condensing large phrases into short, key ideas, and focusing the group on each topic. The leader should not comment, editorialize, or contribute; his or her effort should be concentrated on maintaining an effective and productive record of what has been produced.

Setting

From five to ten students should form a fairly tight semicircle of chairs facing the leader. (Larger groups can be effective at times.) Behind the leader is a wall containing three to five large sheets of paper or newsprint, double-folded to prevent strikethrough marks on the wall (see Figure 6.5).

These sheets, approximately 20 to 34 inches wide and 30 to 36 inches high, should be attached to the wall and placed a few inches apart from each other at a comfortable height for recording. The leader should use a broad-tipped felt marker for instant visibility by the entire group. A timekeeper should be appointed for the two- or three-minute brainstorming segments, but he or she may participate in the brainstorming. It is useful to have additional sheets available and an overhead projector to

Figure 6.5
Brainstorming Format

permit groups to analyze, plan, or to subset brainstorming for specific aspects of general answers.

Rules for Participants

All participants must observe the following rules:

1. Concentrate on the topic: "Storm your brain."
2. Fill the silence: Call out what "pops into your head."
3. Wait for an opening: Don't "step on someone's lines."
4. Record the thoughts in short form.
5. Record everything, no matter how strange.
6. Repeat your contribution until it is recorded.
7. Be positive; no criticisms, body language, or editorial comments.
8. Stay in focus; no digressions.
9. Use short time spans of one to three minutes.
10. Analyze later; add, subtract, plan, or implement.
11. Brainstorm from general to specific subsets.

Examples

The following are examples of topics appropriate for brainstorming:

1. the desirable characteristics of good leaders in any culture
2. all the solutions you can think of to ending physical violence
3. coming up with as many ways as possible for preventing poverty

Next consider the following way to do three-part problem solving through brainstorming.

(Take Three Minutes)	*(Take Three Minutes)*	*(Take Three Minutes)*
What would constitute an ideal energy program?	What might be the obstacles to this ideal program?	What can we citizens do to overcome the obstacles and guarantee adequate energy?

-or-

| Brainstorm the special problems of Native American students in American society. | Brainstorm as many solutions for each problem as possible. | Finally, Brainstorm the obstacles to the solutions that have been generated. |

If you wish to introduce students to the concept of cliches and have them understand what they are and how to parallel the idea on which each is developed, you might try: "List all the cliches that you can think of in three minutes." Then brainstorm each cliche in an action sentence. For example, instead of saying "as quiet as a mouse," try "as quiet as a _____ _____ing."

As students become familiar with brainstorming, they will demonstrate increasing creativity and gradually become skilled in this form of thinking. Once the first person calls out something charming or clever, for example, "as quiet as an eyelid closing" or "as quiet as a heart breaking," or perhaps "as quiet as a thought forming" or "as quiet as blood pressure rising," others will follow suit, taxing their brains for nuances and witty alternatives. Thereafter, many of your students will delight you with their spontaneous giftedness.

Small-group instructional techniques serve multiple purposes, including permitting students to work with peers, to become actively involved in the learning process, to contribute to their own learning, to experience different ways of gathering information, and to develop an appreciation of their own and their peers' contributions. The diversity of these techniques responds to many adolescents' need for variety rather than for routines and patterns.

Case Studies

A case study stimulates and helps to develop analytical skills. Four to five students can spend considerable time discussing and interpreting short, relevant stories that teach them something they need to learn. Case studies provide:

- a strategy for developing material within the student's frame of reference. The characters, situations, and events can, if constructed properly, strike responsive and understanding chords.

- an approach that can be stimulating and meaningful if student identification is fostered and debate is structured to understand different points of view on recognized problems and situations.

- safe, nonthreatening situations for students who can participate in the analysis without direct personal effects.

- training and development in problem solving, analytical skills, arriving at conclusions, and planning for new directions in learning situations and in real life.

Developing Case Studies

Format: Case studies may be written as very short stories, audio- or videotaped dramatizations, minifilms, psychodramas, news events, or historical happenings, real or fictional. The use of chronological sequence aids students in following the flow of events and in analyzing key issues. Flashbacks and other complex approaches should be avoided except for the most advanced students.

Focus: The case should focus on a single event, incident, or situation. Ability to analyze is aided by a high degree of concentration on the factors that precipitated the event, the attitudes prevailing during a given incident, or the sharply defined points of view of those dealing with a problem.

Relevance: Reality or "potential credibility" related to the students' frame of reference is critical to the success of this small-group technique. The participants must be able to recognize, understand, or even identify with the people in the situation because their behavior seems authentic or possible. The study should try to capture the flavor of familiar people and places, and their actions should be at a level that is at, or slightly above, the levels of understanding of the participants.

Increasing Motivation: After initial training in the analysis of case studies, involve students in the actual writing and acting of roles in subsequent cases. Both relevance and motivation will increase as students become involved and develop a sense of ownership of their new creation.

Procedures: Elect, seek volunteers, or appoint a leader and a recorder from among the participants in each case study group. Ask the members in each group to read the case study script at the beginning of the session. As the students become increasingly familiar with this approach, you may wish to assign the materials as prior reading exercises to increase time devoted to their group discussion.

The leader should not dominate the session but should keep the group on target for the allotted time. The recorder should participate and also concentrate on capturing the essence of the group's responses to various analytical questions. He or she must periodically verify all notes with the group to obtain consensus.

Key questions for the case study should be developed in advance, although other questions may be suggested as the group delves into the problem or situation. Questions may begin with factual checkpoints but then should move quickly into possible reasons, alternative motives, and analysis of the subtleties and complexities of the characters' experiences and interactions as well as their values, standards, and other abstractions. Finally, students should be asked to reach conclusions and to apply developing insights to new situations.

Analyzing case studies should build students' ability to interpret, synthesize, describe, observe, perceive, abstract, compare, judge, conclude, make determinations and decisions, solve problems, identify alternatives, and predict.

Sample Case Study

The purpose of this case study is to help students understand emotions and attitudes, cope with a difficult situation, and develop alternative solutions.

The Unwanted Visitor

People of every culture have experienced times during which they were either physically attacked, as in war, or psychologically assaulted, as in South Africa, where blacks were subjected to the rulings of a white government that refused to allow them participation in governance.

In the American colonies during the time of the Boston Massacre British soldiers were feared, despised, and unwanted by many colonists who considered themselves loyal British subjects under the rule of King George III. Nevertheless, the crude, red-uniformed soldiers were housed in Boston's homes, where they ate the colonists' food, used their bedrooms, and sometimes mistreated the local citizens. Their red uniforms earned for them the derogatory name "lobster back."

For their part the British soldiers were not pleased to be far from home among hostile "barbarians." Some students, perhaps of your age, undoubtedly found those red-coated lobster backs inviting targets for snowballs in winter. Because of the hostility generated by the forced intrusion of the soldiers, without the colonists' vote, the young people often took opportunities to steal from them, pelt them with snow, ridicule them with laughter, and mimic their walk. These harassments, added to the irritable confrontations on the streets and commons of Boston, may have led to the accidental, or at least unnecessary, firing by the troops on the unarmed citizens of Boston.

Analysis Questions

- If you had lived in Boston during the American Revolution, how would you have felt about British soldiers taking over and living in your home? Why?
- Why was "lobster back" a derogatory term? Why was this term used instead of another one, such as "red flannel–head"?
- How would you have felt had you been one of the British soldiers?
- What could the elders have done to ease the tension in town and to prevent the massacre and needless loss of life?
- Have there been similar situations in history either before or since the Revolutionary War? (Dunn & Dunn, 1993)

Sample Case Study: English

A series of incidents or consecutive events may be interesting in and of themselves. Consider the following.

What Happens Next?

Gregor Mendel bent over the pea plants in his genetic experiment. He searched every leaf diligently. The muscles rippled across his back and arms. His mind focused even more sharply, and he slowly began to smile as the realization of his finding spread throughout his consciousness like warm waves on a tropical beach. He pulled himself out of the crouched position he had been in for hours and permitted the warm sunshine to bathe his lean body. He walked toward the microscope to confirm what he believed. After another few minutes of further scrutiny, Mendel realized that he had uncovered the secret of genetics. In many ways, the future now belonged to humankind!

Analysis Questions

- How do you know what Gregor Mendel was feeling?
- Do you believe he was feeling well?
- What might have happened in the past?
- How does the passage support your position?
- Have you ever felt the way Mendel did? Explain why.
- Describe what probably happened next in Mendel's life.
- Use the selection to indicate why you believe the next series of events you created is plausible.
- *Bonus Assignment*: Write one paragraph describing (1) who Gregor Mendel was, (2) what he uncovered, and (3) how that knowledge influenced science.

Alternative Case Study Assignments

Select a favorite novel, short story, or narrative poem. Then do one of the following activities.

1. Write the next minichapter.
2. Send a letter to one of the main characters describing how you will control his or her future and what will happen next.
3. Have the main character write a story or journal of succeeding events.
4. Report the next series of events to the newspapers.
5. Write a soap opera scenario for television about the main characters just after the end of the novel or story.

A Final Word on Small-Group Techniques

The five small-group techniques discussed here, as well as other small-group techniques you use or devise, are essential to building independence and for responding to those adolescents whose learning styles clearly indicate a need to work with peers. Each technique has particular benefits:

- *Circle of Knowledge* reviews and reinforces previously learned material.
- *Team learning* introduces new material and uses factual, inferential, and creative questions/assignments.
- *Role playing* develops empathy for and understanding of others and how they cope.
- *Brainstorming* releases creative energy and aids in planning, solving problems, and making decisions.
- *Case studies* develop analytical skills and build empathy and understanding of people as they work together to solve problems or cope with crises.

There are variations and other small-group techniques such as simulations, group analysis, task forces, and research committees (Dunn & Dunn, 1972). Each technique should focus on one or more specific objectives, such as learning new material, developing higher-level cognitive thinking skills, or applying information. Select or develop the technique that best responds to your goals and your students' varied learning styles. Your instructional role will eventually take less effort and will be far more rewarding for you and for your students.

Chapter 7

Designing Tactual and Kinesthetic Resources to Respond to Adolescents' Individual Learning Styles

THE IMPORTANCE OF TEACHING TACTUALLY AND KINESTHETICALLY

Maximally effective instruction introduces new and difficult information through students' strongest perceptual preferences (Carbo, 1980; Dunn, 1990a; Garrett, 1991; Hill, 1987; Ingham, 1990; Martini, 1986; Weinberg, 1983; Wheeler, 1983) and reinforces what was introduced through at least one of the individuals' next two strongest modalities (Bauer, 1991; Kroon, 1985; Wheeler, 1983). Students then apply what they learned by creating a new instructional resource to teach the exact same information to someone else. This process has produced significantly higher standardized achievement and attitude test scores throughout the United States at the elementary level (Andrews, 1990; Klavas, 1993; Lemmon, 1985; Quinn, 1994; Stone, 1992; Turner, 1993), the secondary level (Brunner & Majewski, 1990; Elliot, 1991; Gadwa & Griggs, 1985; Orsak, 1990 a,b), and the college level (Clark-Thayer, 1987; Lenehan, Dunn, Ingham, Signer, & Murray, 1994; Mickler & Zippert, 1987; Nelson, Dunn, Griggs, Primavera, Fitzpatrick, Bacilious, & Miller, 1993).

Students who perform well in school tend to learn by listening and/or by reading. They are well matched with teachers who teach by talking and/or reading assignments. Students who do not achieve well in school tend to be tactual or kinesthetic learners (Dunn, 1990c); their strongest perceptual modalities are neither auditory nor visual. These adolescents acquire and retain information or skills when they handle manipulatives or participate in concrete, real-life activities. Because most instruction in the upper elementary, intermediate, or secondary grades is verbal, most visual, tactual and kinesthetic students become handicapped. Once they begin to achieve poorly, they lose confidence in themselves, feel embarrassed, withdraw physically or emotionally, or begin to resent school because of their repeated failures.

Some parallels exist between age and perceptual strengths. Young children first begin learning kinesthetically—that is, by experiencing. Usually they next develop tactual preferences, followed by visual and ultimately auditory preferences. Generally girls develop auditory strengths earlier than boys. Although some kindergarteners are visual and/or auditory, most students do not evidence auditory preferences much before sixth grade. Eventually, many adolescents develop auditory strengths and function well in a traditional class. However, most secondary students remain unable to learn easily either by listening or by reading.

Gifted students often have two or more perceptual strengths, of which auditory or visual strength is always one. Learning-disabled students usually have tactual and/or kinesthetic preferences or they skip visual development and often reveal tactual/auditory preferences, sometimes mistaken as a strength in both modalities. When development bypasses the normal maturation sequence (for example, the visual does not develop) that student often experiences problems while learning in school. However, it is easier to learn as a kinesthetic/tactual/and/or visual student who never develops auditory strengths than it is to be a tactual-auditory learner who has bypassed visual development. On the other hand, high motivation (LSI scores of 60 or higher) often enables students to bypass the lack of auditory development. Sensory strengths appear to be so individualized that it is important to test each student and to provide instructional resources to complement individual strengths.

Because many adolescents are interested in designing and building tactual and kinesthetic resources, it is not difficult to teach them how to teach themselves through these approaches. The easy-to-follow directions in this chapter can be used to help many multicultural adolescents gradually achieve instructional independence.

LEARNING-STYLE CHARACTERISTICS RESPONSIVE TO TACTUAL AND KINESTHETIC RESOURCES

Because tactual and kinesthetic resources tend to be gamelike, they are usually motivating, particularly for underachievers. However, when tactual and kinesthetic resources are perceived as juvenile, they can embarrass and cause resistance. It is important that the students to whom these resources are introduced are positive about them and therefore willing to follow directions for their use, care, and replacement. When adolescents enjoy learning this way, they become persistent and continue using the materials until they achieve the established goals.

Other than the taped and printed directions for using the resources, little structure is provided for students who use them. Beyond the elements of motivation, persistence, and responsibility, students need have only visual-tactual, tactual-kinesthetic, or visual-kinesthetic preferences. Be certain, however, to emphasize to the entire class that all students will be responsible for learning and mastering the identical objectives, but each will learn the information through his or her learning style strengths (Brunner & Hill, 1992).

LEARNING STYLE CHARACTERISTICS TO WHICH TACTUAL AND KINESTHETIC RESOURCES CAN BE ACCOMMODATED

Because these resources may be used in a classroom, library, corridor, instructional resource center, or at home, they can accommodate each student's environmental and physiological preferences. Because they may be used independently, in pairs, with a small group, or with an adult, they also respond to each student's sociological preferences.

STEP-BY-STEP GUIDE TO DESIGNING TACTUAL RESOURCES

After you have made one or two samples of the resources in this chapter for experimentation and have observed the progress that certain students make with them, you will become committed to their availability for student self-teaching. Developing these resources is easy, and after seeing how yours work, students will duplicate and create sets for themselves.

Students' ability to take difficult information from a chalkboard or a ditto and translate it into resources that facilitate their memory retention is a first important step toward becoming independent learners—a stage that many adults fail to reach. Once students become aware of their perceptual strengths, they can sequence their exposure to their teacher's lectures. Thus, the lecture may be an introductory, intermediary, or reinforcement strategy based on each student's primary, secondary, or tertiary strengths.

Understanding Task Cards

Multipart task cards are easy-to-make tactual and visual resources that respond to adolescents' need to see and to touch simultaneously. Often designed in sets or as part of a unit, each series teaches related concepts or facts. This resource tends to be effective with students who do not remember easily by listening or by reading. Task cards are used to introduce new material as well as to reinforce something to which the youngster has been exposed but did not learn.

The most effective task cards are the ones that are self-corrective. These (1) permit students to recognize whether they understand and can remember the material; (2) allow no one other than the individual who is using the cards to see errors that may have been made, thus preserving the adolescent's dignity and self-image; (3) enable students who err in their responses to find the correct answers without the help of others; and (4) free the teacher to work with other, more dependent or demanding students.

Task cards can be made self-corrective through any one of several methods: color coding, picture coding, shape coding, or answer coding. They may be used by individuals, pairs, or a small group, and they permit self-pacing. Students may use them until they feel secure about their knowledge of the topic. Too, task cards can be reused as a reinforcement when specific data have been forgotten or when preparing for a test. They are gamelike in character and often win and sustain adolescents' attention. They appeal to students who do not learn easily through other available resources, and therefore they are important for tactual-visual learners.

Students who select or are assigned task cards may work with them at their desks, in an instructional area such as a learning station or interest center, in the library, on carpeting, or anywhere in either the school or home environment. They may be used alone by an individual, in a pair, or with a small group, provided that students follow the established rules; for example, "Your learning style must never interfere with someone else's style, your grades must be better than they have ever been before, you need to work quietly and must complete this assignment, and/or you need to be where I can see you."

Designing Task Cards

Begin by listing exactly what you want your students to learn about a specific topic, concept, or skill. Then translate your list into questions and either answers concerning what they should learn or samples of the answers, some true and others false. For example, students need to learn that African Americans have made contributions to society in areas other than sports and music. Challenge students to match the following names with each person's contributions (Tiedt & Tiedt, 1990, p. 125).

C	Matthew Henson	A.	astronomer
A	Benjamin Banneker	B.	first person killed in Boston Massacre (in the Revolutionary War)
D	Charles Drew	C.	went to the North Pole with Admiral Perry

<u>B</u>	Crispus Attucks	D.	invented blood transfusions
<u>G</u>	Shirley Chisholm	E.	poet in colonial America
<u>E</u>	Phyllis Wheatley	F.	led slaves to freedom
<u>F</u>	Harriet Tubman	G.	first female African American in Congress

Students can develop their own two-part set of task cards for this exercise by printing the name of each famous person on the left half of a rectangular index card and the correctly matched information about why that person became famous on the right side. The cards should be irregularly cut into two halves, with the names on the left side and why the person is famous on the right. A picture of the person or his or her deed(s) should be drawn or cut out and then glued to the card. The irregular cutting produces shape coding in that only the two halves that fit together match. By mixing all the card halves, students can first guess which name matches which deed and then see whether they guessed correctly by placing the two halves together. If they fit well, their answer is correct (see Figure 7.1).

A three- or four-part task card set can be made if more information related to the question is available. For example, in a study of regional vocabulary differences, you can point out that many common objects have different names in different parts of the country (Tiedt & Tiedt, 1990, p. 137). Early people who investigated regional pronunciation and vocabulary differences (dialectologists) developed maps that showed the spread of words for particular objects. Direct students to make multipart task cards with a question concerning words that are used either for the same object or for the same action. Each question should be printed onto the first third (left-hand side) of the card. Then they should find all the words, phrases, or expressions that answer the question; those should be printed on the middle third. On the last third, they should draw or cut-out-and-glue-on an illustration of either the word meaning or the action described. Then each card should be cut irregularly into thirds. For example, see Figure 7.2. After some of the students become familiar with the words by using the first set of task cards and then perhaps writing short stories that include their favorite set(s) of descriptors, you might reinforce the words with a second set on which the question is on the front of the card and the answers are on the back, necessitating thinking rather than merely matching. In that way, students who have become somewhat familiar with some of the words may be further challenged to recognize the words without the shape coding or illustrations.

Any factual information lends itself to task card applications. For example, it is easy to explore different languages by developing task cards

Figure 7.1
Sample Two-Part Task Cards to which Drawings Should be Added

with a foreign word on the left side, the name of the country that uses that word in the center, and what that foreign word means in English on the right (See Figure 7.3). Be certain to require that the students illustrate each task card!

Materials for Creating Task Cards

• Colored oak-tag or cardboard
• Black felt pens for printing
• Colored felt pens for illustrations and attractiveness

Directions for Making Task Cards

1. Cut colored oak-tag or cardboard into 3-by-12-inch rectangles; if the topic lends itself to being represented by a shape, then cut the oak-tag or cardboard into shapes of approximately 3-by-12-inches each.

Figure 7.2
Sample Three-Part Task Cards to which Drawings Should be Added

What do you say to stop a game?		time out, times, pax, time, fins
What do you call being absent from school?		play hooky, ditch, bag school, bolt, lay out, lie out, play truant, skip class, cut school
What do you call someone from the country?		hayseed, rube, hick, yokel, hillbilly, hoosier, mossback, cracker, redneck, sodbuster, yahoo
What do you call a thick sandwich?		dagwood, hoagie, grinder, sub, submarine, hero, poor boy

2. On the left side of each rectangle, in large easy-to-read letters print either information or a question about the topic. On the right side of the rectangle or shape, print the corresponding answer. Be certain to leave space between the two facts or the question and answer, or the word and its meaning, or the numeral and the representative illustration. Illustrate the answer. Were you teaching vocabulary, you might place the printed word on one side of the shape and the illustration on the other.

3. Either laminate or cover each rectangle or shape with clear contact paper.

4. Cut each rectangle or shape into two (or more) parts by using a different linear separation for each (to code them according to shape) so that only the matched halves fit together.

5. Package the set in an attractive box, perhaps one you kept from a gift you received. Write a title on top of the box to describe the task cards inside. Take one card from the set, illustrate it, and glue it onto the top of the box next to the title. In that way students will be able to identify the topic of the task cards

Figure 7.3
Sample Three-Part Task Cards that Match Words of "Foreign" Origin with the Country from Which They Were Adopted and the Meaning of the Word in English

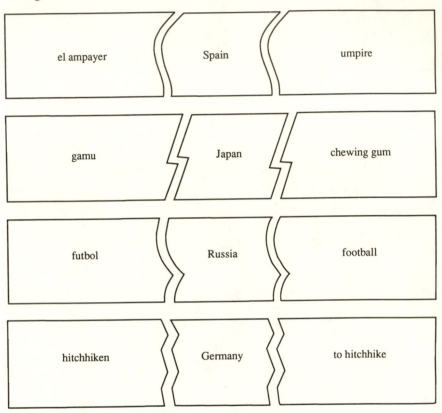

within each box. For example, if the box holds math task cards, place a single sample from the set inside the box on top of the box and laminate the entire top—or the box itself.

6. The best task cards are designed in a shape representative of the topic they teach. Older or more advanced students might consider four- and five-part (or more) task cards. Although you need to introduce students to task cards through the sample cards you create, they will learn more information from designing their own than they will from using the ones developed by the teacher. Thus, teach students to create their own set as early as possible and assign them to beautify or complete it for homework. Allow them to (1) copy the facts that you print on the chalkboard, (2) cut out the set of task cards in a shape related to the topic, (3) divide the facts among the various task card parts, and (4) study the set to help them learn the facts tactually and visually.

Understanding Flip Chutes

Everything that can be taught with task cards also can be taught with a flip chute. We suggest alternating tactual resources to maintain student interest and enthusiasm—particularly if students need variety. For those who prefer to use the same materials repeatedly, this single device will suffice.

Materials For Making Flip Chutes

Flip chutes are made from half-gallon orange juice or milk containers decorated to reflect the topic being studied. Small question-and-answer cards are designed to be inserted into the upper face of the container. As each question card descends on an inner slide, it flips over and emerges through a lower opening with the correct answer face up.

Directions For Making Flip Chutes

1. Pull open the top of a half-gallon milk or juice container.
2. Cut the side folds of the top portion down to the top of the container (Figure 7.4).
3. On the front edge, measure down (a) ½ inch and (b) 2½ inches. Draw lines across the container. Remove that space.
4. Mark up from the bottom (a) ½ inch and (b) 2½ inches. Draw lines across the container. Remove that space.
5. Cut one 5-by-8 index card to measure 6½ inches by 3½ inches.
6. Cut a second index card to measure 7½ inches by 3½ inches (Figure 7.4).
7. Fold down ½ inch at both ends of the smaller strip. Fold down ½ inch at one end of the longer strip.
8. Insert the smaller strip into the bottom opening with the folded edge resting on the upper portion of the bottom opening. Attach it with masking tape.
9. Bring the upper part of the smaller strip through the upper opening with the folded part going down over the center section of the carton. Attach it with masking tape (Figure 7.5).
10. Working with the longer strip, one end is folded down, and the other end is unfolded. Insert the unfolded end of the longer strip into the bottom opening of the container. Be certain that the strip goes up along the back of the container. Push it into the container until the folded part rests on the bottom part of the container. Attach it with masking tape.
11. Attach the upper edge of the longer strip (⅝ inches from the top) to the back of the container creating a slide. Secure it with masking tape. Follow the next illustration (Figure 7.6).
12. Fold down the top flaps of the container and tape them in place, forming a rectangular box.

Figure 7.4
Directions for Designing a Flip Chute

Directions

1. Pull open the top of a half-gallon milk or juice container.
2. Cut the side folds of the top portion down to the top of the container.

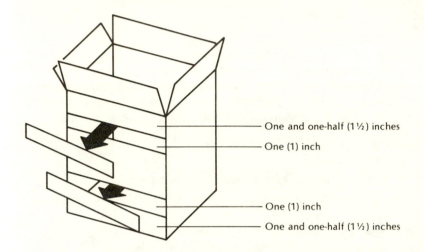

One and one-half (1½) inches

One (1) inch

One (1) inch

One and one-half (1½) inches

3. On the front edge, measure down both (a) 1½ inches and (b) 2½ inches. Draw lines across the container. Remove that space.
4. Mark up from the bottom (a) 1½ inches and (b) 2½ inches. Draw lines across the container. Remove that space.
5. Cut one 5 × 8 index card to measure 6½ inches by 3½ inches.
6. Cut a second index card to measure 7½ inches by 3½ inches.
7. Fold down ½ inch at *both* ends of the smaller strip. Fold down ½ inch at *one* end of the longer strip.

13. Use a small 2 by 2½-inch index card to write the question on one side and the answer on the flip side. Notch each question side at the top right to ensure appropriate positioning when the student uses the cards (Figure 7.7)

(Flip chute directions were developed by Dr. Barbara Gardiner [1983]).

If you want to make the flip chute reflect a particular theme or area of study, add a rounded section at the top to represent a head and elongated extensions for arms, legs, a tail, or other special effects. Paint, color, or cover with colored contact paper or vinyl wall covering and add lettering describing this particular Flip Chute's purpose. When completed, an everyday sample should look similar to the one in Figure 7.8 created

Figure 7.5
Continued Directions for Designing a Flip Chute

7½ inches by 3½ inches	6½ inches by 3½ inches

8. Insert the smaller strip into the bottom opening with the folded edge resting on the upper portion of the bottom opening. Attach it with masking tape.

9. Bring the upper part of the smaller strip out through the upper opening, with the folded part going down over the center section of the carton. Attach it with masking tape.

Step 8

Step 9

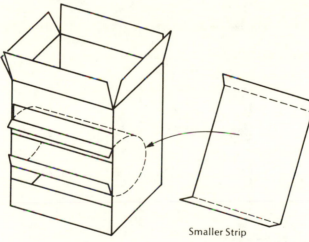

Smaller Strip

10. Work with the longer strip, one end is folded down and the other end is unfolded. Insert the unfolded end of the longer strip into the bottom opening of the container from the outside. Be certain that the strip goes up along the back of the container. Push it into the container until the folded part rests on the bottom part of the container. Attach it with masking tape.

11. Attach the upper edge of the longer strip to the back of the container creating a slide. Secure it with masking tape about ⅛" from the top of the carton.

12. Fold down the top flaps of the container and tape them in place, forming a rectangular box.

Figure 7.6
Continued Directions for Designing a Flip Chute

13. Use small, 2 × 2½ inch index cards to write the question on one side
    and the answer upside down on the flip side. Notch each question side
    at the top right to insure appropriate positioning when the student uses
    the cards.

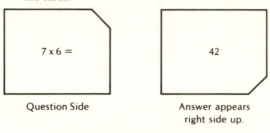

Question Side   Answer appears
                                 right side up.

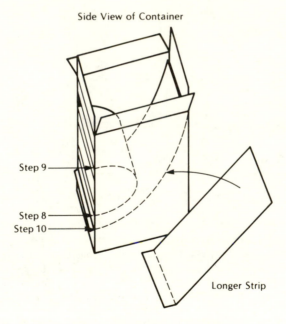

Side View of Container

Step 9

Step 8
Step 10

Longer Strip

(Flip Chute directions were developed by Dr. Barbara Gardiner.)

by Camille Sinatra, Reading Specialist, Manhasset Junior/Senior High
School, Manhasset, New York for a unit on *"The Great Depression: Don't
Let it Get You Down!"* (Dunn & Dunn, 1993).

Flip chutes are a wonderful way of helping tactual adolescents learn
math combinations, particularly simple algebraic equations. You need not
pressure the students; merely make math flip chute cards available and
see how well many begin to teach themselves and others!

Figure 7.7
Sample Flip Chute Cards

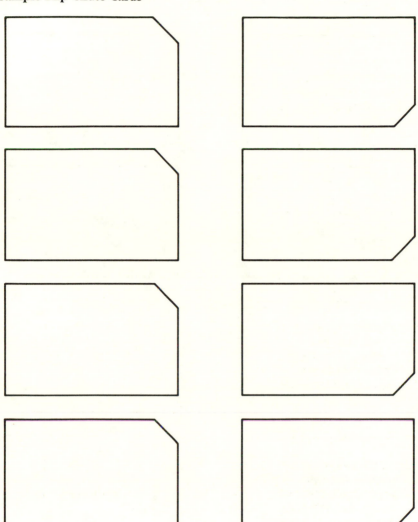

Designing Pic-A-Holes

Tactual students have used pic-a-holes successfully in a variety of subject areas. These directions for constructing them require measuring and cutting accurately, but after you construct the first sample, remember to trace the pattern before you seal the hole. Students will then need only to copy the pattern, so that making several pic-a-holes becomes an easy

Figure 7.8
Sample Flip Chute Cards Created by Sinatra for a Unit on "The Great Depression"

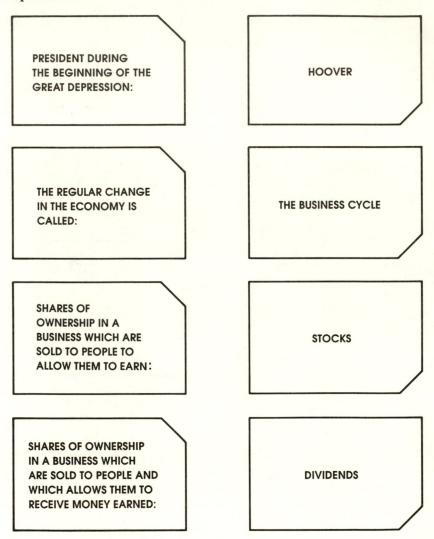

task for them. On the other hand, many tactual-visual youngsters for whom this resource will be effective are capable of measuring and cutting exactly according to directions.

Pic-a-holes can be used either to introduce or to reinforce information. They offer choices from among three options; should a youngster's first or second choice be incorrect, the self-corrective feature of this device ensures eventual success in a private, nonthreatening environment.

Figure 7.9
Pic-A-Hole Example

A Pic-A-Hole may be used to either introduce or reinforce the same information included in task cards or a flip chute. All three may be tactual components of a PLS or a multisensory instructional package. They also may be used as the resource alternatives for a CAP.

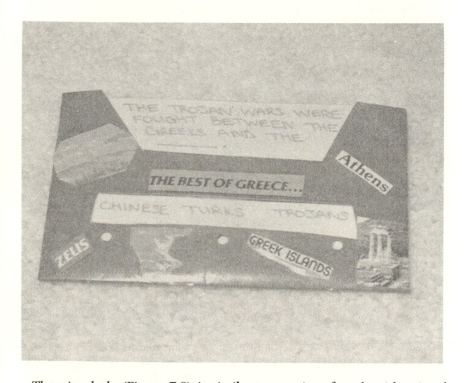

The pic-a-hole (Figure 7.9) is similar to a series of cards with printed questions. Students consider answers and look at three possible options printed at the bottom. Using a golf tee attached with Velcro, yarn, wire, or string, they place the point of the golf tee into a hole directly below the option they believe to be correct. They then try to lift the question card out from its holder. If the answer selected is correct, the card lifts easily and can be removed. If the answer is not correct, the card will not budge (see Figure 7.10).

*Directions for Making Pic-A-Holes**

1. Cut a colorful piece of cardboard or poster board 24⅜ inches by 6½ inches.
2. Following the guide in Figure 7.11 measure and mark the cardboard (on the

*Pic-A-Hole directions were developed by Barbara Gardiner (1983).

Figure 7.10
Sample Pic-A-Hole Cards are Self-Corrective and Can Only be Raised When the Student Chooses a Correct Answer

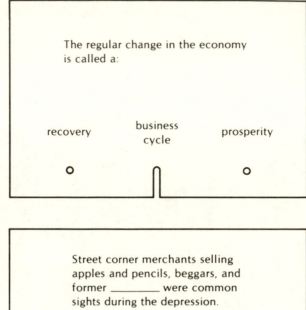

The regular change in the economy is called a:

recovery   business cycle   prosperity

○   ○

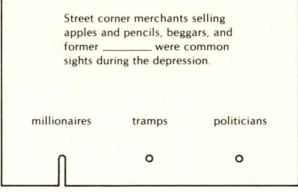

Street corner merchants selling apples and pencils, beggars, and former _____ were common sights during the depression.

millionaires   tramps   politicians

○   ○

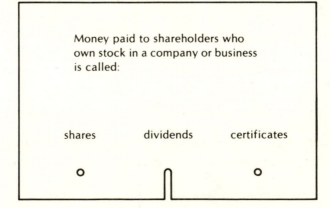

Money paid to shareholders who own stock in a company or business is called:

shares   dividends   certificates

○   ○

Figure 7.11
Directions for Designing a Pic-A-Hole

Directions

1. Cut a colorful piece of cardboard or poster board 24⅜ inches by 6½ inches.

2. Following the guide below, measure and mark the cardboard (on the wrong side) to the dimensions given. Use a ballpoint pen and score the lines heavily.

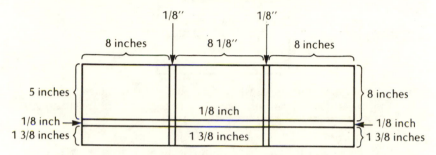

3. Remove the 1 ⅛ inch bracketed areas at right and left. Use a ruler and a razor or exacto knife to get a straight edge. The piece of poster board then should look like the following illustration.

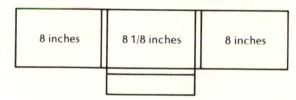

wrong side) to the dimensions given. Use a ballpoint pen and score the lines heavily.

3. Remove the 1⅜ bracketed areas at right and left. Use a ruler and a razor or exacto knife to get a straight edge. The piece of poster board will look like the illustration above.

4. Working on the wrong side of the center section only, follow the measurement guide given in Figure 7.12.

5. Remove the shaded areas with a ruler and razor or exacto knife.

6. Fold on all the drawn lines using a ruler as a guide to obtain sharp, straight fold lines.

7. Punch three holes as shown in the diagram.

8. Place an index card under the center section. Trace the openings onto the card. Remove the same areas from the index card. This will serve as a guide

Figure 7.12
Continued Directions for Designing a Pic-A-Hole

   4. Working on the wrong side of the center section only, follow the measurement guide given below.

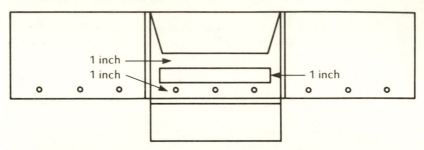

   5. Remove the shaded areas with a ruler and razor or exacto knife.
   6. Fold on all the drawn lines using a ruler as a guide to obtain sharp, straight fold lines.
   7. Punch three holes as shown in the diagram.
   8. Place an index card under the center section. Trace the openings onto the card. Remove the same areas from the index card. This will serve as a guide for placement of questions and answers, which can be written on 5 × 8 inch index cards in appropriate places. Punch holes.
   9. Using 5 × 8 inch index cards, mark holes and punch them out. Use the guide for the placement of information.
  10. Fold over the first side under the center section; then fold up the bottom flap; now fold over the last side. Paste or staple them together, being certain that the bottom flap is in between.

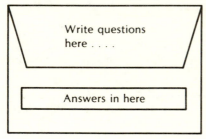

(Pic-A-Hole directions were developed by Dr. Barbara Gardiner.)

for placement of the questions and answers, which can be written on 5-by-8 inch index cards in appropriate places. Punch out the holes.

   9. Using 5-by-8-inch index cards, mark holes and punch them out. Use the guide for the placement of information.

  10. Fold over the first side under the center section; then fold up the bottom flap; now fold over the last side. Paste or staple them together, being certain

that the bottom flap is in between the other two flaps. For sample pic-a-hole cards in social studies and accounting, see Figures 7.13 and 7.14.

Designing an Electroboard

Although most students pay rapt attention to what they are trying to decipher when the tactual component is added, electroboards may be the single resource that consistently holds their attention. Electroboards require less handling than task cards, which merely need to be shuffled, examined, and then placed side by side with their correct half. Electroboards require no more tactile involvement than flip chutes where an answer, once selected, is placed into the upper slot and caught as it emerges from the bottom opening. If anything, the pic-a-hole is more tactual, for students must choose the correct answer and then insert the golf tee into the correct hole, attempt to pull out the card, place it onto a nearby surface, and then reach for the cards and golf tee and repeat the process.

Electroboards, however, have a bulb that lights up whenever the chosen answer is correct, and, as with a slot machine or a computer, that facet appears to mesmerize adolescents with the lighted bulb's immediate visual feedback. This resource takes longer to make but once completed is worth every moment devoted to it.

Questions are listed on one side of the electroboard, whereas answers are listed on the opposite side but out of sequence, so that the questions and their correct answers are not adjacent to each other. Students hold a two-prong continuity tester in their hands. They attach one prong to the question they are trying to answer, and after reading the list of possible responses on the opposite side of the board, they touch what they believe is the correct answer to that question with the second prong of the continuity tester. If they are correct, the bulb lights up. On certain electroboards the continuity tester makes a bell ring, but that ringing sound can be disconcerting to some students.

Electroboards and all other tactual resources are particularly attention holding when their outer shapes are in harmony with the subject matter they teach. For example, an electroboard on whales could be designed in the shape of a whale, or one on a foreign nation could be designed either in the shape of that country or in the shape of an item generally associated with that nation. An Electroboard on "Foods From All Nations" could be in the shape of a bottle of wine or a quiche (France), a sturgeon or salmon (Russia), a sleigh (Holland), a kimono (Japan), pasta or macaroni (Italy), wild rice or squash (Native American), or a ketchup bottle (Malaysia).

Figure 7.13
Sample Pic-A-Hole Cards in Social Studies

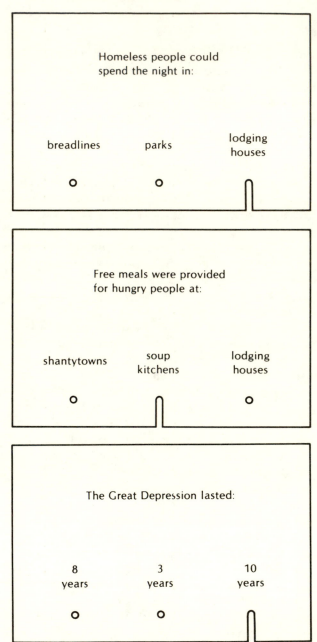

Figure 7.14
Sample Pic-A-Hole Cards for Accounting Designed by Karen Robinson

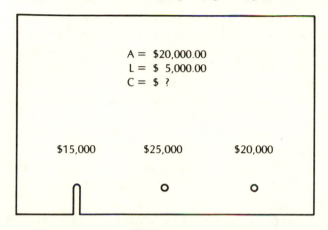

A = $20,000.00
L = $ 5,000.00
C = $?

$15,000 $25,000 $20,000

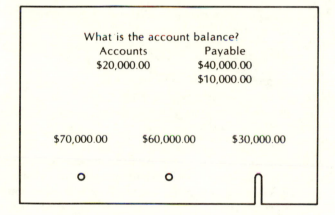

What is the account balance?
Accounts   Payable
$20,000.00 $40,000.00
$10,000.00

$70,000.00 $60,000.00 $30,000.00

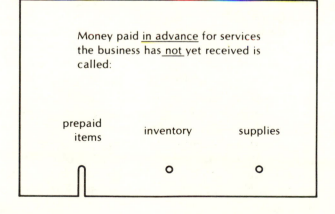

Money paid in advance for services
the business has not yet received is
called:

prepaid
items   inventory   supplies

Directions For Making Electroboards

Creatively vary the outer dimension of each electroboard to reflect the theme or unit being studied and to make it is easy for students to locate the one they need without assistance. For example, they will learn that when looking for an electroboard dealing with a unit on outer space, its outline is likely to be in the shape of a rocket, planet, or constellation. Thus, when they are focusing on a specific theme, all the tactual resources for that theme should have the same shape. Resources for a unit on Mexico could all be in the shape of the country or a sombrero, adobe, or burro, whereas resources on Greece might be in the shape of Greece, the Pantheon, an urn, or an Olympic stadium. Thus, a pic-a-hole, an electroboard, a set of task cards, a flip chute, and any other tactual resources for that unit or topic would all be in the identical shape.

1. Begin with two pieces of poster board or oak-tag cut into exactly the same size and shape (12 by 10 inches to 24 by 10 inches).

2. List the exact questions you want the electroboard to ask; then list their answers. Count the number of questions and divide the face of the left side of the electroboard into evenly divided spaces so that the questions all fit on the left side.

3. Use a paper hole puncher to make one hole on the left side of the face of the Electroboard for each question you developed. Then punch corresponding holes on the same horizontal level as the beginning of each question—but on the right side; those holes are for the answers to the questions (½ inch in and 1–2 inches apart).

4. Print the questions and each answer separately in large, black, capital letters either directly on the oak-tag or poster board or, to secure very neat, attractive lines, onto double-line (2-by-8-inch) opaque correction tape, which can be obtained in most large stationery stores. When you are satisfied with the printing of the questions and their corresponding answers, peel the correction tape from its base. Carefully place each question next to one of the pre-punched holes on the left side of the developing electroboard's face and each answer next to one of the pre-punched holes on the right side. Be certain that each question and answer is placed on a horizontal plane with the other and that even spaces remain between. It is important to randomize the answers so that no answer is on the same horizontal level as its matched question.

5. Turn the oak-tag or poster board face over and on its back create circuits made with aluminum foil strips and masking tape. One at a time, place ¼-inch wide strips of aluminum foil connecting each question and its correct answer. Then use masking tape that is wider than the foil strips, cover each foil strip with ¾-inch-wide to 1-inch-wide masking tape. Be certain to press both the foil and the masking tape cover so that they completely cover the punched holes and remain permanently fixed. An easy way to be certain that the foil is covered

involves laying the appropriate length of masking tape on a desk or table sticky side up and then placing the foil on the tape.

6. Note the positions of each question and its answer so that you can prepare a self-corrective guide in case one is necessary for substitute teachers or aides. Write the name and number of the electroboard at the top of the code. Place the answer key into a secure place where access is available when necessary.

7. Using a continuity tester, which can be purchased in any hardware store, check every circuit to be certain that each is working correctly. Do that by touching each question with one prong of the circuit tester and the related answer with the other prong. If the circuits are attached correctly, the tester's bulb should light each time the prongs touch the correct answer and its matched question. Experiment with touching several questions and incorrect answers, one at a time, to be certain that the bulb does not light. Remove sharp points if any exist.

8. Next tape the second, identically shaped and identically sized piece of oak-tag or poster-board to the back of the first piece on which you have been doing all this tactile work. The second piece will serve as a cover to conceal the circuits so that your students do not know which questions are paired with which answers. Then tape the entire perimeter of both cards together, or connect the cards using double-faced tape.

Electroboard Variations

It is efficient to develop multiple Electroboards by inserting blank circuit boards with room for question-and-answer cards to be placed in the middle and attached by using one of the following:

1. Velcro
2. Plastic binder spines
3. Pocket made of oak-tag

Further, additional circuit patterns are presented by turning the Electroboard upside down, turning it over (where the holes have been punched through and show on both sides), or using both sides as well as the top and bottom.

Figure 7.15 is a sample Electroboard designed by Wendy St. John for a unit on France. Laminate or use clear contact paper on all boards after questions and answers are completed but before holes are punched. Insert a paper fastener into each hole for permanence.

Crossword Puzzles

Emphasizing what is important in each unit helps students to focus on what they need to memorize. Thus, in a unit on dinosaurs, placing questions that require specific answers on the chalkboard or on a ditto and

Figure 7.15
Sample Electroboard on French Expressions Designed by Wendy St. John, a Graduate Student

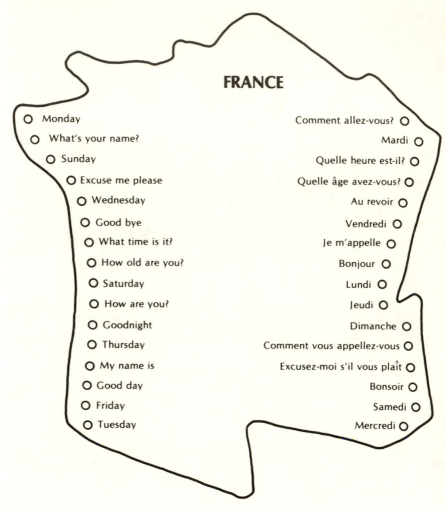

then requiring that the adolescent find the answers and then convert those answers into a crossword puzzle serves several purposes. It

- emphasizes what needs to be remembered.
- provides different types of activities for adolescents who prefer to learn in several ways and therefore tend to become bored with routine teaching and learning.
- permits the students to concentrate in their learning-style strengths rather than in predetermined ways. For example, they may seek the answers from printed

material, ask for the information, use tactual resources to gather it, or learn it through a kinesthetic floor game.

* enables students to learn in any sociological grouping that is best for them (For example, alone, in a pair, in a small group, or with their teachers).
* allows reflective learners to think critically and impulsive learners to get their answers down immediately without disturbing others.
* makes it possible to learn in any environment that most appeals to the student.
* increases motivation.
* permits options and choices for the nonconformist.
* entails structure for those who are externally motivated and choices for those who are internally structured.

Example of a Crossword Puzzle

Find the answer to as many of these questions as you can. As you find the answer to each question, count the number of alphabetical letters in it and the number of spaces in the blank crossword puzzle attached to it. If the number of alphabetical letters and the number of spaces on the same numbered item are the same, neatly print the answer into the correct space, one letter on each space. In this way, you will be "doing" a crossword puzzle, just as many adults do!

1. The word *dinosaur* means _____.
2. Which dinosaur was called the "King of Tyrants"?
3. Dinosaurs were like reptiles because they *laid* _____.
4. We know about dinosaurs because we saw their footprints and body prints in special rocks. What are those prints called?
5. Dinosaurs lived _____ 200 million years ago.
6. Dinosaurs are *different* from reptiles because they do not drag their _____ on the ground.

As you find each answer, write it onto the crossword puzzle.

STEP-BY-STEP GUIDE TO DESIGNING KINESTHETIC ACTIVITIES

Some adolescents can learn only by doing; for them, real-life experiences are the most effective way of absorbing and retaining knowledge. It is easy to teach students to convert pints to quarts and quarts to gallons through baking and cooking, or to teach them inches and feet by helping them to build a model car or antique doll house, but it is not simple to teach all the skills and information that must be achieved through reality-oriented activities. Such activities are time consuming and many require supervision. Finally, we are not used to teaching that way, and to do so requires an endless source of creative suggestions. There is, however, a new kind of kinesthetic (whole-body) game that you can design for classroom use and ongoing learning by your kinesthetic students.

Designing Floor Games

Now is the time to locate all the large plastic tablecloths, shower curtains, carpet and furniture coverings, and sails that may be hidden away in the basements, attics, and garages of your acquaintances, friends, and family. Old sheets and bath towels may also be pressed into service, but they are not as durable as plastic, and when they are washed, the printed matter on them often fades and occasionally disappears altogether. If you are not a collector of old valuables, you may need to solicit castoff materials from others or purchase a large sheet of plastic from your neighborhood bargain store.

Materials for Making Floor Games

You will require the following items:

- one large sheet of plastic or other material, approximately 4 by 5, 5 by 5 or 5 by 6 feet or within that size range
- smaller pieces of multicolored plastic that can be cut into decorations and illustrations and then glued or sewn onto the larger sheet
- black, thin-line permanent-ink pens
- black and brightly colored permanent-ink felt pens
- glue that will make plastic adhere to plastic
- assorted discarded items to use as part of the game you design
- pad and pencil for sketching ideas

Directions for Making Floor Games

1. Identify the information or skills you want your students to learn.
2. Consider ways in which you can either introduce that information or reinforce it through a kinesthetic floor game in which selected students can hop, or jump, or merely move from one part of the large sheet to another as they are exposed to the major (or finer) points of the topic.
3. Sketch a design on a sheet of paper to work out your plan before you begin cutting, pasting, or sewing.
4. When you are satisfied with your conceptualization of the game, plan a layout of the various sections on the plastic sheet you will use; consider the placement of articles, and list the additional items you can use, noting the ways in which you can use them.

5. In pencil, lightly sketch on the large sheet where you will paste each item, the dimensions you must plan for and where you will place key directions.

6. Cut the smaller plastic pieces into appropriate shapes or figures and glue them onto the larger sheet.

7. With a felt pen that will not wash off, trace cover those penciled lines you wish to keep.

8. Develop a set of questions and answers or tasks students can complete as they use the floor game. Then either develop an answer card so that students can correct themselves or color code or picture code the questions and answers so the game is self-corrective.

9. If you teach poor readers or students who have not yet mastered English, develop a tape that will tell them how to play the game, what the game will teach them (the objectives), and how they can recognize when they have learned whatever it is the game is designed to teach (the test).

10. If your students are capable of reading and following printed directions, print or type and illustrate a set of directions for them and attach them to the sheet (perhaps in a pocket that you cut out and glue or sew onto the underside of the sheet).

Examples of Floor Games

For an instructional package entitled "*Heredity: The Genes We All Wear*" (Arcieri, 1994), a kinesthetic floor game was designed to teach students the vocabulary and the information required by the topic's objectives. The floor game included the following directions for "Mendel's Punnet-square":

Let's see how much you know about what makes people the way they are—their heredity!

1. Remove the floor game (large colored plastic sheet) from the box labeled "Heredity: The Genes We All Wear!" Carefully spread it out on the floor in a section of the room where it is not likely to be stepped on by anyone not playing this game. Then take the yellow and white index cards and the black die from the same large box.

2. Place the same-colored index cards into a stack and place the (a) yellow cards in the box with the big Y and (b) white cards in the box with the big W on the plastic sheet.

3. Each player, in turn, must roll the die to see how many places he/she can move. The square moved to will have either *white* or *yellow* printed on it.

4. If the square says *white*, the player must take a white question card; if it says *yellow*, the player must take a yellow question card. Players must answer the question on the card they take.

5. After answering the question, the player must follow the directions on the question card. There will be one set of directions if the player's answer is

correct and a different set of directions if the answer is incorrect. Whatever the answer, players must follow the directions—forward or backward—on the question card.

6. Players must wait for their turn to roll the die. Each player gets one turn and then waits until all the other players have had one turn before taking a second turn.

7. The player who finishes first wins. However, if players wish to pair or team, the game can be played by groups who confer to determine their answers.

A Final Word On Teaching Tactually and Kinesthetically

Obviously, extensive time and effort is needed to develop tactual and kinesthetic games. But if you find that students who rarely achieved before, suddenly begin to learn and to enjoy learning when exposed to this method, you will agree that the results are worth your effort. We encourage you to do something very different for the next unit you teach. Begin the unit with the flip chutes, task cards, electroboards, and pic-a-holes for the tactual students. After they have had a chance to become familiar with the concept and vocabulary by working with these resources twice, perhaps for 20 minutes each time, then teach them by talking. We are certain that you will see the difference in their levels of understanding, attention to the topic, attitudes, and behaviors. If not, you have lost little. If we are correct, you have gained a great deal.

USING TACTUAL AND KINESTHETIC RESOURCES IN COUNSELING

When addressing the content of counseling in such areas as career education, the development of life skills, and the use of problem-solving and decision-making approaches to resolve personal concerns, the same resources described previously as used for teaching can be used to accommodate students with strong tactual and/or kinesthetic perceptual strengths. For example, when learning about trends in the world of work, occupational groupings, and identification of the basic sources of occupational information, tactual adolescents can utilize task cards, flip chutes, electroboards, and crossword puzzles to become knowledgeable about careers. Additionally, counselors can expose tactual students to computerized career guidance systems, such as the System of Interactive Guidance and Information (SIGI) (Educational Testing Service), Guidance Information System (GIS) (Houghton Mifflin), or Computer-Linked Exploration of Careers and Training (C-LECT) (Chronicle Guidance Publications), which direct the student in (1) assessing themselves, (2) exploring occupations, (3) searching for occupations congruent with personal interests, skills, values, and education, (4) learning about a delimited number of occupations in-depth, and (5) making educational choices.

Kinesthetic approaches are particularly attractive to adolescents who like to be involved in active, experiential learning. Kinesthetic interventions frequently used in counseling include modeling, game therapy, and systematic relaxation.

Modeling and Role Play

Modeling is a technique by which a person can learn through observing the behavior of another and then attempting to demonstrate that skill or activity. Group counseling is an optimal forum for using this technique because peers can serve as live models. The greater the similarity between the model and the counselee in terms of age, gender, and cultural background, the more likely the counselee will be motivated to acquire the new behavior. Also, it is helpful if the model has had similar concerns, problems, or setbacks to those experienced by the counselee. Finally, the model should be perceived not as perfect but, instead, as someone who is coping effectively in the area of concern.

The types of issues amenable to modeling include learning assertive behaviors such as saying no to an unwelcome request, responding with thank you to a compliment, or effectively challenging someone who cuts in line. Interpersonal areas such as communicating effectively with peers, parents, or authority figures, also lend themselves to modeling. In addition, developing competence in specific areas, such as learning job interviewing skills, and learning to identify and label feelings and respond to others cognitively as well as emotionally may be effectively accomplished through modeling.

Steps to follow in using live modeling in group counseling are listed below.

1. The counselor identifies a group member who is experiencing an issue that lends itself to role play, such as friend who consistently makes unreasonable demands.

2. The counselor invites the member to experiment with a technique that will provide a different, more effective way to deal with her demanding friend—role play.

3. After the group member consents to the role play, the counselor solicits participation from other group members who have effectively dealt with persons making unreasonable requests.

4. The role play is introduced, with the following suggestions:
   (1) The group member who has difficulty in the demanding situation plays the friend and is instructed to assume the stance, facial expression, voice tone,

and general demeanor of the person. (2) The volunteer who plays the model, ideally someone with whom the group member can identify, is instructed to express thoughts and feelings of the group member who is displeased with the demands.

5. The role play is implemented and might take the following form:

> *Demanding friend*: Joan, I'm doing poorly in algebra. I need to copy your homework tonight and to have you pass the answers during the class quiz tomorrow!
>
> *Model*: [Briefly hesitates and appears to want to please her friend but is uncomfortable]: Sally, I don't feel comfortable with helping you to cheat on homework and tests. I can't be a party to that kind of deception, because it hurts you more than anyone and our friendship is important to me.
>
> *Demanding friend*: If our friendship is important to you, you'd help me pass algebra!
>
> *Model*: You're right! I will help you, but not in the way you suggest. Instead, I'll tutor you in algebra for an hour after school each day until you understand it.
>
> *Demanding friend*: Well, perhaps that would be the better way to go.

6. The counselor facilitates an evaluation of the role play through a series of questions: How did it feel to be in the shoes of the demanding friend? Did the model accurately express your thoughts and feelings about this situation? Was there anything that seemed phony or unreal in the role play? If you don't want to commit to tutoring Sally, what other responses might be appropriate?
7. A second role play is conducted with the model playing the demanding friend and other group member playing herself as a more effective, assertive person.
8. Again, the counselor facilitates a discussion of the second role play by asking questions: How did it feel to express your thoughts and feelings to Sally? Is this something you will be able to say directly to Sally? Do you have any reservations about taking a more assertive approach with Sally? How do other members of the group feel about how this situation was handled?
9. The counselor encourages Joan to spend time outside the group, reflecting on her desired response to Sally, rehearsing what she will say, planning when she will meet with Sally, and finally verbalizing and acting out the desired behavior.
10. During the next group counseling session, the counselor follows up with Joan to determine how she responded to Sally and how she felt about behaving differently in the relationship.

To summarize the role of the counselor in using modeling and role play with adolescents: Identify interpersonal concerns that are amenable to role play; facilitate the role play by explaining purpose, procedures, and roles; coach the participants before the role play; evaluate the role play; and elicit feedback on the counselee's thoughts and feelings about implementing the desired behavior.

Game Therapy

Games provide a vehicle for enhancing the learning of tactual and/or kinesthetic adolescents because such learners require involvement—frequently through hands-on activities or total body movement. Additionally, games provide interesting experiences, and allow for creativity, self-expression, and affective involvement. Game therapy in counseling:

1. Provides a vehicle for trying out new social roles and activities.
2. Has rules and is competitive. Hence, it provides a means for learning about teamwork, success, and failure.
3. Allows for motor activity and can enhance communication and self-expression;
4. Can provide adolescents with insight into themselves and help them to achieve many counseling objectives (Nickerson & O'Laughlin, 1982).

Games can be either commercial or counselor-made. Commercial games that can be used in counseling include Monopoly ©, which can be used to teach about power, security, helplessness, and economic principles and Scruples (Milton Bradley, 1986), which is designed to encourage provocative discussion of ethical dilemmas. Usually, between five and eight adolescents can play one of these games and the therapeutic value is found in processing the experience, that is, using the counselor and observers to record what transpires among individuals during the game playing and to facilitate a discussion of the personal and interpersonal insights gained from the game.

Counselor-made games can be found in books on family counseling, group counseling, and specialized areas. Bradshaw (1992) described an exercise on conflict resolution that can be used with up to 12 adolescents who work together in dyads. The counselor provides the following directions:

Pair off so that each of you is sitting in a chair and facing one other person. I am going to give each pair an 8½-by-11-inch sheet of white paper that represents something very valuable. There is only one piece of paper and each of you wants it very badly, but only one of you can keep the paper. Each person begins by holding two corners of the paper, using thumbs and forefingers. At the word "start," you each have five minutes to try to get the paper from the other person using any method you know of, but if the paper is torn or damaged in any way, you both lose. After ten minutes the group reassembles for discussion.

This exercise can provide insight into how adolescents negotiate conflict. For example, some members might give up, turn their backs, and pout, whereas others may trick their partners by distracting their attention. Sometimes, gender differences are evident: Boys may try to over-power their partners, whereas girls sometimes use seduction to get the paper. Discussion should center around such themes as willingness to compromise, accepting real differences, winning and losing, and learning to confront another person with respect.

Another game that is particularly appealing to adolescents is the co-operation versus competition game described by Napier and Gershenfeld (1973). The objectives of the game are (1) to experience some of the aspects of cooperation, (2) to have data for evaluating one's own behavior in a cooperative and competitive situation, (3) to become aware of be-haviors that help or hinder group problem solving, and (4) to develop sensitivity to others in the group in order to be more helpful. Up to 30 adolescents can be involved in this game, working in teams of five mem-bers with one or two adolescents assigned to observe each team. The counselor arranges the teams of five members so that they are seated together in a small circle of desks. Observers are instructed separately to notice who shares first, who completes the square first, whether there is a leadership pattern, whether all share the work or one person is given or accepts responsibility, and which members surrender their pieces and are not given any pieces. The participants are provided with the following directions:

Each of you will receive an envelope with pieces of cardboard inside. Among the five of you there are enough pieces for each person to complete a square that is approximately 6 inches by 6 inches. This is a nonverbal exercise—you may not ask a member for pieces to complete your square. Instead, the other person must see that he or she has a piece that is essential for you to complete the square and give it to you. You may not take the piece. The object of the game is for all members of the group to complete their squares before the other groups complete their squares. Are there any questions about the task? If not, you may begin!

The time required to complete the exercise may vary from a few minutes to as long as 40 minutes. As each group finishes, the counselor checks that there is a square before each member and requests that mem-ber remain quiet while the other teams complete the nonverbal game. Direction for making a set of squares are provided in Figure 7.16. When a group completes the task, request that members place the cardboard pieces back into the envelopes as follows:

Envelope A: i, h, e
Envelope B: a, a, a, c
Envelope C: a, j
Envelope D: d, f
Envelope E: g, b, f, c

Figure 7.16
Directions for Creating Materials for Cooperation Versus Competition Games

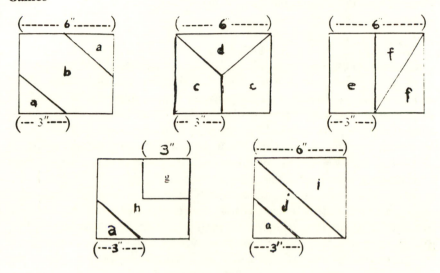

After all groups have completed the exercise, the counselor requests that the observers provide feedback on their findings regarding the way individual members and the group overall proceeded with the exercise; the counselor then involves individual members in expressing their feelings about the task and facilitates group discussion. Questions for guiding the discussion are listed below.

1. How did members who were given only a few pieces feel about the initial unfairness concerning the distribution of resources? (Analogies might be drawn to the gifts or talents that each is given at birth.)
2. How did you feel about giving pieces? receiving pieces?
3. How did you react when someone holding a key piece did not see the solution?
4. Were you able to "read" the reactions of other group members based on nonverbal cues?
5. What evidence did you see of members trying to help one another?
6. How did members of the first group to complete the task feel? How did members of the last group feel?
7. Did you conclude that members of the group were working more as a team or as separate individuals?
8. Which members and teams appeared to be the most competitive?

Creative counselors can devise a wide variety of games that challenge adolescents to gain insight into such areas as peer pressure, independence versus submission to group pressure, decision making, creative problem solving, dealing with interpersonal conflict, risk taking, and the interdependence among family members.

Systematic Relaxation

Adolescents experience stress as a result of daily frustrations and pressures that result from too many things to do in the course of a day. Petty annoyances, frustrations, and unexpected events are termed "hassles," and coupled with the stress of life changes, they have the potential to affect mental health and well being negatively. Life events that are stressful for adolescents include such things as a delinquency charge; the death of a close family member; personal injury or illness; suspension from school; pregnancy; a sibling leaving home; trouble with a teacher; a change in living conditions; or positive events such as a vacation, winning an award, or excelling in a particular sport. Research on stress in youth indicated that the relationship to psychiatric disorders is influenced by the number of stresses the adolescent is experiencing concurrently; by the pervasiveness of the stress and the degree to which it affects the individual's daily life; by the adolescent's ability to cope with problems; and by the social support available to the adolescent from parents, extended family members, and key persons in the school and community (Berger & Thompson, 1994).

Through an exploration of adolescents' concerns and problems expressed during group counseling, the counselor is able to identify youth who are experiencing high levels of stress. Referral for mental health services may be indicated if students lack adequate social support systems and coping ability. All adolescents experience daily hassles with the resulting anxiety and can benefit from learning relaxation techniques. Baldwin (1988) outlined some strategies to help individuals learn to relax:

1. Focus on experiencing through your senses. Take a few minutes each day to study the beauty around you and the sensations it produces—the sights, smells, and the feelings evoked by a walk through the park or a jog through an attractive neighborhood.

2. Allow unstructured time for yourself. Set aside an interval after school or in the evening to spend in whatever way you choose—with someone or alone— making decisions spontaneously.

3. Soften your communication. When you are stressed and anxious, communication often becomes fast, hurried, and abrasive. Take time to listen intently to others and respond with understanding and empathy.

4. Work on developing patience. You can save emotional energy by accepting things that can't be changed, such as traffic delays that make you late for a sporting event.

5. Learn to play for fun. Engage in activities that are noncompetitive and ego enhancing.

6. Make time for contemplation. Take a few minutes each day to reflect on yourself and your priorities. Thinking about what is really important to you will help you identify the meaningless things that fill your day and need to be eliminated.

7. Put some spontaneity into your life. Doing things on impulse can be interesting and fun for many people. Seeking out pleasure and fun is one of the pillars of sound mental health.

8. Spend time on physical activities that produce relaxation. Engaging in muscle relaxation can help you sleep better at night and wake up more relaxed and energetic.

Systematic relaxation training is a kinesthetic activity that adolescents can engage in to facilitate relaxation. The procedure involves learning to tense and relax different muscle groups in the body and can be taught in an individual or group counseling setting. The counselor can begin by modeling and demonstrating the exercise focusing on a specific muscle group, such as the biceps. The counselor many start with either the right or left hand, make a fist, and hold it for ten seconds, and then let go and relax. Students then are directed to stand and the counselor guides them through the exercise, progressing from the feet and toes up to the head. Tape recordings with muscle relaxation instructions can be given to students so that they are able to engage in this activity at home—ideally in a prone position and scheduled close to bedtime. Students should be encouraged to engage in these exercises for 15 to 20 minutes daily and to maintain a homework log sheet to record the degree to which they are gaining control over stress and anxiety.

Chapter 8

Designing Programmed Learning Sequences to Respond to Adolescents' Individual Learning Styles

A second method for responding to adolescents' individual learning styles is to program curriculum content so that it can be learned in small, simple steps without the direct supervision of an adult. Like any other method, programmed instruction is responsive to only selected learning-style characteristics and should not be prescribed for all students. The special type of programming described in this chapter is called programmed learning sequences (PLS).

PLSs are designed around curriculum objectives that should be mastered by each student. Objectives range from simple to complex and are sequenced so that after taking a pretest students need to concentrate only on the content that they did not know as evidenced by their pretest score. All students proceed through the identical sequence but pace themselves and study in the section of the classroom that is most responsive to their environmental preferences for sound, light, temperature, and seating.

Programs that have been commercially produced have had only limited effectiveness because they are solely visual—similar to workbooks—and therefore appeal most to students who either read fairly well or who can retain information by seeing.

In actual practice students are each given a PLS for which they are responsible; and as the various objectives and their related tests are completed, gradual progress is made toward completing the curriculum requirements. Unless learners need and seek assistance, they work through the PLS by themselves without adult or peer interaction. The PLS tape may be played aloud while the student is directed to listen carefully, read along, think of answers, and then record them. The answers are self-corrected by the material; thus there is little danger that erroneous guesses will not be corrected.

There are, however, adolescents at each grade level who are peer oriented; they learn better with a friend than they do alone. When the Learning Style Inventory (LSI) score indicates that certain students prefer to learn with a classmate, allow each pair to work together with the PLS. Teachers across the United States have permitted peer-oriented learners to work in pairs or in small groups of three and have reported no inappropriate behaviors or poor grades (Andrews, 1990, 1991; *The Bridge to Learning*, 1993; Klavas, 1991, 1993; Orsak, 1990a, 1990b; Stone, 1992). Indeed, extensive research indicates that peer-motivated adolescents achieve statistically higher achievement and attitude test scores when they are permitted to work with a classmate (DeBello, 1985; Dunn, 1989c; Dunn, Giannitti, Murray, Geisert, Rossi, & Quinn, 1990; Fleming, 1989; Miles, 1987; Perrin, 1984; Review of Research, 1991).

ADOLESCENTS' LEARNING-STYLE CHARACTERISTICS RESPONSIVE TO PROGRAMMED LEARNING SEQUENCES

Because PLSs were designed for use independently or in pairs, it is important that those students to whom this resource is assigned enjoy working alone or with one other student. They should also be persistent and continue working with the PLS until the entire program has been completed. Should they find the content difficult, they need to review previous frames before trying to progress or they should seek assistance from appropriate sources.

By organizing everything that should be learned so that only one item at a time is presented, the sequenced materials in each program provide a great deal of structure. A student should not proceed until the content included on each frame has been understood. Adolescents who need structure—who prefer to be directed and told exactly what to do—will feel at ease with PLSs. Creative students may find them boring and unchallenging.

PLSs are a perfect match for students who prefer learning (1) in a pair or by themselves, (2) by hearing a tape or seeing or reading print and illustrations, (3) through touching (4) with structure, and (5) in small stages followed by frequent reinforcement. Finally, because a PLS always begins with a short story, they also match the style of global students.

If you know students who are neither motivated nor persistent, only average or slow achievers, visual or tactual, independent or pair motivated, and in need of structure, experiment with PLS to determine if this approach keeps them on task. Because this strategy presents concepts and skills simply, gradually, and repeatedly and may be used by students individually or paired, without causing embarrassment or pressure, many youngsters often become motivated, persistent, or responsible when using a PLS. When the "right" method is matched correctly with the "right" student, increased academic achievement and improved attitudes toward learning are likely to result. Include a tape recording of your voice reading each frame slowly for students who do not read well.

Because a PLS can be used in a classroom, in a library, in a corridor, or in a resource center as well as at home, it can accommodate each student's environmental and physiological preferences. For example, the PLS can be taken to a silent area if quiet is desired, or it may be used in the midst of classroom activity when the learner can block out sound. It can be moved to either a warm section of a room, near a radiator perhaps, or to a cool area. It can be studied at a desk or on a carpet, in either a well-lit space or away from the bright sunshine. A student may snack or not as he or she works, may use the package at any time of day that is convenient, and may take a break or two if mobility is necessary. Since the PLS is visual, it will utilize the perceptual strengths of students who learn best by reading or seeing. For auditory youngsters, add a tape that reads orally what the text teaches visually. Hearing and seeing the words simultaneously will help struggling readers.

BASIC PRINCIPLES OF PROGRAMMED LEARNING SEQUENCES

PLSs are designed on the basis of several important principles that increase achievement for students with specific learning-style elements. All programs tend to follow a pattern that includes each of the characteristics that follow.

1. Only one item is presented at a time, in a format called a frame. A single concept or skill that should be mastered is introduced through a simple written statement. After reading the material, the learner is required to answer a question or two to demonstrate that what was introduced on that frame is understood. This procedure prevents the lesson from advancing faster than the student and does not permit the student to fall behind. Individuals may learn as quickly as they can or as slowly, and with as much repetition, as they need. Students should not continue into a subsequent frame or phase of the program until each previous frame has been mastered.

Presenting one item at a time is effective for the analytic youngster who wants to learn (is motivated), who will continue trying (is persistent), and who wants to do what is required (is responsible/conforming). For students who are not persistent, exposure to one item at a time divides the content into small segments and the process into short steps that can be mastered gradually. Global students will respond positively to PLS when the frames are illustrated and the introduction is a brief story or anecdote that summarizes the content and attracts their interest. A series of PLSs is inappropriate for students who need diversity and variety. For such students, a PLS should be followed for the next few units or lessons by an entirely different method—perhaps by tactual and kinesthetic activities, a Contract Activity Package (CAP), and/or a Multisensory Instructional Package (MIP). In addition, the PLS is a method that does not attract and hold many creative students who want to add their own knowledge and special talents to what is being learned before they have accomplished the entire task.

Unlike large-group instruction, where a student may merely sit and appear to be listening, a PLS requires that a response be made to questions related to each introduced item. Youngsters cannot progress through the program without responding, and only accurate answers permit continuation of this instructional process.

2. Students are required to be active, rather than passive, learners.

3. Students are immediately informed of the correctness of each response. As soon as youngsters read each frame, they are required to answer a question based on the material just read. The moment that response is recorded, the frame may be turned over to show the back, where the correct answer is stated. Students are immediately made aware of the accuracy or inaccuracy of each response. This strategy of immediate feedback is highly effective with many average or below-grade-level learners.

4. Students may not continue into the next phase of a PLS until each previous phase has been understood and mastered. When the program reveals that their responses to the questions related to each frame are correct, students are directed to continue to the next frame. When their responses are not correct, students can be directed either to restudy the previously read frames or to turn to another section of the program that explains differently the material that was not understood. Because each phase of the program must be mastered before students are permitted to continue into the next phase, learners do not move ahead aimlessly while grasping only parts of a concept or topic. Their knowledge base is solid before they are exposed to either new or related ideas.

5. Students are exposed to material that gradually progresses from the easy to the more difficult. Frames are written so that the first few in a series—after the initial global introduction, directions for usage, and vocabulary—explain in an uncomplicated, direct manner the curriculum objectives that need to be learned. Gradually, as correct answers demonstrate the students' understanding of what is being taught, more difficult aspects of the topic are introduced. Through this technique students are made to feel comfortable and successful with the beginning phases of each program and their confidence in their own ability to achieve is bolstered.

6. As students proceed with the program, fewer hints and crutches are provided. Programming uses a system of "fading," or gradually withdrawing easy questions or repeated expressions, illustrations, color coding, and similar learning aids. This technique enables teachers to assess accurately student progress and mastery of the curriculum content.

STEP-BY-STEP GUIDE TO DESIGNING A PROGRAMMED LEARNING SEQUENCE

Developing a PLS is not difficult, but it does require organizing the topic to be taught into a logical, easy-to-follow sequence. Begin with Step 1 and gradually move through each of the remaining steps until you have completed your first program. Each consecutive program will be easier and easier to design. By the questions they ask of you and the answers they give to the questions at the bottom of the frames, your students will provide direct feedback on how to revise and improve your first PLS development efforts.

Step 1: Begin by identifying a topic, concept, or skill you want to teach. A good choice would be the next difficult lesson or unit your students need to learn. Since all students are not capable of learning at the same time, in the same way, and with the same speed, a PLS is one way of permitting individuals to self-pace at the time of day they are most able to achieve. Thus, some youngsters may use a specific program early in the day, whereas others can use it later. Some will use it to learn before the entire class is exposed to the material, and others will use it to reinforce an idea that you previously taught but they did not master.

Step 2: Write the name of the topic, concept, or skill that you want to teach as a heading at the top of a blank sheet of paper. Add a subtitle that is humorous or related to the experiences of the adolescents you teach. Design the cover—or the entire PLS—in a shape that represents the topic to appeal to visual/tactual students. If you can include some humor, it will appeal to global students.

Examples of PLS Titles

- Exploring the Planets: Give Me Some Space!
- All about Insects: Don't Bug Me!
- Inference: I Don't Have a Clue!
- Numismatics: A Penny for Your Thoughts! (Alternatives: Numismatics: Money Talks! or Numismatics: To Coin a Word!)
- Aerodynamics: Wind Beneath My Wings!
- Travel: A Moving Experience!
- Congress: A Capital Offense!

- Gravity: Coming down to Earth!
- Death and Dying: A Grave Matter!
- Graphing: Get the Point?
- Weather: You're All Wet!
- Learning Styles: No Fault Insurance
- Philately: Don't Stamp on Me!
- Shooting Stars: Celestial Gunfire
- The Rain Forest: It's Da-Vine! (Alternative: The Rain Forest: A Swinging Place!)
- Pronouns: Up Front and Personal!

Step 3: In one or two simple declarative sentences, explain to the students who will use this PLS exactly what they will need to do to show you that they have mastered the curriculum objectives that this PLS was designed to teach. For example, in "The Great Depression: Don't Let It Get You Down!" Camille Sinatra (1993) of the Manhasset Public Schools wrote: "By the time you finish this Programmed Learning Sequence, you should be able to explain each of the following terms and classify them as either "Words/Phrases Associated Only with the Great Depression Era" or "Words/Phrases in Use Today."

Step 4: List all the prerequisites for using the program effectively.

Examples of Prerequisite Information

- "On the following frames, answer questions by filling in the blanks or circling, underlining, or matching answers. The correct answers will be on the back of each frame. You may use a marker or wipe-off crayons to write your answers."
- "Be certain that you begin reading this PLS either on or near a large table so that you have ample room to use the booklet, its materials, and the tape recorder at the same time."
- "If you would like to hear the material you are reading, use the tape in the plastic box attached to the back of this PLS. Be certain to rewind the tape when you have completed this entire PLS."

Because you may realize that certain knowledge or skills are prerequisites to mastering the curriculum objectives in this PLS after you have moved beyond Step 4, leave space on your paper so that you can insert additions as they come to mind.

Step 5: Create a short global story, fantasy, cartoon, or humorous beginning that relates to the topic. Place this global opening just before the teach-and-then-question frames begin.

Example of Global Story Openings

Fon Lan, Federico, Friedreich, and Frank were all in deep trouble! Their principal had sent each home with a note complaining that none of the boys had done yesterday's homework. The mothers of all four boys told them they could not attend the football game that weekend. Instead, they had to make up this assignment and do next week's assignments in advance on Saturday. All four promised to do their homework every week of the entire year if they could only attend the game on Saturday.

Fon Lan's mother said, "Talk does not cook rice!"

Federico's mother said, "It is one thing to cackle and another to lay an egg!"

Friedreich's mother said, "Fancy words don't butter cabbage!"

Frank's mother said, "Actions speak louder than words!"

Why did their mothers say different words with the same end result? What did their mothers' words really mean?

This PLS on "Proverbs: Say What You Mean and Mean What You Say!" will show you that many people in different cultures feel exactly the same way about certain things; they just express their feelings differently.

Step 6: Decide exactly what needs to be taught in this PLS curriculum unit. What needs to be taught becomes the PLS's objective. Teach to the objective directly and clearly in small segments—whatever fits onto each frame without crowding. Leave room for an illustration or two and one or more questions related to what you have taught on that frame. At the bottom of each frame ask a question about whatever was taught on that frame. Turn the frame over and write the answer(s) to the question(s) on the top of the back side.

This type of programming presents material in a highly structured sequence. Each part of the sequence is called a frame, and each frame builds upon the one immediately preceding it. Each frame ends with an item that requires an answer, either in completion, matching, or multiple-choice format. Prior to the introduction of each subsequent frame, the answer to the previous frame should be printed and/or illustrated. The PLS becomes increasingly motivating when the correct answer is accompanied by an explanation and a humorous comment or cartoon. Additional comprehension is developed when the incorrect answers also are accompanied by explanations.

Vary the way students need to respond to the questions on the frames. Their concentration remains alert when different types of responses are required; example, students may be directed to circle the correct answer, match the correct answer to each question by connecting it with a line, pick up the Velcro cloud shapes and place the correct cloud onto the phrase that correctly describes it, write the correct answers, or fill in the missing letters.

Step 7: Outline how you plan to teach the topic. Use short, simple sentences, if possible.

Most people have two different vocabularies: One is used for speaking, the other for writing. When you begin to outline your program, pretend you are speaking to the students who will have the most trouble learning this material. Use simple words and sentences. Then write the words that you would use if you were actually talking to that youngster. In other words, use your speaking vocabulary instead of your professional writing vocabulary to develop the PLS.

Step 8: Divide the sentences in your outline into frames. Frames, which are equivalent to pages, are small sections of the topic that teach part of the idea, unit, skill, or information. After listing the sentences that teach the information, ask a question that relates to that material. Students' answers will demonstrate their developing understanding of the subject. Think small! Most people who begin to write programs try to cover too much in one frame. Keep each frame simple and a small part of the total amount of knowledge that should be included in the PLS curriculum.

Pose fairly easy to answer questions in the first two or three frames to build student self-confidence, to demonstrate to the students that they can learn independently with the PLS, and to provide them with successful experiences in at least their first five or six PLS frames.

Step 9: Cut five-by-eight-inch (or larger) index or oak-tag cards into an outline of a shape related to the concept of this curriculum unit. Make a pattern for the cover, and cut out as many shaped frames as are needed to teach everything you want the students to learn.

Step 10: Reread what you wrote and refine what will be printed on each index card frame before you actually transfer the teaching material from your papers to the card frames.

Step 11: Review the sequence you developed to be certain it is logical and does not teach too much on each frame. Add the answers to the questions you posed on the front of each frame to the back of it. After you place the answers on the back of the frame, add a humorous or "corny" comment, joke, or remark to relax the user.

Step 12: Check the spelling, grammar, and punctuation of each frame.

Step 13: Review the vocabulary you included to be certain that it includes all the important words in this unit and is understandable by the slowest youngsters who may use the PLS. Avoid colloquialisms that are acceptable in conversation but are less than professional in written form. Remember to use good oral language as opposed to good written language.

Step 14: Reread the entire series to be certain that each frame leads to the next one, and so on, that you did not forget to teach something you consider important, and that your students can really learn from what you have written.

Step 15: When you are satisfied with the content, sequence, and questions on the frames, add colorful illustrations to clarify the main point on each index card. If you do not wish to draw, use magazine cutouts or gift-wrapping paper, or you can ask some students to do the illustrating for you (If students do the illustrations, cite them as illustrator somewhere in your text). The illustrations should relate directly to the PLS content.

Step 16: When you are satisfied with the text of the PLS, read the written material of each frame onto a cassette so that poor readers may listen to the frames being read to them as they simultaneously read along.

Step 17: Ask three or four of your students to try the PLS, one at a time. Watch the youngsters as they use the material and see whether any errors, omissions, or areas of difficulty exist. Correct anything that requires improvement.

Step 18: If necessary, revise the PLS based on your observations of your students' usage.

Step 19: Laminate each of the index cards that comprise the program or cover them with clear contact paper. Use will cause the index cards to deteriorate unless they are protected by a covering. Laminated programs last for years and can be cleaned with warm water and soap. They can be written on with grease, pencils, or water-soluble felt pens and then erased for use by another student.

Step 20: Every seven or eight frames, add miniature tactual activities (pic-a-holes, task cards, or electroboards) to reinforce the most important information covered to that point in the PLS. As designed through Step 14, the PLS will respond only to youngsters who learn through their visual or auditory strengths. The tactual reinforcements provide youth who need to learn by touching and handling with a method appropriate for them. The tactual reinforcement will add to the effectiveness of the PLS and increase the number of students who can learn with it successfully.

Step 21: Ask additional students to use the PLS. Again observe the students' reactions, but this time assess how much they are learning as they work through it.

Step 22: When you are satisfied that all the "bugs" have been eliminated from the PLS, add a front and back cover in the shape related to the topic.

Step 23: Place the title and a global subtitle of the program onto the front cover, which should be in the shape of and illustrated to represent the subject matter. Bind the covers to the index card frames. You may use notebook rings, colored yarn, or any other substance that will permit easy turning of the index cards. Be certain that the answers to each frame, which appear on the back of the previous frame, are easily readable and are not upside down.

When the program has been completed, make it available to students whose learning styles are complemented by this resource.

Figure 8.1
Cover of Programmed Learning Sequence, "Looking at Colleges: A Mirror of Self"

SAMPLE PROGRAMMED LEARNING SEQUENCE

Examine the PLS sample that follows—one developed for school counselors. Counseling content can be learned in the same way curriculum content is mastered. For example, a PLS can address career education, goal setting, stress management techniques, problem solving, and aspects of drug education and prevention. A PLS on college choice, "Looking at Colleges: A Mirror of Self," is presented here to provide a model for school counselors to use with students interested in pursuing higher education. Counselors are encouraged to duplicate this material and use it with students in a wide variety of ways that complement their learning-style preferences in sociological, emotional, physiological, and environmental domains. Some of the content of this PLS deals with personal preferences, values, interests, and academic achievement; thus there are no right or wrong responses. *Counseling for College* (Matthay, 1991) was a valuable resource in developing this PLS.

Frame 1

WHERE TO BEGIN?

You are in your junior year of high school and are beginning to ask yourself, "What comes next—after high school graduation?" You are leaning toward continuing your education after graduation, but you are undecided about many things.

After completing this program, you will be able to

- identify your reasons for wanting to go to college;
- list factors to consider in selecting a college;
- describe the college admission process;
- use your perceptual strengths in learning about colleges;
- compute the costs at various colleges and identify sources of financial aid;
- narrow your choices by matching your needs and interests with the characteristics of selected colleges;
- monitor the college application process.

Information you will need for making college choices will be presented step by step. Proceed at your own pace and return to earlier frames if you do not recall some of the information presented.

Frame 2

SELF-KNOWLEDGE

When you try to visualize the ideal college, what is it like? Do you picture a rural environment with a campus situated on rolling hills or a thriving metropolis in an urban setting with lots of activity? Do you envision yourself living in a college residence hall or ensconced at home amid family and friends? Do you dream of a small institution with a median class size of 25 or a large university with lecture sections for over 500 students? Have you made a career choice or do you plan to pursue a liberal arts program before deciding on a major area of study? Will you seek out a competitive college with high admission standards or would you be more comfortable enrolling in a local community college with an open admissions policy?

Take time now to jot down what you prefer in each of the following categories:

Size of College _____

Residential or Commuter _____

Rural or Urban Environment _____

Median Class Size _____

Career Choice: Known or Unknown _____

Highly or Minimally Competitive _____

Frame 3

WHY DO YOU WANT TO GO TO COLLEGE?

Why do you want to go to college in the first place? You will probably benefit more from college if you can take ownership for having made the decision yourself—rather than because other people think that it's beneficial.

Some typical reasons students give for going to college include the following. Check the reasons that most closely reflect your own thinking:

- to get a high-paying job
- to get it over with
- to learn more
- to work in a profession that requires a degree
- to get out of the house
- because my friends are going to college
- to meet men (or women)
- because my parents, brothers, or sisters went to college
- to become independent
- to fulfill personal goals
- to avoid going to work after high school graduation

Frame 4

OPTIONS IN HIGHER EDUCATION

Institutions of higher learning have unique personalities, just as people do. There are more than 3,500 colleges and universities in our nation, but they can be classified as to type based upon resources, curriculum, and student life. Different categories of higher education institutions are listed as follows:

1. *Universities* are institutions of higher education comprised of a number of "schools" or "colleges," each of which emphasizes a general area of study such as business, pharmacy, law, engineering, or liberal arts. They are characterized by an emphasis on research and graduate education.

2. *Liberal Arts Colleges* focus on the education of the "whole" person. A liberal arts and science curriculum includes literature, foreign languages, philosophy, history, art, music, sociology, psychology, chemistry, biology, physics, and so on. Students who are undecided about a college major sometimes select a college of this kind in order to acquire knowledge in many discipline areas before declaring a major area of study.

Frame 5

OPTIONS IN HIGHER EDUCATION CONTINUED

3. *Professional Colleges and Institutes* are specialized institutions that offer associate (two-year) and baccalaureate (four-year) degrees in such fields as nursing, business, engineering, and music. Students who have strong aptitude and interest in a specialized area may select this type of setting.

4. *U.S. Service Academies* prepare individuals to become career officers in the army, navy, air force, merchant marine, or coast guard. The academies have a rigorous academic curriculum and a challenging athletic program. Although there are no tuition, board, and room costs, graduates are expected to serve in the military a minimum of five years following graduation.

Frame 6

OPTIONS IN HIGHER EDUCATION CONTINUED

5. *Community Colleges* are two-year institutions that offer (a) technical, occupational training, (b) general education, and (c) remedial programs to compensate for academic deficits. Students who elect to live at home and commute to college and/or pursue a technical area of study—such as electronics technician, landscape architect, or human services—may select this type of institution.

Frame 7

QUIZ ON OPTIONS

Match the terms in Column 2 to the statements in Column 1.

Column 1	Column 2
_____ 1. Prepares students in specialized professional areas.	A. University
_____ 2. Emphasizes research and graduate education.	B. Liberal Arts College
_____ 3. No tuition or room and board costs	C. Professional College/Institute
_____ 4. Committed to educating the "whole" person.	D. U.S. Service Academy
_____ 5. Prepares individuals to become career military officers.	E. Community College
_____ 6. Provides remedial programs to compensate for academic deficits.	
_____ 7. Comprised of a number of different "schools" or "colleges."	
_____ 8. Provides a strong, four-year liberal arts curriculum.	

[Back of Frame 7]

Key: 1.C   2.A   3.D   4.B

       5.D   6.E   7.A   8.B

Frame 8

NARROWING THE OPTIONS

There is no such thing as "one perfect college." The truth is that you can be perfectly happy at a number of different colleges. The key to making a sound choice is understanding yourself and what you are seeking.

Knowing what is most important to you means that if you feel you need to be within three hours from home (by car or by plane), a college thousands of miles away is not for you, no matter how great it appears to be. Having some idea about the occupation you plan to enter after college can narrow your choice and help you to identify colleges that prepare students in that field. However, college students frequently change their major area of study, so don't be concerned if you don't yet know whether you want to be a teacher, pharmacist, computer programmer—or whatever!

You may have special needs that not every college is prepared to meet. For example, you may have limited proficiency in English or a learning disability that requires special services.

Turn the page to record your preferences.

Frame 9

NARROWING THE OPTIONS

Take some time, think, and then write down what you think you want in a college within the following categories:

Size of college _____

Two-year community college; four-year liberal arts college; or university with graduate programs _____

Distance from home _____

Rural, Suburban, or Urban _____

Climate _____

Commuter or Residential _____   Public or Private _____

co-ed versus single sex _____

Fraternities/Sororities or None _____

Strong or Limited Extracurricular Program _____

Religious Affiliation or None _____

Academic Majors _____

Special Needs _____

Frame 10

HOW DO YOU RATE?

By now you have a pretty good idea of where you stand in your class and how you feel about it. You may like the way it feels to be at the top of your class. You may like "fitting in with the majority of the group" and feel comfortable about being in the average, middle group. You may be near the bottom of your class—either because you haven't applied yourself or you have some academic deficiencies that will need to be remediated before you can pursue higher education.

Ask your high school guidance counselor to provide you with the following information about yourself:

Class Rank: _____ out of _____ students

Grade Point Average: _____

[Back of Frame 10]

According to *Peterson's Guide to Four-Year Colleges*, you are most likely to be considered for admission by a

- "most difficult" college if your grade point average is B+ or better and you are in the top 10 percent of your class;
- "very difficult" college if your grade point average is B or better and you are in the top 20 percent of your class;
- "moderately difficult" college if your grade point average is C+ or better and you are in the top fourth of your class;
- "minimally difficult" college if your grade point average is C or better and you are willing to work at earning good grades;
- "noncompetitive" college if you are willing to apply yourself and prove that you are capable of doing college work.

Frame 11

COLLEGE ADMISSION: LEVEL OF DIFFICULTY

Colleges and universities use a selection process in which some applicants are accepted and others are rejected. Of the more than 3,500 institutions of higher education, fewer than 50 deny admission to half or more of their applicants.

Peterson's Guide to Four-Year Colleges, which is published annually, classifies colleges according to an annual self-assessment of entrance difficulty. The categories are as follows:

- "Most difficult" colleges accept up to 30 percent of applicants
- "Very difficult" colleges accept up to 60 percent of applicants
- "Moderately difficult" colleges accept up to 85 percent of applicants
- "Minimally difficult" colleges accept up to 95 percent of applicants
- "Noncompetitive" colleges accept virtually all applicants

Based on your class rank and grade point average, cite the college types most likely to admit you.

Frame 12

COLLEGE ADMISSION TESTING

A majority of colleges use admission tests to (1) provide an objective measure of a student's reasoning ability or knowledge in specific areas, (2) predict an applicant's chances for academic success within the institution, in addition to other information about the student's academic achievement, and (3) help students compare themselves with other students who were enrolled at the same institution the previous year.

Two major testing programs used by colleges are the American College Testing Program (ACT) and the College Board Admissions Testing Program, which includes the Preliminary Scholastic Assessment Test/National Merit Scholarship Qualifying Test (PSAT/NMSQT) and the Scholastic Assessment Test (SAT).

Frame 13

PREPARING FOR ADMISSION TESTING

Visit the guidance center in your school and/or talk with your guidance counselor about the following items:

- the dates when admission tests are scheduled
- ways to prepare for the admission tests
- how test results are used by colleges
- whether to take specialized tests such as the Test of Standard Written English or particular subject achievement tests
- special testing procedures if you are a student with a visual, hearing, or learning disability

After receiving your test results, schedule another session with your counselor to understand and interpret the scores.

Frame 14

HOW COLLEGES MAKE ADMISSION DECISIONS

Colleges are interested in identifying applicants who possess the background and potential to be successful students at their institution. Each applicant is evaluated individually, and usually many of the following factors determine the admission decision:

- high school grade point average
- rank in graduation class
- quality and competitiveness of the academic course of study
- results of standardized admission tests
- legal obligation of state-funded institutions to enroll a certain percentage of students from within the state

- anticipated major and/or career plans
- academic honors received while in school
- extracurricular activities and achievements
- work experience and/or volunteerism
- teacher, counselor, and personal recommendations
- student essays and personal statements

Overall, some colleges attempt to select a diverse student body that represents a range of freshmen with different ethnic, geographical, and socioeconomic backgrounds.

Frame 15

USING YOUR PERCEPTUAL STRENGTHS TO LEARN MORE ABOUT COLLEGES

Each of us perceives the world around us in different ways! We learn from our experiences and through our senses. Our favorite mode of learning is termed our *perceptual strength*, which might be auditory, visual, tactual, or kinesthetic.

If you are an *auditory* learner, you learn by listening, talking, discussing, or interviewing people. A *visual* learner retains information by seeing printed words, graphic or illustrated materials, and mental pictures. *Tactual* persons require a "hands-on" approach to learning—they need to use their fingers and be involved through such activities as writing or touching. *Kinesthetic* individuals need to be involved in learning through experience and by using "whole-body" approaches.

Frame 16

IDENTIFY YOUR STRENGTHS

Now look at your Learning Styles Inventory profile sheet to identify your perceptual strength(s). If your score is 70 or higher, you have a strong preference. Scores of 60 to 69 indicate a preference. Scores of 41 to 59 are average; you can learn this way when you are interested in what you are learning. Scores of 40 or below indicate that this is not a good way for you to *begin* learning. You should always begin learning material through your strongest modality! Record your scores below:

_____ auditory

_____ visual

_____ tactual

_____ kinesthetic

[Back of Frame 16]

Ranking your perceptual strengths below with number 1 being the highest and number 4 the lowest score, indicate next to each score whether it is high (60 or above) average (between 41 and 59), or low (40 or under).

1. _____
2. _____
3. _____
4. _____

Frame 17

AUDITORY APPROACHES TO LEARNING ABOUT COLLEGES

If you are an auditory learner, you acquire knowledge and understanding by listening, talking, discussing, and interviewing people. College representatives will visit your high school to meet with students who are interested in their institutions and to respond to questions. It might be helpful to you to tape record the presentation of the college official; then you can hear it again to help you make a decision. *Ask permission before recording the presentation.*

Interviews with current students, graduates, and alumni in your community from colleges of interest to you may be formal or informal. Prepare for the interview by jotting down questions about (1) the academic environment, such as the size of the freshman classes or the adequacy of the library; (2) the social environment, including the extracurricular program, cultural events, and the influence of fraternities and sororities on campus life; (3) the student services, such as academic advisement, counseling, and health services; and (4) other concerns such as campus rules and security, orientation programs, and student housing.

[Back of Frame 17]

Prepare for an interview with a college senior and write down questions that are important to you in each of the following categories:

1. academic environment
2. social environment
3. student services
4. quality of campus life
5. other concerns

Frame 18

VISUAL APPROACHES TO LEARNING ABOUT COLLEGES

If you are a visual person, you retain information by reading printed words, viewing and perusing materials, and retaining mental pictures. You can read about colleges that are of interest to you by (1) securing recruitment materials printed by the college, including bulletins, college newspapers, and view-books; (2) obtaining reference publications such as college manuals, texts that rank colleges, and how-to-get-into-college guides; and (3) using test preparation books to assist in preparing for college admissions. Additionally, you can view videotapes from individual colleges and laser disks produced by the Learning Resource Network of Durham, North Carolina or the Info-Disk Corporation (College USA) of Gaithersburg, Maryland. These present visual material on many different types of colleges and universities. Your high school and local library have a "College Resource Center" that contains these printed materials and visual resources.

Write the name of the library section where you are likely to find printed materials and visual resources about colleges:

C _ _ _ _ _ _ R _ _ _ _ _ _ _ _ _ C _ _ _ _ _ _

[Back of Frame 18]

The *College Resource Center* is where you are likely to find visual materials that will help you to choose a college suited to your special style.

Frame 19

READING ABOUT COLLEGES

Visit the College Resource Center in your high school or local library and check out at least two (2) reference books from the following list. Then read about any ten (10) colleges that may interest you in any of the following books.

Barron's *Profiles of American Colleges,* 2 volumes (annual)

Carris, J. D., McQuade, W. R., & Crystal, M. R. (1987). *SAT Success.* Princeton, NJ: Peterson's Guides.

Cass, J., & Birnbaum, M. (1985). *Comparative Guide to American Colleges.* New York: Harper & Row.

College Handbook. (annual) New York: College Entrance Examination Board.

Fiske, E. B. (1989). *The Fiske Guide to Colleges.* New York: Random House.

Gourman Report: A Rating of Undergraduate Programs in International Universities. Naperville, IL: Longman Trade USA.

Matthay, E. R., & Comer, J. P. (1991). *Counseling for College.* Princeton, NJ: Peterson's Guides.

Moll, R. (1987). *The Public Ivys: A Guide to America's Best Public Undergraduate Colleges and Universities.* New York: Penguin.

Munger, S., Burtnett, F., & Moulton, W. (1988). *Selecting the Right College.* Alexandria, VA: National Association of College Admission Counselors.

Peterson's Guide to Four-Year Colleges. (1991). Princeton, NJ: Peterson's Guides.

Frame 20

TACTUAL APPROACHES TO LEARNING ABOUT COLLEGES

If you are a tactual learner, you require a "hands-on" approach to learning. The computer may prove to be a meaningful technological resource for you. A number of software programs are designed to assist in your search for the "right" college. Most search programs provide the following information database: (1) selectivity level (competitiveness), (2) geographic location, (3) size of school and nature of the community, (4) available majors, (5) type of institution (public, two-year, religious affiliation), (6) availability of housing, (7) tuition costs, (8) athletic and recreational programs, and (9) makeup of student body as to gender and ethnicity.

Make a note of the databases *you* will examine before you apply to specific colleges.

[Back of Frame 20]

Check the databases you decided to examine.

1. selectivity level (competitiveness)
2. geographic location
3. size of school and nature of the community
4. available majors
5. type of institution (public, two-year, religious affiliation)
6. availability of housing
7. tuition costs
8. athletic and recreational programs
9. makeup of student body as to gender and ethnicity

Frame 21

COMPUTER ASSISTANCE

Most high schools and local libraries have computer facilities and college-search programs. An assistant may be available to help you delimit your search by placing parameters around the nine variables in the database. Most programs provide you with a printout of a listing of colleges that meet your criteria.

Frame 22

COLLEGE SEARCH PROGRAMS

Visit your high school or local library computer center and work with one (1) of the following college search programs, identifying and listing ten (10) colleges that meet your selection criteria.

1. *The Guidance Information System* (GIS) provides occupational information on two- and four-year colleges, the armed services, graduate and professional opportunities, and financial aid. GIS is published by the Educational Software Division of Houghton Mifflin in Lebanon, NH.
2. *Peterson's College Selection Service* uses *Peterson's Guide to Four-Year Colleges* as a database and includes 20 criteria for students to consider in college selection. It is published by Peterson's in Princeton, NJ.
3. *College Explorer* uses the database of the College Board's *College Handbook* for describing two- and four-year institutions. The program includes a section that describes the policies of many colleges regarding the Advanced Placement Program. The program is published by the College Board in New York.
4. *Discover* is both a career planning and college-search program with separate versions for middle school, high school, and adult users. It is available through the American College Testing Program in Hunt Valley, Maryland.

Frame 23

KINESTHETIC APPROACHES TO LEARNING ABOUT COLLEGES

If you are a kinesthetic person, your preferred way of learning about colleges is through total involvement—using yourself as a vehicle for learning. Plan to look at some colleges within easy driving distance from your home. Take a walk around the campus, observe student life, stay in a residence hall overnight, attend some classes, and meet with students and faculty. Try to get a feel for the size of the college and whether it seems right for you. Take notice of the students. Is the student body comprised of a multicultural population? Do students seem friendly, helpful, enthusiastic, and responsive? Are the facilities conducive to studying? Are the computer centers, laboratories, and libraries utilized by students? Are the recreational facilities and student union attractive?

Frame 24

ATTENDING COLLEGE FAIRS

You may have the opportunity to attend a college fair in which hundreds of institutions of higher education are represented. For the colleges that interest you, obtain literature, ask questions at the booth, and meet with college officials and alumni.

Try to do as much of the legwork as possible *beforehand*. Many colleges inform students of admission around April 15. Your decision is usually expected by May 1.

Frame 25

LEARNING ON YOUR OWN

Keeping in mind *your* perceptual strength(s), list at least three (3) ways you can learn more about colleges on your own.

1. _____
2. _____
3. _____

(Be responsible! Check back and be certain you are correct!)

Frame 26

THE COST OF COLLEGE

As of 1995, the total cost of attending public colleges ranged from $3,000 to $15,000 a year. Total cost at private institutions ranges from $12,000 to $29,000 annually. Before you begin to narrow your choices of colleges, you need to have a serious talk with your parents. *This is important!* You need to know how much money your family can afford to spend, and you need to consider your siblings as well— they might want to go to college too!

If finances are not a concern, then you can feel free to look into a broad range of colleges. However, the majority of students who attend college require some type of financial aid. There are four ways to meet college costs, including (1) grants or scholarships that do not have to be repaid, (2) loans, which have to be repaid—but often at more favorable rates than noneducational loans, (3) work either on or off campus, and (4) family financing. In general, most students who receive financial aid work part time and their parents are expected to take out loans.

Question: List four ways to pay for the cost of college.

[Back of Frame 26]

1. grants or scholarships that do not have to be repaid—but you need to be a good student;
2. loans, which have to be repaid—but often at more favorable rates than noneducational loans;
3. work either on or off campus; and
4. family financing.

Your high school counselor and the financial aid officers of colleges are excellent resources for finding out more about meeting college costs. *Peterson's College Money Handbook* and *How to Pay for College*, both published by Peterson's Guides, are helpful reference books.

Frame 27

APPLYING FOR FINANCIAL AID

What is financial aid and who gets it? Financial aid is assistance with the cost of attending college, and you *must* apply for it to get it. To do this, you and your parents should fill out the Financial Aid Form (FAF). Important terms follow.

Demonstrated need: many colleges claim that they fulfill 90–100 percent of their students' "demonstrated need." This is the amount, based on your FAF, that the college determines you need (in addition to what you have) that will enable you to attend that institution;

Financial aid package: a composite of work-study (a job), loans, and sometimes grant money (gift from the school);

Athletic scholarships: money awarded for excellence in a particular sport. The scholarship is awarded annually and may cover part or, on rare occasions, all of your college costs;

Merit scholarships: money given based on your academic ability and high school performance on certain tests;

Armed Services Support: hundreds of colleges offer Reserve Officers' Training Corps (ROTC) scholarships through the navy, army, air force, and marines. Students compete for scholarships and agree to serve in the armed services for a specified period in exchange for financial support.

Question: your family's "demonstrated need" is based on information supplied in the _____.

[Back of Frame 27]

Answer: Financial Aid Form
(It is important to have your parent(s) complete this form!)

Frame 28

ARE THERE OTHER SOURCES OF FINANCIAL AID?

You need to contact local, state, and federal organizations to identify additional sources of aid. Labor unions and employers often provide financial aid to the children of members. Local organizations such as Jaycees, B'nai B'rith, and the Rotary Club also provide scholarship money.

Philanthropies, foundations, and state governments often award grants and loans. The federal government gives grants to students and money to colleges to distribute to students. If you are a student with a disability, apply directly to your state office of vocational rehabilitation.

Frame 29

LOCATING SOURCES OF FINANCIAL AID

A number of *people* can help locate sources of financial aid: (1) your parents, (2) the personnel director at your parents' place(s) of employment, (3) officials of unions your parents have membership in, (4) officers of local community service groups, (5) directors of foundations, (6) state departments of education and commissions on higher education, (7) regional offices of the U.S. Office of Education, (8) your high school guidance counselor, and (9) the financial aid officer at prospective colleges.

Frame 30

IDENTIFYING OTHER SOURCES

If you need financial assistance to attend college, visit your school or local library College Resource Center. Check out two (2) of the following reference books and identify at least three (3) possible sources of financial aid:

Deutschman, A. (1987). *Winning Money for College: The High School Student's Guide to Scholarship Contests.* Princeton, NJ: Peterson's Guides.

Krefetz, G. (1988). *How to Pay for Your Children's College Education.* New York: The College Board.

Leider, A. J. (1989). *Don't Miss Out: The Ambitious Student's Guide to Financial Aid, 1990–1991.* Alexandria, VA: Octameron Press.

Peterson's College Money Handbook. (annual). Princeton, NJ: Peterson's Guides.

Peterson's State and Federal Aid Programs for College Students. (annual). Princeton, NJ: Peterson's Guides.

Schlachlter, G. A. (1987). *How to Find out about Financial Aid: A Guide to Over 700 Directories Listing Scholarships, Fellowships, Loans, Grants, Awards, and Internships.* Redwood City, CA: Reference Service Press.

Frame 31

CALCULATING NEED AND THE FINANCIAL AID PACKAGE

College financial aid officers frequently "package" financial aid, which involves (1) computing college expenses, (2) identifying family resources, and (3) calculating need. The following example is provided to clarify this procedure:

Expenses		*Family Resources*	
Tuition, Room, Board, Fees	$10,000	Parent's Contribution	$4,000
Books, Personal Expenses	2,000	Student's Income	2,000
Travel	1,000		
Total	$13,000	Total	$6,000
Student's Need		*Financial Aid Package*	
Total College Expenses	$13,000	Work	$3,000
Total Family Resources	−6,000	Loan	2,000
	$7,000	Grant	2,000

Question: Compute a student's financial need at three (3) colleges given family resources of $5,000:

College A: (High cost) College expenses are $22,000.

College B: (Medium cost) College expenses are $11,000.

College C: (Low cost) College expenses are $4,000.

[Back of Frame 31]

Answers: Student's financial need is as follows:

College A:	$17,000
College B:	6,000
College C:	0

Frame 32

TAKE TIME OUT FOR A REVIEW!

You and this PLS have covered a great deal of information about college and about yourself. Let's take a moment to review what you have learned to date.

- You have identified your reasons for wanting to go to college.
- You know the differences among the various types of colleges.
- You know the things to consider when selecting a college.
- You have looked at college admission criteria.
- You have reviewed college admission tests.
- You know your learning-style perceptual preferences and how to use them when obtaining information about various colleges.
- You have discussed college costs with your parents and know about your family resources.
- You have considered sources of financial aid.

[Back of Frame 32]

If you are unclear about any of these topics, go back and review selected material in Frames 3 through 29. Remember that your high school counselor is available to help you understand the process of knowing yourself and identifying colleges that will meet your needs.

Frame 33

DECISION MAKING

Decision making is a five-stage process; it involves

- identifying the decision that has to be made;
- listing the alternatives to be considered;
- gathering information related to each alternative;
- weighing the pros and cons of each option; and

- making a choice from among the best options.

Other factors to consider when making a decision include:

- your economic, social, and psychological needs;
- your values and beliefs;
- the degree of risk you are willing to take; and
- how your decision will affect significant other persons in your life.

Question: What stage are you in, in the process of deciding about the college you want to attend?

[Back of Frame 33]

Answer: You have probably completed Stage 1—you need to make a decision about choosing a college.

Frame 34

IDENTIFYING THE ALTERNATIVES

So far you have been actively involved in assessing both yourself and college environments. It is now time to narrow the field to identify viable alternatives.

You need to find a match between your talents, abilities, values, and expectations and the academic programs, extracurricular offerings, and campus life that certain colleges offer. Narrowing the number of alternatives is frequently guided by your probability of gaining acceptance into various colleges. We can categorize these alternatives in three ways:

First-level colleges may meet your criteria for the ideal undergraduate experience. However, their admission standards may be highly competitive, and they may accept a relatively small number of students who apply. These colleges are sometimes termed "reaches."

Second-level colleges meet many of your criteria for the ideal college. They are less competitive, and your academic background may closely match that of most entering students. These colleges are termed "target" institutions.

Third-level colleges are "safety" schools for you because your credentials exceed those of the majority of entering students. However, these colleges lack some of the elements you are seeking in a college.

Question: What are colleges that closely match your academic background with that of entering students called?

[Back of Frame 34]

Answer: Second-level or "target" colleges.
List the choices that are *your* target colleges!

_____	_____
_____	_____
_____	_____

Frame 35

LISTING THE ALTERNATIVES

Most students apply to between three and six colleges. You might want to identify at least one "reach" college and one "safety" institution. Most of your choices should be in the middle or "target" range. Spend most of your energy identifying and researching those institutions in the middle range—colleges with selectivity that matches your grades and admission test scores. Your guidance counselor is an expert and will help you to determine your chances for admission to a particular college.

List three (3) to ten (10) colleges that are either *first* (rating 1), *middle* (rating 2), or *last* (rating 3) choices and place one of these numbers next to each institution.

[Back of Frame 35]

Listing of Colleges   Ratings (1, 2, or 3)

 1.
 2.
 3.
 4.
 5.
 6.
 7.
 8.
 9.
10.

Frame 36

GATHERING INFORMATION ON EACH COLLEGE

You have now developed a listing of from three to ten colleges that you want to research thoroughly. Furthermore, you have identified (1) factors important in the college experience, including the academic and social environment, quality of campus life, and student services (Frame 9), and (2) variables when choosing a college, including selectivity level, (Frame 10), geographic location, size, type of institution, and costs.

You are now ready to peruse the resources that provide in-depth descriptions of your delimited listing of viable institutions of higher education. Develop a listing of the "pros" and "cons" of *each* institution. For example, the positive aspects of College A might be that it is a good match between your academic background and the degree of selectivity, within the desirable geographic range, and an optimal size; the negative aspect might be that it is beyond your price range.

Assignment: List each of the colleges in your delimited list and note the pros and cons of each institution.

[Back of Frame 36]

Delimited College Choices	Pros	Cons
1.		
2.		
3.		
4.		
5.		
6.		
7.		
8.		

Frame 37

WEIGHING THE "PROS" AND "CONS"

Now you are close to making a decision! You have listed the pros and cons of your delimited list of possible colleges on the back of Frame 37. Your next task is to identify those colleges where you plan to apply for admission. Now is the time to actively involve your parents and your high school guidance counselor in making your final choices. Remember that you want to select at least one institution from each of the following categories: (1) "reach" colleges, (2) "target" colleges, and (3) "safety" colleges.

Discuss the positives and negatives of each of the colleges in your delimited list. You need to weigh the importance of each factor—some may be "very important," some "important," and others "minimally important." For example, college costs might be "very important" for you to consider, whereas the athletic program might be "minimally important"—unless you are an outstanding athlete, in which case you may be in the reverse situation.

Frame 38

COMPARING YOUR CHOICES

After rating the importance of each factor, rank each institution for the extent to which it meets your "very important" criteria. Your parents need to be involved in helping you with these decisions because they are aware of their financial capabilities. Your school counselor needs to be involved because he or she is an expert on colleges and the degree of match between you and the institution.

Task: On the back of this frame, rank the colleges that most meet your criteria from highest to lowest.

[Back of Frame 38]

Ranking the colleges I plan to apply to:

1.
2.
3.
4.
5.
6.

Frame 39

MAKING A DECISION—TYPE OF ADMISSION

Various colleges have different admission plans termed *early admission, regular admission, rolling admission,* or *open admission,* each with different deadlines and response dates. Consult your ranking of colleges on the back of Frame 39. If your first-choice college has an *early decision* policy, it may be a binding commitment that is made to accept you early in your senior year of high school and implies that you do not plan to apply to any other college, or it may be a nonbinding admission that does not commit you to enrolling in that institution and allows you to apply to other colleges.

Institutions with *regular admission* policies expect you to apply in January or February and notify the institution by May 1 if you plan to enroll in the next fall semester. This system implies that your application is carefully compared with those of other applicants; it is a *competitive process.*

Frame 40

FURTHER TYPES OF ADMISSION

Institutions with *rolling admissions* evaluate applications on a first-come, first-served system. Your application is reviewed upon receipt, and you are notified of acceptance or rejection within a short period of time.

Open-enrollment institutions are usually community colleges or state-funded colleges that accept all applicants who meet their published admission standards.

Frame 41

QUIZ ON TYPES OF ADMISSION

Place the correct letter from Column B next to the number of the correct definition in Column A.

Column A

_____ 1. Institutions that usually allow four months between application and the decision to accept or reject because they are competitive

_____ 2. Institutions that make early, nonbinding decisions

_____ 3. Colleges that accept all applicants who meet the published admission standards

_____ 4. Colleges that evaluate each application on a first-come, first-served basis

Column B

a. early decision commitment

b. early decision noncommitment

c. regular admission

d. rolling admission

e. open enrollment

[Back of Frame 41]

1. c   2. b   3. e   4. d

Frame 42

THE COLLEGE APPLICATION FORM

Most college applications are comprised of five (5) sections that need to be completed carefully and thoughtfully. These sections include (1) the information form, (2) the secondary school report, (3) the school profile, (4) counselor, teacher, and other personal recommendations, and (5) student essays and personal statements.

The *information form* requests background data on the applicant's (1) educational preparation, (2) family members' occupations and educational backgrounds, and (3) major academic interests, honors, and so on. The *secondary school report* is usually completed by the school counselor and includes the student's official transcript, class rank, and grade point average. The *school profile sheet* is generally prepared by your school administrators and counselors and includes information on the school, community, faculty, grading system, and curriculum features.

Frame 43

MORE ON COLLEGE APPLICATIONS

It is your responsibility to request *letters of recommendation* from teachers, counselors, and community leaders, such as members of the clergy or employers who know your academic potential and/or personal strengths, aspirations, and character.

Your *essay* or *personal statement* needs to be carefully prepared and should provide the college admissions officials with an understanding of your personality, values, ideas and opinions, interests, and aspirations. This statement also provides you with an opportunity to address reasons why you excelled or may have performed poorly in certain academic areas.

Frame 44

KEEPING TRACK OF YOUR APPLICATIONS

You need to develop a management system that keeps you on target in terms of deadlines. Develop a chart now that will record the following information and dates:

College 1   College 2   College 3

Admission Plan:
Application Deadline:
Secondary School Report:
Letters of Recommendation:
    Counselor_____
    Personal_____
    Teachers_____
Standardized Tests:

	College 1	*College 2*	*College 3*

Required tests:

Dates taken:

Scores sent:

Notification Date:

Financial Aid:

  Deadline:

  Sent to College:

Interview:

  (Required?)_____

  Date Scheduled:

Frame 45

A FINAL WORD

If you have persevered and completed this program, you are terrific! You now have a sound, overall picture of the process related to selecting a college that meets your individual needs and requirements.

Best wishes for success at whichever college or university you attend!

A FINAL WORD ABOUT PROGRAMMED LEARNING SEQUENCES

Programmed Learning Sequences are the closest thing we know to a tape-recorded story book. They may be based on segments of the curriculum or on the curriculum as a whole rather than on literature alone. They enable learning to occur globally—in a processing style many adolescents reflect. They are structured but normally do not cause students tension or pressure. They may be used in any environment or sociological pattern responsive to individuals' strengths. In short, PLSs stimulate interest. They can be used without direct adult involvement, free the teacher or counselor to work with those who require immediate adult interaction, and can be designed by parents, students, aids, and interested noneducators, as well as by teachers.

You may duplicate the PLS in this chapter and ask students to use it. You will, however, need to read the text onto a tape so that your students can hear the contents read—quietly and in relative privacy. We hope you will decide to make at least one PLS for a unit you can use. If you do, check the following features to be certain that you created a PLS that can teach effectively.

The PLS should include the following elements:

1. an attractive cover in a shape related to the content
2. an analytic and global title (with humor, if possible, or a clever play on words)
3. clearly stated objectives
4. specific directions for adolescents to follow (e.g., read, answer, check, wipe off, erase, put back, then use the accompanying tape, carefully handle)
5. a global beginning
6. when possible, the story woven through the entire PLS
7. interesting, upbeat phrases rather than academic directives
8. step-by-step sequencing
9. actual teaching; identical concept/material repeated in different ways on several frames
10. answers on the back of the frame accompanied by humor, jokes, and illustrations
11. illustrations related to the text, in color
12. varied types of questions (e.g., circle, write in . . . , fill in the missing letters, draw a line from the right side of the sheet to . . .)
13. an accompanying tape
14. answers provided in incomplete statements
15. no "yes" or "no" answers
16. an interdisciplinary theme for global students
17. appropriate review frames
18. built-in tactual reviews
19. neatness, attractiveness, legibility
20. correct spelling and grammar
21. original and creative touches
22. themes or ideas related to students' interests, lifestyle, or talents
23. a choice of two, at times
24. laminated, easy-to-handle frames
25. frames that turn in the correct position (not upside-down)

STUDENT DEVELOPMENT OF PROGRAMMED LEARNING SEQUENCES

Adolescents can create a PLS based on a chapter in any of their textbooks—particularly if you allow them to work on the project with one or more classmates. After your students have experimented with using two or three PLSs, offer them the opportunity of developing a PLS instead of taking the unit test—if they include all the items listed above (1 through 25). Allow two or three students to work together if they wish to do so. You will be pleased with many of the PLS units your students produce. In addition, they will have focused on the curriculum's objectives and learned the content as they created this instructional resource.

Chapter 9

Designing Contract Activity Packages to Respond to Adolescents' Individual Learning Styles

WHY CONTRACT ACTIVITY PACKAGES ARE EFFECTIVE

Contract activity packages (CAPs) are one of three basic methods for individualizing instruction. The other two methods, programmed learning sequences (PLSs) and multisensory instructional packages (MIPs), are effective for students with different learning styles. CAPs, PLSs, and MIPs teach exactly the same information, but each teaches it differently. That is why it is so important to assign adolescents, whose learning-style patterns and ability levels differ, to the single instructional strategy that best accommodates their individual strengths. However, for a student who scores 60 or above on the Dunn, Dunn, and Price (1979) Learning Style Inventory (LSI) on Learning in Several Ways, who therefore needs a lot of instructional variety, first assign the approach that best matches his or her style and then offer the second best approach occasionally as an alternative.

CAPs are most appropriate for independent average, above-average, and gifted students because they permit self-pacing for motivated adolescents who want academic knowledge (LSI score of 60 or above on Motivated) or who are interested in the topic (LSI score of between 41 and 59 on Motivated). For such students, CAPs provide objectives, resources, activities, and small-group interactions through a variety of perceptual and academic levels to accommodate different learning-style preferences; they also foster independence for learning-alone preferents (LSI score of between 20 and 40 on Learning Alone) and peer interaction for students who want to learn with a friend or two (LSI scores of between 60 and 80 on Learning With Peers). Independent students gradually develop self-confidence through the success they experience because of the CAP's resource, activity, and reporting alternatives, which build in the repetition and application that contribute to information retention. Further, CAPs reduce the frustration and anxiety experienced by competent learners in traditional classrooms, where they are often required to progress at the class's, group's, or underachievers' rate. CAPs can be designed to capitalize on the interests and talents of individual students; for example, a CAP on memorizing basketball plays or tennis rules simultaneously increases reading and mathematics skills. Finally, because of the many options they include, CAPs are also effective with nonconformists (LSI scores of 40 or below on Responsibility) (Dunn & Dunn, 1992, 1993).

LEARNING-STYLE CHARACTERISTICS ACCOMMODATED BY CONTRACT ACTIVITY PACKAGES

CAPs can be used flexibly to accommodate learning-style characteristics.

1. When sound is needed (LSI score of 60 or above on Sound), earplugs may be used to provide recorded music to block out the environmental noises many adolescents actually do not consciously hear. When discussion and interaction are important to individuals (the same LSI score of 60 or above on Sound), an instructional area such as a learning station or an interest center can be established; a section of the classroom can be blocked off by perpendicular cardboard dividers to provide a sanctuary for its occupants and simultaneously protect classmates from being distracted by the movement or talking that occurs within it. Rules for discussion need to be established so that no one outside the instructional area hears the words of anyone inside it, but setting such rules is a management strategy that will be necessary when you redesign the classroom to accommodate adolescents' diverse learning styles.

Youngsters who require silence (LSI score of 40 or below on Sound) should use a distant section of the classroom where no one may speak and where the adjacent dens or alcoves are used for essentially quiet, learning-alone or well-disciplined learning-in-pairs activities.

2. When students are permitted to work on their CAP anywhere in the classroom (as long as they work quietly, do not interfere with anyone else's learning style, and respect the rules that have been established), they adapt available illumination, temperature, and seating to their special learning-style traits. LSI scores of 60 or above on Light, Temperature, and Design suggest that the individual will function best with bright light, warmth, and a formal design. In contrast, LSI scores of 40 or below on these elements suggest that the individual will function best with soft light, cool environment, and an informal design.

Areas near a window or directly beneath a bulb provide better illumination than areas away from such sources of light. Caps with a brim or sunglasses protect the light-sensitive adolescent from excessive illumination (as revealed by LSI scores of 40 or below on Light.) Students may be allowed to wear sweaters or appropriate extra garments for warmth, as indicated by LSI scores of 60 or above on Temperature. They should be advised to wear lightweight fabrics when they need a cool environment in which to concentrate (LSI scores of 40 or below). A pillow placed on the seat of a chair, or carpeting, a rug square, or a bean bag on the floor of a classroom corner are likely to provide sufficient informal seating; and conventional desks and seats suffice for formal preferents.

3. Motivated, persistent, and responsible students are given (a) a series of objectives to complete, (b) a listing of the resources they may use to obtain information, (c) suggestions for how and where to get help should they experience difficulty, and (d) an explanation of how they will be expected to demonstrate their mastery of the assigned objectives. They should then be permitted to begin working and to continue—with only occasional spot-checking and encouragement for those who need either—until their tasks have been completed. Unmotivated, less able, and less persistent adolescents should be encouraged to work with either a PLS or a MIP, or to study the material with tactual or kinesthetic resources. If the students strongly prefer learning with a CAP and you are willing to experiment to see whether this method increases their motivation or persistence, in the beginning assign only a few objectives, gradually adding objectives as the students evidence ability to follow through and complete their tasks successfully. Circulate among the students, keeping an eye on adolescents for whom a CAP does not initially seem to be appropriate. Ask questions, check that students understand what they are learning, and comment favorably when you observe positive effort. Were you to treat motivated students thus, you would be interrupting their concentration and diverting them. But if you don't check on unmotivated adolescents, when they experience difficulty with the assignment they may become frustrated, involve themselves in diversionary activities, or give up.

4. Sociologically, CAPs permit students to work alone, with a friend or two, or as part of a team using small-group techniques. Youngsters may also work directly with their teacher when difficult objectives require adult assistance or direct teaching.

5. The resource alternatives of the CAP include auditory, visual, tactual, or kinesthetic learning approaches at different academic levels. The varied approaches permit students to learn initially through their strongest perceptual preference and to reinforce the information to which they have been exposed through their next strongest modality. The CAP may be used at any time you allow—early in the morning, before, after, or during

lunch when no class is scheduled, or as homework after school in the afternoon or evening—to match each learner's best biochronological time for concentrating and producing.

Adolescents are in the largest age group for which intake while learning is important (Price, 1980). CAPs permit snacking on raw vegetables or other nutritious foods while studying—as long as classroom rules are followed; for example, no student's snacking may interfere with another student's learning, and thus eating must be unobtrusive and unoffensive; all assignments must be completed; and individuals' grades must be better than they ever have been before (or this procedure is not working and there is no need to continue).

Students may also take short, one-minute breaks for relaxation, as long as they return to their objectives and work on them until completed within the time frame allocated. As suggested previously, experiment with CAPs for students who have the potential for mastering objectives either alone or with a classmate or two. However, should youngsters using a CAP not perform well on the final assessment of the CAP topic, immediately transfer them to a different instructional approach, (e.g., a PLS, an MIP, tactual and kinesthetic resources, or direct instruction). CAPs are best for motivated auditory or visual learners, but they are also responsive to nonconformists.

THE PARTS OF A CONTRACT ACTIVITY PACKAGE AND THE PURPOSE OF EACH PART

A CAP is an individualized educational plan for independent and able students. It facilitates learning because it includes the following elements:

1. Simply stated *objectives* that itemize exactly what the student is required to learn.

2. *Multisensory resource alternatives* that teach required information through each student's perceptual preferences.

3. *Activity alternatives* students develop immediately after they have used the multisensory resource alternatives to learn the information itemized in the CAP objectives. These activities require students to apply the information to which they have been exposed. The activities may require converting the information into (a) a flip chute, a pic-a-hole, task cards, an electroboard, a floor game, or other tactual or kinesthetic resource; (b) an original composition, poem, play or script, or song; (c) a drawing, dance, pantomime, or other original resource to show that the student has actually mastered the required objectives and to reinforce the information or teach it to classmates. Such application of what has been learned increases its retention.

4. *Reporting alternatives* that require students to share with classmates the creative activity alternative each makes. Thus, students are (a) told what they must learn by the objectives, (b) permitted to learn

through multisensory resource alternatives that match their perceptual strengths, (c) required to apply the new information by engaging in an activity alternative, therein creating a new instructional resource, and (d) directed to share the activity they created with a classmate or two through the reporting alternative. The sharing of the completed activity alternative serves as either an introduction or a reinforcement of the material for the person who uses it and then checks or corrects it. It also provides the creator of the activity with reinforcement and a sense of accomplishment. This sharing, or reporting, increases retention of what has been learned and, in addition, provides a sense of accomplishment for some.

5. Three *small-group techniques* that permit students whose LSI printout indicates they learn well with peers, in a pair, or in a small group (score of 60 or above on Learning with Peers) to complement their style by working with classmates. These instructional strategies are not mandated for every youngster. Rather, they are suggested for students who prefer learning with others or find it difficult to complete complex tasks by themselves.

6. *A pretest, a self-test, and a posttest.* Each CAP includes a single test administered before the CAP is assigned to assess the student's knowledge of the information required in the CAP's objectives. This pretest eliminates the possibility that students will spend time relearning previously mastered material. This same pretest may also be used as a student self assessment at any time to identify how much the individual still needs to learn. Self-testing reduces stress and promotes self-confidence.

A single assessment can be used to determine how much the student knows about this topic before study has been undertaken and how much has been learned since the unit was begun. In the second case, testing will occur after (a) multisensory resources have been initially used to learn the required information, (b) students have applied the information they learned through the resources by creating activity alternatives and sharing them with selected classmates, (c) peer-oriented students—or those who wish to work on a difficult objective with a classmate or two—have reinforced the information through the CAP's three small-group techniques, (d) the self-test has been taken, and (e) either the objectives have been mastered or the time allocated to this unit of study has been expended.

If you wish, you may develop three separate assessment devices. However, three assessments are usually unnecessary because the test questions are directly related to the CAP's objectives. However, when using a CAP on mathematics, change the examples in the tests. When seeking other specific information, the same questions can be maintained for all three assessments. For example, consider the following CAP objectives:

• Describe how the Christian holiday Christmas is celebrated in at least three (3) different countries.

- Explain the origin of at least three (3) different practices such as the piñata, the Christmas tree, the Yule log, the Menorah, Santa's elf helpers, or the sleigh pulled by reindeer on Christmas Eve.
- Conduct library/media research and learn at least twenty (20) interesting facts about Australia. Then memorize the song "Waltzing Matilda" and explain the words and meaning of the song. Explain why the words are not "English" as you know the language and explain why people speak English differently in other countries.

In these instances, the statements need not be rephrased for the culminating test; they are explicit and students will know exactly what they must learn and do.

This approach clearly identifies what has to be mastered, provides choices of resources through which the material can be learned, builds in reinforcement and application for long-term memory, permits individualized, pair, or peer learning, removes some of the anxiety associated with testing, and fosters in many adolescents the motivation and ability to teach themselves—a skill that will stand them in good stead in their post–high school and adult years. Should you become concerned about the rote memorization of answers, change the order of the questions on the final CAP test or require higher-level cognitive responses. But if you tell students they will need to explain specific vocabulary, you need to require them to explain that specific vocabulary on the test.

STEP-BY STEP GUIDE TO DEVELOPING CONTRACT ACTIVITY PACKAGES

The first CAP you design will take time because you will need to use several relatively unfamiliar techniques. The second CAP will be much less difficult to write, and by the time you embark on the third, you will be assisting colleagues by explaining the parts. Furthermore, most secondary students are capable of designing their own CAPs after they have worked successfully with three or four. Before you assign CAP development to the students, however, you may want to list the objectives required for that unit and permit the students to design the remaining parts as they sociologically prefer, that is, alone, in pairs, or in a small group. In a short time they will be able to create complete CAPs, whether alone or with a friend or two; eventually they will be able to convert their textbook chapters into CAPs for teaching themselves difficult content when necessary.

Step 1: Identify a topic, concept, or skill your entire class is required to learn.

Step 2: Write the name of the topic, concept, or skill as a title at the top of blank sheet of paper.

Step 3: Develop a humorous or clever global subtitle. For example:

- The Brain (Alternative: Getting Your Head Together)
- Life in the Universe: Give Me Some Space
- DNA: The Double Helix is Not a Roller Coaster Ride
- Mitosis: Breaking up is Hard to Do!
- Electricity: The Shocking Truth
- (Alternative: Electricity: Lightning Strikes!)
- Photosynthesis: Light up My Life!
- Indexing: Finding Your Notch!
- Rocks: A Hard Topic (Alternatives: Rocks: Heavy Thinki. ₀! or Rocks: My Sediments Exactly!)

Step 4: List which information about this topic is so important that every student in your class should learn it. Then list the information about this topic that may be important but is not required. Finally, consider the information about this topic that would appeal to certain students but not necessarily to all. For example, musically, artistically, or writing-talented students might undertake one or more objectives related to their special focus on this topic, as might students who enjoy traveling, building, engaging in sports, cooking, and so on. List these as special-interest objectives and make them optional based on choice.

Examine your developing list of objectives. Be certain that the most important objectives are placed first. These should be followed by objectives of consequence that not everyone need necessarily master. Finally, add the special objectives that might be of interest to only selected students. Objectives concerning sports, dance, drama, music, or the culinary arts often generate enthusiasm when related to subject matter content.

The most important objectives will be required for all students. Many of the secondary list of important items will be required, but students should be given some options among them. The way you assign the objectives will help you personalize the CAP according to individual achievement and/or interest levels. Because options often increase motivation, permit students to make choices among some objectives. When you do, you will observe nonconformists evidencing interest in their assignments. For example, you might say, "The class must master any ten of the following twelve objectives." Some teachers suggest, "Complete the first eight and any additional four you choose." Another alternative would be, "Do any five objectives in the first group, numbers 1 through 3 and any additional two in the second group, and any two in the third group." Before you know it, some students will complete either all the objectives or the most difficult ones, design two or three objectives of their own, and/or create an entire CAP for their next unit (especially if the CAP is an alternative to doing homework assignments for that unit or taking the test). Many nonconformists who normally perform only marginally or complete the least amount of work necessary will become very involved with their studies, vie for your praise concerning their completed activity alternatives, and demonstrate a level of creativity and persistence that you did not anticipate from them.

Step 5: Write the objectives clearly so that students understand exactly what they are required to learn. These become the students' short-term instructional goals for that unit or topic. Years ago Mager (1962) suggested that a behavioral objective should include identification of the overall behavioral act, the conditions under which the behavior is to occur, and the criterion for acceptable performance. When all three items are included, however, the objectives become too lengthy and complicated for most students to fully understand and follow, are not individualized—and therefore do not respond to diverse learning styles, interests, ability levels, or talents—and are used neither as efficiently nor as humanistically as is possible.

Therefore, in the CAP, objectives are written in a generalized way, as shown in the example that follows, and mastery of the knowledge or skills is made *optional* through a series of activity alternatives. Furthermore, each objective starts with a simple verb (e.g., list, divide, collect, identify, predict).

Example: Explain the point of view that Martin Luther King, Jr., was arguing (a) for and (b) against in his "I Have A Dream" speech.

This objective clearly indicates what must be learned, but it does not restrict learners to showing their mastery in a single everybody-prove-it-in-the-same-way approach. Martin Luther King's point of view was fairly explicit, and what he was for and against can be explained in a composition, poem, drawing, play, time chart, pantomime, three-dimensional clay, plaster of paris, or wood sculpture, and so forth. Thus, students choose how to show they have learned the answer. They show their knowledge by completing one alternative from a group of activity alternatives listed directly below each objective.

Step 6: Design at least three or four activity alternatives for each objective or for a group of related objectives so that students may choose how they demonstrate that they have learned the information required by their objectives. In effect, the activity alternatives permit students to choose the condition under which they will demonstrate mastery, enabling them to capitalize on their personal talents, interests, or perceptual strengths. For example:

Objective: The following phrases normally associated with Christmas originated in a variety of different countries throughout the world. (a) Explain the meaning of at least ten (10) of the phrases, (b) pronounce those ten (10) correctly and with confidence, and (c) name the country/countries from which each was derived.[1] (See Note 1 for correct answers.)

Joyeux Noel
Glaedelig Jul
Stretan Bozic
Feliz Navidad
Merry Christenmass
Nodlaig Mhaith Dhuit
Wesolych Swiat
Vrolyk Kertsmis
Happy Christmas

Kala Hrystoughena
Froeliche Weihnachten
Buon Natale
God Jul
Um Feliz Natal
Boldog Karacsony Unep
Kung ho shen tan
A Rozhdestvom Christovom

Activity Alternatives

1. Dramatize or roleplay the meaning of at least ten (10) of the above phrases, name the country from which each was derived, and say the words correctly and with confidence in your performance.

2. Make a tape-recording to explain at least ten (10) of the phrases, name the country from which each was derived, and say the words correctly and with confidence on your tape.

3. Draw a map of the world on which you will write at least ten (10) of the phrases, placing each on the correct country. Be prepared to read the phrases correctly and with confidence when you point out the words and the country.

4. With a friend or two, write a television quiz program on which all the words, their meaning, their pronunciation, and the country from which they were derived are questions. Put on the program and see how many "classmate contestants" get at least ten (10) words correct.

Step 7: Create a reporting alternative for each of the activity alternatives designed.

The activity alternative permits students to choose how to apply the information they have learned. When students complete an activity alternative, they must share it with classmates. Sharing an activity alternative with classmates or friends provides a review for the person who created it; an introduction of new material *or* a reinforcement of previously studied material for the students who serve as listeners, viewers, players, or participants; and another way of demonstrating the acquired knowledge or skill.

Objective: State at least one (1) important date and event in the life of any ten (10) of the following famous African-Americans and explain how each contributed to society.

1. Duke Ellington
2. Ralph Bunche
3. Booker T. Washington
4. Marian Anderson
5. Carter G. Woodson

6. Mary McLeod Bethune
7. Bessie Smith
8. Langston Hughes
9. Dizzy Gillespie
10. Sidney Poitier

11. Shirley Chisholm
12. Lena Horne
13. Willie Mays

14. James A. Baldwin
15. Nat Turner
16. Martin Luther King, Jr.

[If you can complete this assignment for twelve (12) of the above people, you have excellent potential for becoming an historian!]

Activity Alternatives

1. Make a timeline listing the dates and events in the lives of the ten (10) or twelve (12) people that you choose.

   Through illustrations, show how each contributed to society.

2. Write a poem or produce a record that describes how each of the ten (10) people contributed to society and at least one (1) important date and event in each of their lives.

3. Write an original story, play, or radio or television script that describes a date and event in the life of each of the people about whom you chose to learn. Explain how each contributed to society.

4. If you can think of an activity you would prefer instead of the ones above, write it on a piece of paper and show it to your teacher for possible approval.

Reporting Alternatives

1. Mount the timeline in our room and answer any questions your classmates may ask about it.

2. Read your poem or play your record that describes one important date and event in the lives of each of the ten (10) famous African-Americans.

3. Read the story or play, or radio or television show. Rehearse the script with classmates and ask a few students to observe it and comment in writing. Add their comments to your CAP folder.

4. If your original activity is approved, develop a reporting alternative that complements it.

The following list of activity and reporting alternatives may be used to develop options for your students. Identify those activities you believe would be most motivating, adapt and rewrite them so that they are appropriate for the specific CAP objectives you are designing, and use them as some of the choices you permit. They may also be used as homework assignments to add interest to and provide application of required knowledge. The development of an original resource through each student's perceptual strengths contributes substantially to the retention of difficult information.

Activity Alternatives

1. Make a poster "advertising" the most interesting information you have learned.

Reporting Alternatives

1. Display the poster and give a two-minute talk explaining why the information was interesting.

2. Develop costumes for people or characters you have learned about.

2. Describe to a group of classmates how you determined what the costumes should be, how you made them, and the people who would have worn them.

3. Prepare a travel lecture related to your topic.

3. Give the lecture before a small group of classmates. You also may tape-record it for others who are working on the same topic.

4. Describe in writing or on tape an interesting person or character you learned about.

4. Ask a few classmates to tell you what they think of the person you portrayed.

5. Construct puppets and use them in a presentation that explains an interesting part of the information you learned.

5. Display the pictures and the puppets. Do the presentation.

6. Make a map or chart representing information you have gathered.

6. Display the map or chart and answer questions about it.

7. Broadcast a book review of the topic as if you were a critic. Tape-record the review.

7. Permit others to listen to your tape and tell you if they would like to read the book.

8. Make a mural to illustrate the information you consider interesting.

8. Display the mural and answer questions that arise.

9. Make a timeline listing important dates and events in sequence.

9. Display the timeline and be prepared to answer questions.

10. Write a news story, an editorial, a special column, or an advertisement for the school or class newspaper explaining your views concerning any one aspect of your topic.

10. Mail your writing to the paper. Ask three students to write "letters to the editor" praising or chastising you as a reporter.

11. Write an imaginary letter from one character to another. Tell about something that might have happened had they both lived at the time and place of your topic.

11. Display the letter.

12. Keep a make-believe diary about your memorable experiences as you lived through the period concerned with your topic.

12. Read a portion of your diary to some of your classmates. See whether they can identify the period concerned with the topic. Add the diary to the resource alternatives available to other people who are studying the topic.

13. Try to find the original manuscripts, page proofs, first editions of books, book jackets, taped interviews with authors or other interesting persons in the community, autographs of authors, or any other documentation related to your topic. If the material cannot be brought to school, organize a small-group trip to visit the place where you found the items.

13. Take a group trip concerned with your topic. Either write or tape-record something of interest that you learn.

14. Search the library card index and/or bring photographs and a description of new materials concerned with your topic to class.

14. Add the information to the resource alternative for your topic.

Step 8: List all the resources students can use to master the information required by their objectives. Be certain to include tactual-visual and kinesthetic-visual resources if they are available. Categorize the materials into separate sensory or multisensory groups. For example: *Visuals*: books, transparencies, or magazines; *Auditory*: tapes, records; *Kinesthetic-Visuals*: floor games; *Multisensory*: PLSs, MIPs, television programs, videodiscs; *Visual-Tactuals*: pic-a-holes, flip chutes, electroboards, task cards, or learning circles. List the name or title of each resource next to it. For example:

Multisensory:
Programmed Learning Sequence: Brotherhood Week
Multisensory Instructional Package: Brotherhood Week
Television program: "The Way It Was," CNBC, April 4, 1994 (one hour)
Videodisc: "The Way It Ought to Be: Brotherhood Week," Museum of Natural History (rental available third and fourth week in April; see Miss Ewing, school librarian, rooms 203–205).

Students may use additional materials if they wish, but they should either obtain your approval or reference their sources in their work. Because students may select which resources to use, these materials are called resource alternatives.

If available, include materials on the CAP topic but at different reading levels to provide suitable information for students of varied ability levels. For example, a CAP on biological systems may require readings at the seventh through twelfth-grade levels for a heterogeneous ninth-grade class in health.

Step 9: Add at least one team learning, circle of knowledge, brainstorming, and/or case study exercise to the developing CAP (see Chapter 6).

Step 10: Develop a test that is directly related to each of the objectives in your CAP. An assessment instrument or examination that is directly related to stated objectives is called a criterion-referenced test. Questions for such a test are formed by restating the objective or by phrasing it in a different way. For example, if the objective is "List at least five (5) major causes of racial rivalry," then the question on the examination should be "List at least five (5) major causes of racial rivalry."

You may, of course, be creative in the way you test your students. The test can include maps, puzzles, games, diagrams, drawings, and photos for those who can demonstrate knowledge best in such ways.

Step 11: Design an illustrated cover for the CAP (see sample CAP that follows).

Step 12: Develop an informational top sheet. On the page directly after the illustrated cover, provide information that you believe is important. Some items that may be included are the following:

- the CAP name
- the student's name
- the student's class
- the objectives that have been assigned to and/or selected by that student
- the date by which the CAP should be completed
- the date that selected parts of the CAP should be completed (for students in need of structure)
- a place for a pretest grade (optional)
- a place for a self-test grade (optional)
- a place for a final test grade
- the names of the classmates who worked on this CAP as a team
- directions for working on or completing the CAP

Step 13: Reread the CAP parts to be certain that each is clearly stated, well organized, in correct order, and grammatically correct. Check your spelling and punctuation.

Step 14: Add illustrations to the pages so that the CAP is attractive and motivating.

Step 15: Duplicate the number of copies you will need.

Step 16: Design a record-keeping form so that you know which students are currently using the CAP, which have previously used the CAP, and how much of it each has completed successfully.

Step 17: Try the first CAP with the entire class to show everyone how to learn with this approach. Be prepared to guide and assist students through their first experiences with a CAP. Establish a system whereby youngsters can obtain your assistance if it is needed. Placing an "I Need You" column on the chalkboard or a chart and having students sign up for help when they are stymied may be effective for your group. Direct students to print their names beneath the caption and return to their places until you are free to assist them. They should not interrupt you; rather, they should busy themselves on other objectives or tasks—or get help from a classmate—until you can get to them. After one whole-class experience, assign the next CAP to those students who functioned well with the first one and who enjoyed learning that way.

GUIDELINES FOR PERFECTING A CONTRACT ACTIVITY PACKAGE

Although it is not incorrect to state repeatedly, "You will be able to . . . ," doing so does become repetitious and often provokes humor. It is suggested, therefore, that you use such a statement only once as an introduction to the specific objectives. For example:

Behavioral Objectives
By the time you have finished this contract, you will be able to complete each of the following objectives:
List at least five (5) ways in which the media protects us.
Name at least three (3) ways in which the media controls us.

Any time that you use a number in the objectives, spell out the number and then in parentheses write its numeral. This technique is used to accentuate the number for youngsters who may overlook specific details. For example: List at least three (3) tools archaeologists use in their work.

Use complete and grammatically correct sentences. Do not capitalize words that should not be capitalized. Contracts should be excellent examples of good usage, spelling, and grammar for students. If you wish to emphasize a word that may be new to the student's vocabulary, underline the word or set it in italics. Make sure each objective begins with a verb.

Use the phrase "at least" before any number of required responses to motivate selected students to achieve more than is required. For example: List at least five (5) events leading up to the use of nuclear power over Hiroshima. Can you think of a sixth?

Be certain that the objective does not become an activity. The objectives state what the student should learn. The activity enables the youngster to demonstrate what he or she has learned by making a creative, original product using the information. For example:

Objective: Identify five (5) nontraditional (less than 20 percent) occupations for women.

Activities: Locate one (1) of these occupations in the 1994 *Occupational Outlook Handbook* and outline the job description, functions, educational preparation, and working conditions. Alternatively, interview a woman in one (1) of these occupations, focusing on areas of job satisfaction and job dissatisfaction.

Never ask an adolescent to report to the entire class. Instead, have an activity shared with one, two, or a few classmates or the teacher. It is difficult for a student to hold the entire class's attention, and if one member is given the opportunity, it should be offered to all. Instead, have the students each report to a small group of two, three, or four classmates at most. If the activity is outstanding, ask that student to share it with a second small group. You may either assign students or ask for volunteers to listen to the report.

The title of each of the major parts of the CAP should be underlined. For example, Objectives or Activity Alternatives.

Be certain that you used the following:

- both an analytic and a global title
- clearly stated objectives that require no further explanation
- a new page for each objective
- multisensory resources for the resource alternatives
- "at least" statements so that motivated students can respond to more than the minimum requirement
- numbers written with both symbols as well as words
- related activity and reporting alternatives for each objective
- activity alternatives that require students to develop an original creative resource
- reporting alternatives that correspond with their related activity alternatives
- choices for students
- team learning for each difficult objective and a circle of knowledge to reinforce what the team learning introduced
- three different types of questions (factual, higher-level cognitive, and creative) concerned with what was taught in each team learning
- one or more circles of knowledge
- a third small-group technique, such as case study or brainstorming
- assessment directly related to the objectives
- pictures, illustrations, or graphs directly related to the CAP content throughout the CAP
- easy-to-read type
- no spelling or grammatical errors

Make sure the CAP provides some choices for the student. And finally, evaluate the CAP. It is attractive and easy to use?

SAMPLE CONTRACT ACTIVITY PACKAGE

The follow sample CAP was created by D. T. Arcieri (1994), an instructional support technician and adjunct professor in the Department of Biological Sciences at the State University of New York at Farmingdale.

If this is your students' first experience with a CAP, assign only a few objectives to introduce them to the process. Give them an opportunity to begin to feel secure with this method before deciding whether it is effective for each individual. When the CAP stimulates their thinking and expands their knowledge, continue its use. If certain students do not respond well to it (even if they are permitted to work with one or two classmates), set aside the CAP system for those adolescents and introduce either PLSs or MIPs. The later method is potent for students who require multisensory resources and structure and who learn essentially through tactual or kinesthetic resources.

CAPs are most effective with youngsters who are motivated and either auditory or visual, or are nonconforming. You will note that the CAP is an especially well organized system, although it does permit flexible learning arrangements and give students options.

HEREDITY: THE GENES WE ALL WEAR[2]

Introduction and Objectives

From the colors of eyes to the colors of flowers, genes control much of the variation seen in living things. Most of your own personal characteristics are the result of how the genes you inherited from your parents are expressed. What are some of the basic rules that guide the inheritance and expression of genes? This contract is filled with many interesting activities to help you answer that question!

First, take the pretest on the last page and answer all the questions that you can. Ask your teacher to check your answers. Everyone must complete (a) any six (6) of the first seven (7) objectives and (b) at least one additional objective to be chosen from among the two optional objectives cited—a total of seven objectives. In addition, complete one (1) *Activity* and one (1) *Reporting Alternative* for each objective. You may work alone, with a classmate or two, or check in with your teacher as frequently as you wish. Should your teacher be busy when you need attention, print your name on the "I Need a Little Help" list on the pad. You will get help as soon as possible. In the meantime, work on another objective, project, or assignment.

When you have completed this CAP, if you wish, you may retake the pretest to see how many of the objectives you have mastered and whether you still need to work on more. On *date*, the entire class will take the posttest for this topic. At that point, we will decide (a) how much you learned using this method, (b) whether you should study the next unit with a CAP, or (c) whether you should try a different method.

If for any reason you have difficulty working with the CAP system, don't wait until you fall behind. Let your teacher know as soon as you suspect that CAPS may not be the best approach for you!

In the next section, please keep track of your progress. Most of these activities will be completed in class, although some may be done as homework. All of the resources you will need are in the classroom or in the library. If you wish, you may use books, films, filmstrips, tapes, tactual or kinesthetic games, or other museum, library, or public domain materials that you locate elsewhere.

Progress Report on CAP, Heredity: The Genes We All Wear

Name: _____   Date: _____

Objectives: After reading the objectives, list below the ones you elect. Write in the date you expect to complete them.

1.

2.

3.

4.

5.

6.

7.

Pretest Score: _____ Self-Test Score: _____
Team Members (if working with others): _____, _____, _____.

Objective 1: Using B (brown eyes) and b (blue eyes), explain how alleles are variations of genes. Choose one (1):

Activity Alternatives
1. Cut out a large capital B and color it brown. Cut out a large b and color it blue.

Reporting Alternatives
1. Display these large letters and explain to at least three (3) other students how they represent variations of the gene for eye color.

2. Find a brown-eyed classmate and a blue-eyed classmate, and put them together in a convenient location.

3. Write a limerick about alleles and variations.

4. Make a list of five (5) funny make-believe characteristics for people, then invent alleles that could be responsible for them (example: pink hair, wings, etc.).

2. Present the concept of alleles to a small group of classmates using these two (2) students as an illustration of genetically based variation.

3. Read the limerick to three (3) friends.

4. Show the list to at least four (4) other students and ask them to add one funny characteristic to the list.

(Reader: Add picture of blue-eyed baby)
Human progeny possessing blue eyes alleles (translation - a baby with blue eyes!).

Objective 2: Describe the difference between a dominant allele and a recessive allele. Choose one (1):

Activity Alternatives

1. Pantomime with a friend a dominant allele and a recessive allele.

2. Search the library card index for the subject "genetics," and bring to class at least two (2) books that contain references to dominant and recessive alleles.

3. Write a funny letter from a recessive allele to a dominant allele complaining about their relationship.

4. Create a "wanted poster" for the B (brown-eyed) allele and one (1) for the b (blue-eyed) allele, describing the characteristics of each. Be sure to include a brown B "mug shot" on one (1) and a blue b "mug shot" on the other.

Reporting Alternatives

1. Let a few classmates guess which one of you is dominant and which is recessive.

2. Add these books to the Resource Alternatives listed in this contract.

3. Display the letter.

4. Display the letter.

Objective 3: Explain the meanings of the words *homozygous* and *heterozygous*. Choose one (1):

Activity Alternatives

1. Cut out two (2) large Bs and color them brown. Cut out two (2) bs and color them blue. Identify which is homozygous and which is heterozygous.

Reporting Alternatives

1. For a group of three (3) students, show possible color combinations of these alleles.

2. Describe in writing or on tape the basic differences between being homozygous and heterozygous.
3. Ask at least five friends about the color of their parents' eyes.

2. Share this work with at least three (3) other students.

3. Identify parents and friends who are heterozygous, then explain what that means.

(Reader: Add picture of a lady with blue eyes)
Human female who is homozygous with respect to eye color.

Objective 4: Describe how to use a Punnett-square. Choose one (1):

Activity Alternatives
1. Use masking tape to create a Punnett-square on the floor. Direct four (4) students to act as alleles (combinations of B and b) and do crosses.
2. Design a poster showing the use of Punnett-squares for the following crosses: BBxbb, BbxBb, and Bbxbb.
3. Write a song touting the merits of the Punnett-square.
4. On a sheet of paper compare the "cross" method with the Punnett-square method for the crosses Bbxbb and BBxBb. Explain the differences in a written narrative on the same sheet.

Reporting Alternatives
1. Demonstrate the use of a Punnett-square by directing "alleles" for at least four (4) other students.

2. Display your poster.

3. Sing the song or record on tape for a small group of friends.
4. Display the sheet.

(Reader: Add picture of a Punnett-square!)

Objective 5: Describe the pea plant characteristics that Gregor Mendel analyzed genetically. Choose one (1):

Activity Alternatives
1. Make believe you are Gregor Mendel and get interviewed by another student posing as a TV newsperson. Answer questions about your genetics experiments.
2. On a poster illustrate four (4) characteristics of pea plants, including the alleles, that Mendel considered responsible.

Reporting Alternatives
1. Get interviewed in front of five (5) other students.

2. Display the poster.

3. Create a make-believe lab notebook for Mendel in which he has recorded his experimental data. Be sure to use Punnett-squares and illustrate it.

3. Display the notebook.

4. Write a news article about Gregor Mendel as if you were a journalist when he made his famous discoveries.

4. Have three (3) students read the article and then post it.

(Reader: Add a picture of Gregor Mendel)

Objective 6: Gain a working knowledge of the terms *genotype* and *phenotype*. Choose one (1):

Activity Alternatives

1. Make a task card set matching human eye color and pea plant genotypes with their respective phenotypes.

2. Provide written definitions of the words *genotype* and *phenotype*, and give six (6) examples of each.

3. Develop a matching quiz with two (2) columns. Column 1 will have five (5) human and pea phenotypes, and Column 2 will have five (5) matching human and pea genotypes.

4. Write a rap song using human and pea genotypes and phenotypes.

Reporting Alternatives

1. Have at least three (3) friends use the task cards, and then include them on the Resource Alternatives list in this contract.

2. Have two (2) friends read the definitions and examples, and then have them quiz you verbally on the material.

3. Give the quiz to two (2) classmates who have already completed this contract.

4. Perform the rap in person or on tape for at least five (5) friends.

(Reader: Add a picture of a female with brown eyes)
Human female with the dominant eye color phenotype (translation: a lady with brown eyes!).

Objective 7: Using pea plant characteristics, show 3:1 phenotypic ratios from monohybrid crosses. Choose one:

Activity Alternatives

1. On a poster do the following flower color crosses using Punnett-squares:
   $P_1Pp \times pp$
   $F_1Pp \times PP$
Show the F 3:1 ratio.

2. Make a flip chute with monohybrid crosses on one side of the card,

Reporting Alternatives

1. Display the poster.

2. Challenge three (3) classmates to use the flip chute.

and the appropriate 3:1 ratios on
the other side.
3. Do the following human eye color
crosses on a sheet of paper:
P₁Bbxbb
F₁BbxBb
Make five (5) copies and hand out
to interested students.

Introduce each cross with a written explanation of the genotypes and phenotypes involved, then explain the 3:1 ratio of the F_2.

4. On a poster do the following pea   4. Display the poster.
color crosses
P₁ YYzyy
F₁ YyxYy
Illustrate the genotypes with yellow
and green peas. Show the F_2 3:1 ratio!

Resource Alternatives

Books

Carlson, Elof. *Human Genetics*. Lexington, MA: D.C. Heath, 1984, pp. 80–105.
Fraser Roberts, J.A., & Marcus E. Pembrey. *An Introduction to Medical Genetics*.
    Oxford: Oxford University Press, 1985, pp. 9–69.
Jenkins, John B. *Human Genetics*. Menlo Park, CA: Benjamin/Cummings Publish-
    ing, 1983, pp. 79–114.
Mader, Sylvia. *Human Biology*. Dubuque, IA: Wm. C. Brown Publishers, 1992,
    pp. 357–372.
Starr, Cecie. *Biology: Concepts and Applications*. Belmont, CA: Wadsworth Pub-
    lishing, 1991, pp. 117–142.

Video cassettes

Introducing Genetics (Wards Natural Science Est., Rochester, New York).
Genetics and Heredity (Wards Natural Science Est., Rochester, New York).

Additional Teacher-Made Materials

Task Cards
Programmed Learning Sequence
Flip Chute
Pic-a-Hole
Floor Game
Genetics Crossword Puzzle (see Figure 9.1)

Genetics Crossword Puzzle

Across
1. unit of genetic instruction
2. father of classical genetics
3. genes are found on these

Down
1. variation of a gene
2. not recessive
3. location of a gene

Figure 9.1
Genetics Crossword Puzzle

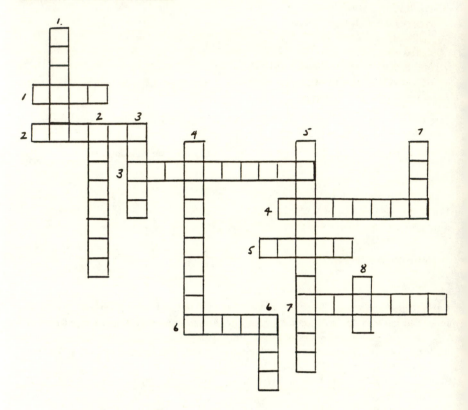

4. the genetic makeup
5. dominant over blue eyes
6. recessive pea stem length
7. study of heredity

4. two (2) similar alleles
5. two (2) different alleles
6. dominant pea stem length
7. brown is dominant over ____
8. Mendel's favorite plant

Team Learning for the Genetics of the ABO Blood Grouping

Directions: Write the names of the team members and then answer the questions below.

1. _____   2. _____
3. _____   4. _____

Recorder _____

The surfaces of red blood cells contain genetically determined proteins. Various blood-grouping classifications are based on the presence or absence of such proteins.

The ABO blood grouping is based on the two (2) proteins A and B. Individuals whose red blood cells manufacture only protein A are said to have blood type A. Those who produce only protein B are type B. Individuals who manufacture both A and B are type AB, and those who manufacture neither are type O.

In this ABO blood group system, a single gene can exist in any of three allelic forms: I, I, and i. The alleles I and I code for proteins A and B, respectively. These alleles are codominant, while the allele i is recessive. Refer to the table below to relate genotypes to ABO blood group phenotypes.

phenotype (blood type)	genotype (allele combinations)
A	
B	I, I
AB	I, I
OO	I
	ii

As the table indicates, people with type O blood always have the homozygous recessive genotype ii. Type AB individuals always have the heterozygous genotype I^AI^B. Type A individuals may have the genotype I^AI^A or I^Ai, and those with type B can have either the I^BI^B or I^Bi.

The four (4) blood types are not equally distributed. The incidence in the white population in the United States is 41 percent type A, 10 percent type B, 4 percent type AB, and 45 percent type O. Among American blacks the frequencies are 27 percent type A, 20 percent type B, 7 percent type AB and 46 percent type O.

Team-Learning Questions

1. On which cells are the ABO blood-grouping proteins located?

2. An individual who is heterozygous type A (I^Ai) has children with an individual who is heterozygous type B (I^Bi). What are the possible blood types of the children? Use a Punnett-square to find your answer.

3. What is the probability that a type O man and a type O woman can have a type A baby?

4. What percentage of the black population in the United States has type AB blood?

5. Write one of the following demonstrating your knowledge of the genetics of the ABO blood grouping: (a) a song; (b) a rap; (c) a limerick; (d) a haiku poem.

Circle of Knowledge

1. _____   2. _____
3. _____   4. _____
           Recorder: _____

List as many words having to do with this unit as you can. Take two (2) minutes.

_____   _____

_____   _____

_____   _____

_____   _____

_____   _____

_____   _____

Group Analysis

1. _____   2. _____
3. _____   4. _____
           Recorder: _____

Discuss these three (3) questions and record your answers.
1. How and why did Gregor Mendel use pea plants in his genetic experiments?
2. How can doctors and medical geneticists use information concerning dominant and recessive alleles to help families with genetic diseases?
3. If the brown-eyed allele (B) is dominant over the green-eyed allele (G), and the green-eyed allele is dominant over the blue-eyed allele (b), what are the chances that a blue-eyed child will be born to the following brown- and green-eyed couple: BbxGb? Use a Punnett-square to explain your answer.

The Pre- and Post-test

Name _____
Date _____

1. Define the word *allele*.
2. Describe the difference between a dominant allele and a recessive allele.

Match the following (3–7):

3. homozygous   a. two (2) of the same alleles
4. genotype   b. observable trait
5. phenotype   c. two (2) different alleles

6. heterozygous   _____d. the genetic makeup
7. 3:1 ratio   _____e. monohybrid F_2 phenotypes

8. Who was Gregor Mendel?
9. Using Punnett-squares, track flower color through two (2) pea plant generations. Start with P_1 PPxpp (P = purple, p = white). What are the genotypes
   and phenotypes of the F_1? Solve the F_1 to find the genotypes and phenotypes
   of the F_2. What is the phenotypic ratio of the F_2?
10. What do all plants and animals have in common given the laws of inheritance?
11. Make a list of the ABO blood-grouping phenotypes and their respective gen-
    otypes.
12. Using a Punnett-square, show the phenotypes and genotypes of the children
    of parents with the blood types AB and O.

INDEPENDENT CONTRACTS

Individual CAPs may be designed for and by gifted, bright, and/or creative students just as described in this chapter. Sometimes students need
to pursue a specific interest unrelated to the required subject matter
curriculum. Students need only think through and respond to the following curriculum questions.

1. What would I like to learn about a topic?
2. Is there something that really interests me that I could study on my own?
3. Which resources should I use to respond to my perceptual strengths?
4. How can I use what I need to learn in a creative, original way that I can
   eventually share with others?
5. If I rewrite the objectives (what I need to learn), how can I translate them into
   a self-assessment?

Building a library of CAPs on varied topics will provide an expanding
resource for schools and districts. Gifted students, parents, aides, and
education majors at local colleges can assist in the effort to stock a central
bank of effective CAPs. Once a bank has been established locally, the CAPs
included in it may be duplicated for use by teachers throughout the system at any level. St. John's University's Center for the Study of Learning
and Teaching Styles provides excellent primary, elementary, intermediate, and secondary samples for a minimal cost to practitioners who prefer
to use existing CAPS rather than create their own.[3]

NOTES

1. All the phrases mean "Merry Christmas" (Tiedt & Tiedt, 1990, p. 290).

Joyeux Noel: France
Kala Hrystoughena: Greece

Glaedelig Jul: Norway
Froeliche Weihnachten: Germany, Austria
Stretan Bozic: Yugoslavia
Buon Natale: Italy
Feliz Navidad: Spain, Mexico
God Jul: Norway
Merry Christenmass: Scotland
Um Feliz Natal: Portugal
Boldog Karacsony Unep: Hungary
Wesolych Swiat: Poland
Kung ho shen tan: China
Vrolyk Kertsmis: Holland
A Rozhdestvom Christovom: Russia
Happy Christmas: England

2. D. T. Arcieri, *Heredity: The genes we all wear*. New York: SUNY, Farming-dale, 1994.

3. For a free resource brochure listing intermediate and secondary CAPs, write to Center for the Study of Learning and Teaching Styles, St. John's University, 8000 Utopia Parkway, Jamaica, NY 11439.

Chapter 10

Designing Multisensory Instructional Packages to Respond to Adolescents' Individual Learning Styles

Can you observe a group of students and tell which do not like school, do not achieve well, and are not likely to improve without drastic intervention? To determine if you have that insight, check the statements below that you believe describe such adolescents. They

- rarely seem interested in learning;
- have short attention spans;
- remember little of what they hear;
- don't read much;
- often fidget and play with items while listening;
- prefer playing to learning;
- like interacting with classmates;
- can't work independently;
- won't learn cooperatively;
- often snack or eat;
- hum, whistle, or talk while working;
- squirm a lot; can't sit still;
- don't stay in their seats.

If you check any five or more items, you can identify those students for whom conventional teaching does not work. Now, if you were a betting person, on which of the following statements would you put your money? These learners are likely to

- become dropouts;
- become adult failures;
- become criminals;
- "grow up" some day;
- be successful in business, a profession, or career that interests them;
- surprise us some day in some good way.

There is no way to predict how students' behaviors in school will affect their lifestyle in the future—with one exception: We can predict that poor readers often become dropouts, though some dropouts become successful in their lives away from school. Nevertheless, if you are not ready to give up on these students, or if you are willing to try one last thing, it probably should be (check one)

- more of the same kind of schooling;
- hands-on manipulatives that permit students to begin learning tactually (see Chapter 7);
- Programmed learning sequences (PLS), effective for students who need structure and are visual or tactual and motivated (see Chapter 8);
- Contract activity packages (CAPS), effective for highly achieving or nonconforming students ((see Chapter 9);
- Multisensory instructional packages (MIPs) designed for unmotivated learners with short attention spans who cannot sit still or remember uninteresting information and that include many short, hands-on, and kinesthetic manipulatives.

Whether you were guessing or reasoning, only MIPs are likely to work for these learners. Why? Because the MIP (choose all appropriate answers)

- allows unmotivated, fidgety, low-auditory and low-visual students to work without disturbing the teacher or their classmates;
- permits poor learners to remain on task for relatively long periods of time by keeping them involved with a series of short, gamelike hands-on activities;
- enables slowly achieving students to learn independently or with a peer;
- provides clearly stated objectives, teaches to those objectives through multisensory resources, and tests directly to those objectives at the end of the package;
- is tape-recorded thus allowing poor readers to follow along and learn at their own pace;
- can easily be made by many adolescents if they are permitted to work in pairs or groups of three or four;

- can be used to introduce a topic or unit to some students and to reinforce it for others.

All the above answers are accurate. In fact, MIPs should be (choose all appropriate completions)

- used by gifted students when they are having difficulty mastering a specific topic or unit;
- used by underachievers who need to learn in an enjoyable way;
- made by teachers, student teachers, aides, and/or gifted students in conjunction with those who are "good with their hands," parents, and/or concerned community members who need only follow directions for adapting subject matter content from a book;
- kept in the classroom or school library so that students who want to use them can.

All the completions above are correct! We urge you to experiment with MIPs for students who have not learned easily in the past and/or who believe they are incapable of achieving. You and they will appreciate the difference in attitude and achievement that results.

STEP-BY-STEP GUIDE TO DESIGNING MULTISENSORY INSTRUCTIONAL PACKAGES

Step 1: Identify a curriculum topic that your class needs to master. Consider the following areas and topics: for example,

- language arts: how and when to use quotation marks or Haiku poetry
- literature: Chaucer's *Canterbury Tales*; folktales from many nations
- science: the skeletal system; how our environment affects nations across the world
- mathematics: fractions; estimating mileage in different systems
- social studies: locating capital cities; how climate affects industrial growth;
- mathematics: finding the perimeter of right triangles; dividing food equitably among humanity
- career education: identifying personal strengths and preferences; locating resources to learn about the world of work.

Step 2: Develop an analytic and global title for the MIP. (See Chapter 8 for a description of how to design two-part titles.)

Step 3: List the important information your students need to learn about this topic. Translate the important information into objectives. (See Chapter 9 for an in-depth description of how to write objectives.)

Step 4: Pretend you are teaching auditory students who need to master the MIP's objectives. Outline what you would say to teach the information required by each objective. After outlining what you would say, follow the outline and teach the information by recording it onto a tape.

Teach your class the information in one or more lessons, as you prefer, but record each lesson in its entirety. The tape will become the *auditory* component of the multisensory MIP, which permits students to learn the information through their individual perceptual preferences.

Step 5: Develop visual, tactual-visual, and kinesthetic-visual resources to teach the same information required by each of the MIP's objectives. Locate one or more textbooks, transparencies, films, movies, or videotapes for essentially visual students.

Step 6: Follow the directions in Chapter 7 for making a pic-a-hole, an electroboard, a flip chute, and task cards to teach the same information in various ways to teach the tactual learner. Do these for each MIP objective, thus developing a variety of multisensory activities to accommodate differing learning styles.

Step 7: Follow the directions in Chapter 7 for making a floor game for each MIP objective to accommodate the style of kinesthetic and activity-oriented learners.

Step 8: Use Chapter 8 to develop a PLS for visual-tactual students in need of structure, and Chapter 9 to develop a CAP for nonconforming adolescents. The PLS and the CAP should teach the same information required by each of the MIP's objectives.

Step 9: On respective labels type the directions for using the tactual materials, the floor game, the PLS, and the CAP. Attach the appropriate label to each resource tape. Paste or draw a picture of the resource each tape matches. For example, the tape that describes how to use the floor game should have a drawing of the floor game on it; the tape describing how to use the task cards should have a drawing of task cards on it.

Step 10: Make an introductory tape that explains how to use the MIP. Try to keep the directions simple. For example:

If you follow these directions carefully, you should be able to master all the objectives in this MIP. Check your Learning Style Profile to be certain you know your strongest perceptual preference. To do that, find lines 12–15, which say "auditory," "visual," "tactual," and "kinesthetic." Examine these four lines together. Which is closest to the right? Which has the highest number? Which is closest to 80? The one closest to 80, even if it is only 41, is your highest number. It is your "perceptual strength."

Find the tape in the MIP that best matches your perceptual strength. If your highest number is tactual, begin with the tape marked "Tactual." You will recognize the Tactual tape by the pair of hands illustrated on the cover. If your highest number is kinesthetic, begin with the tape marked "Kinesthetic." On this tape you will see a picture of a student using a floor game. If your highest number is visual, find the tape with a picture of eyes on it. If your highest number is auditory, use the Auditory tape, which has a picture of an ear on the cover.

Check your Learning Style Profile again. Find your *second* perceptual preference. To do that, look at the four lines, 12 through 15, again. Which of these—auditory, visual, tactual, or kinesthetic—is *next* closest to the right? That is, which has the second-highest number? Which is the next closest to 80? The second-highest number, even if it is only 40, is your "secondary perceptual strength."

Find the tape in the MIP that best matches your secondary perceptual strength. Use that tape next. After you follow the directions of the first and then the second tape, you may reinforce the information by using any other resource in this package.

Use this package either alone or with a classmate or two. You are required to master at least 12 of the 14 objectives. You may choose which 12 to master. Use the self-test at the bottom of the package—the one in the red envelope—to see how much you have learned after you follow the directions on the first two tapes. After you have tried the self-test, you will know if you need to do some more studying.

If you find this package interesting, use the remaining resources too.

Good luck! Ask questions if you need help!

Step 11: Make up a short test that can show whether students have actually mastered the skills and content while using the MIP. This test should be printed as well as tape-recorded, and it should carefully match the objectives. Suggest that students check through the resources in the MIP to see whether their answers are correct.

Step 12: Use a colorfully decorated box to house the multisensory resources and the short tapes that explain how to use them. Cover each activity and the entire box with clear contact paper or laminate everything so that they last for years.

Step 13: List the objectives for this MIP and attach them to the top inside cover of the MIP box.

Step 14: Explain that all students in the class must learn the same material, but each will learn it differently based on individual style preferences.

Organize the PLS, the tactual and kinesthetic resources, the CAP, and each of their related tapes into a single package that many students can use and share according to their perceptual and sociological preferences. Variety of resources permits choice and allows less-interested or less able students to reinforce their learning in a variety of interesting ways.

HINTS FOR FACILITATING THE DEVELOPMENT OF MULTISENSORY INSTRUCTIONAL PACKAGES

When you read about all the parts of an MIP, it must seem like a lot of work to develop one. However, the following ideas may help you gradually increase the number of different multisensory packages available to you.

During the first semester teach the topic of a future MIP just as you always do. However, assign homework that will eventually provide the parts of an MIP. For example, give your students homework such as the following:

- Make a pic-a-hole, an electroboard, or a set of task cards to teach objective 3 in this unit.
- Make a mini-PLS to teach Objective 3 in this unit.
- Make a mini-CAP to teach Objective 4 in this unit.

The day after the homework assignment is due, ask each student to share the resource developed with at least two other students. The two must "correct" any information that may not be clear or correct. This must be done before you see the resource. In that way students will be (a) correcting each other's materials, (b) reinforcing what they learned about this objective, and (c) learning how to create materials to teach themselves. During the *next* semester package the materials, have students make the tapes, and experiment with the package.

Offer the students a choice of either taking the final in the unit *or* developing an MIP on it and accepting a grade for the finished product. Establish criteria for each of the parts of an MIP so that you can demonstrate that your grading system is fair. (See the criteria for tactual and kinesthetic materials, a PLS, and a CAP in their respective chapters.) Add the following:

- a clearly enunciated tape to explain how to use each of the resources in the MIP (e.g., how to determine each person's perceptual strengths and which resources to use first, second, etc.);
- a clearly enunciated tape for each perceptual resource to explain how to use that resource;
- the self-test; and
- the neat, attractive box to house the MIP resources (CAP, PLS, tactual and kinesthetic materials, tapes, etc.).

Many students or student pairs would rather develop instructional resources than take a test. They will learn and retain more from translating their knowledge into a creative resource than they would from studying for a test.

Obtain the assistance of parents or community residents. Each community houses skilled and gifted people; some would willingly become involved in developing instructional materials based on information in a textbook. You could provide the objectives to be included in the MIP and the guidelines included herein, and then request a first draft. Many contributors will develop superior materials. If that does not happen, improve on what *is* submitted. If you dislike what is submitted, discard it.

Ask colleagues involved in teacher education programs or with gifted students to include the development of MIPs in their coursework. Excellent materials can be duplicated, borrowed, or shared.

Write a proposal to elicit grant monies to reimburse colleagues for developing MIPs for your subject matter.

A FINAL WORD ON MULTISENSORY INSTRUCTIONAL PACKAGES

Often teachers have neither the time nor the patience to teach and reteach each adolescent who needs special attention. We sometimes misinterpret why many students learn neither well nor easily in our classes. MIPs can teach and reteach students who do not learn through traditional methods. It isn't that traditional teachers, whose role is that of an intelligent authority figure who shares knowledge by speaking, questioning, advising, or consistently assigning individual or group work, are not good; they just are not good for every learner.

When you find that adolescents of any group, cultural, ethnic, or otherwise, "turn off" or are resistant, do not try more of the same. Instead, develop at least one MIP and experiment with its effectiveness with students whom you heretofore perceived as apathetic, disinterested, unable, or emotionally disturbed. Be prepared to observe better behaviors, grades, and attitudes. If we are correct, you will have broken through the wall of blocked learning for at least some of your students, and you then will find a way to develop more of these MIP stepping stones to help others.

Epilogue

We began this book with the Questionnaire on Learning Style and Multiculturalism to assess your perceptions of the similarities and differences among diverse groups. We then shared the findings of many studies that had examined the learning styles of people in different cultures. Next we explained the 21 elements of style, the instrumentation used to identify it, and how to interpret an individual's learning-style printout.

Following that introduction, we described the adaptation of learning-style theory to counseling adolescents in various stages of their development. We then discussed the major cultural groups within the United States and reviewed the research on the learning styles of African-Americans, Asian-Americans, Hispanics, European-Americans, and Native Americans. Finally, we introduced a variety of instructional and counseling strategies that respond to adolescents with varying learning-style strengths and suggested how these could be altered based on *individual*, rather than cultural-group, differences.

It is the intent of this book to share the research concerning multiculturalism essentially because it has been widely misinterpreted. There is no such thing as a cultural-group style. There are cross-cultural and intracultural similarities and differences among all peoples, and those differences are enriching when understood and channeled positively. By recognizing the wealth of diversity among us and our students and clients, educators and counselors can enhance learning and living for those adolescents with whom we come into contact—and for all the people with whom each of them interacts forever thereafter.

Appendix

CONTRACT ACTIVITY PACKAGES AVAILABLE THROUGH THE CENTER FOR THE STUDY OF TEACHING AND LEARNING STYLES

Intermediate CAPs

Classification
Folktales
Poetry
The Crusades

The Metric System
Volcanoes
The People's Choice
Old Age

Secondary CAPs

The Civil War
Parade of Passing Species
Perimeter, Area, Surface Area, Volume
Haiku Poetry
Congruent Triangles
Cell Regulation
Introduction to Foreign Language

Solution of the Right Triangle
The Universality of War
Julius Caesar
Poetry of Robert Frost
The Power of the Presidency
The Ancient Greek World
The Great Gatsby
AIDS

Matched CAPS and Programmed Learning Sequences (PLS)

Animals with a Backbone: Club Rib (grades 5-8)
The Mind and The Brain: Getting Your Head Together (grades 7-12)

Learning About Learning Style: What's Fashionable May Not Suit You (grades 9-12)

The Skeletal System: Have I Got a Bone to Pick with You (grades 5-8)

Order of Operations: Is There a Doctor in the House? (grades 6-8)

Fractions: A Partial Experience (grades 4-6)

Introduction to Greek Tragedy: No Laughing Matter (grades 7-12)

The Environment: Do You Have Earth Sense? (grades 6-8)

Chaucer's Canterbury Tales: Geoff's Fireside Chats (grades 9-12)

Health Impairment: Physical Disabilities (grades 11-adult)

Edgar Allen Poe: A Grave Matter (grades 7-12)

Naming Chemical Compounds: Calling NACL (grades 7-12)

All CAPs are available through the Center for the Study of Learning and Teaching Styles, St. John's University, 8000 Utopia Parkway, Jamaica, New York 11439.

References

Adler, S. (1993). *Multicultural communication skills in the classroom*. Boston, MA: Allyn & Bacon.

Alberg, J., Cook, L., Fiore, T., Friend, M., Sano, S., et al. (1992). *Educational approaches and options for integrating students with disabilities: A decision tool*. Triangle Park, NC: Research Triangle Institute, Post Office Box 12194, Research Triangle Park, North Carolina 27709.

Amodeo, L. B., & Brown, D. (1986). Students from Mexico in U.S. schools. *Educational Horizons*, 64(4), 192–196.

Anastasi, A. (1988). *Psychological testing* (6th ed.). New York: Macmillan Publishing Company.

Andrews, R. H. (1990, July-September). The development of a learning styles program in a low socioeconomic, underachieving North Carolina elementary school. *Journal of Reading, Writing, and Learning Disabilities International* (New York: Hemisphere Publishing Corporation), 6(3), 307–314.

Andrews, R. H. (1991). Insights into education: An elementary principal's perspective. *Hands on approaches to learning styles: Practical approaches to successful schooling*. New Wilmington, PA: Association for the Advancement of International Education.

Annotated Bibliography. (1995). Jamaica, NY: St. John's University Center for the Study of Learning and Teaching Styles, 11439.

Arcieri, D. T. (1994). *Heredity: The genes we all wear*. New York: St. John's University.

Arrendondo, P. (1991). Chapter 11: Counseling Latinos. In C. C. Lee & B. L. Richardson (Eds.), *Multicultural issues in counseling: New approaches to diversity* (pp. 143–156). Alexandria, VA: American Association for Counseling and Development.

Asher, C. (1987). *Trends and issues in urban and minority education: Trends and issues series*, 6. New York: ERIC Clearinghouse on Urban Education, Teachers College, Columbia University.

Atbar, N. (1975, October). Address to the Black Child Development Institute annual meeting. San Francisco.

Atkinson, S. L. (1988). A longitudinal study: The effect of similar and non-similar student/teacher learning styles on academic achievement in fourth- and fifth-grade mathematics. Doctoral dissertation, Temple University, 1988.

Atkinson, S. L. Morten, G., & Sue, D. W. (1993). *Counseling American minorities: A cross-cultural perspective* (4th ed.). Madison, WI: Brown & Benchmark Publishers.

Avise, M. J. (1982). The relationship between learning styles and grades of Dexfield junior and senior high school students in Redfield, Iowa. (Doctoral dissertation, Drake University, 1982). *Dissertation Abstracts International 43*, 2953A.

Axelson, J. A. (1993). *Counseling and development in a multicultural society,* Second edition. Pacific Grove, CA: Brooks/Cole Publishing Company.

Bailey, G. K. (1988). Examination of the relationship between hemispheric preferences and environmental characteristics of learning styles in college students. (Doctoral dissertation, University of Southern Mississippi, 1988). *Dissertation Abstracts International, 49* 2151A.

Baldwin, B. A. (1988). Relearning relaxation. *Piedmont Airlines,* 16–18.

Banks, J. A. (1988). Ethnicity, class, cognitive, and motivational styles: Research and teaching implications. *Journal of Negro Education, 57*(4), 452–466.

Baptiste, H. P., Jr. (1988). Multicultural education. In R. A. Gordon, G. J. Schneider, & J. C. Fisher (Eds.), *Encyclopedia of school administration and supervision* (pp. 174–175). Phoenix, AZ: Oryx Press.

Baron, A., Jr. (1991). Chapter 13: Counseling Chicano college students. In C. C. Lee & B. L. Richardson (Eds.), *Multicultural issues in counseling; New approaches to diversity* (pp. 171–184). Alexandria, VA: American Association for Counseling and Development.

Bauer, E. (1991). The relationships between and among learning styles perceptual preferences, instructional strategies, mathematics achievement, and attitude toward mathematics of learning disabled and emotionally handicapped students in a suburban junior high school. Doctoral dissertation, St. John's University, 1991. *Dissertation Abstracts International, 53,* 1378.

Beaty, S. A. (1986). The effect of inservice training on the ability of teachers to observe learning styles of students. (Doctoral dissertation, Oregon State University, 1986). *Dissertation Abstracts International, 47,* 1998A.

Bennett, C. I. (1990). *Comprehensive multicultural education: Theory and practice.* Boston, MA: Allyn & Bacon.

Berger, K. S., & Thompson, R. A. (1994). *The developing person through the life span* (3rd ed.). New York: Worth Publishers.

Biggers, J. L. (1980). Body rhythms, the school day, and academic achievement. *Journal of Experimental Education, 49*(1), 45–47.

Billings, D., & Cobb, K. (1992). Effects of learning style preference, attitude, and GPA on learner achievement using computer-assisted-interactive videodisc instruction. *Journal of Computer-Based Instruction, 19*(1), 12–16.

Black, C., Paz, H., & De Blassie, R. R. (1991). Counseling the Hispanic male adolescent. *Adolescence, 26*(101), 223–232.

Bonham, L. A. (1987). Theoretical and practical differences and similarities among selected cognitive and learning styles of adults: An analysis of the literature

(Vols. 1 & 2). (Doctoral dissertation, University of Georgia, 1987). *Dissertation Abstracts International, 48,* 2530A.

Bouwman, C. (1991). *Vive la difference: A guide to learning for high school students.* New York: Center for the Study of Learning and Teaching Styles, St. John's University.

Bradshaw, J. (1992). *Creating love: The next great stage of growth.* New York: Bantam Books.

Branton, P. (1966). *The comfort of easy chairs* (FIRA Technical Report No. 22). Herefordshire, UK: Furniture Industry Research Association.

The Bridge to Learning. (1993). Videotape available from St. John's University's Center for the Learning Styles Network, Utopia Parkway, Jamaica, NY 11439.

Brennan, P. K. (1984). An analysis of the relationships among hemispheric preference and analytic/global cognitive style, two elements of learning style, method of instruction, gender, and mathematics achievement of tenth-grade geometry students. (Doctoral dissertation, St. John's University, 1984). *Dissertation Abstracts International, 45,* 3271A.

Brodhead, M. R., & Price, G. E. (1993). Chapter 12: The learning styles of artistically-talented adolescents in Canada. In R. M. Milgram, R. Dunn, & G. E. Price (Eds.), *Teaching and counseling gifted and talented adolescents: An international learning-style perspective* (pp. 187–196). Westport, CT: Greenwood Press.

Brown, M. D. (1991). The relationship between traditional instructional methods, contract activity packages, and mathematics achievement of fourth-grade gifted students. (Doctoral dissertation, University of Southern Mississippi, 1991). *Dissertation Abstracts International, 52,* 1999A–2000A.

Brunner, C. E., & Majewski, W. S. (1990, October). Mildly handicapped students can succeed with learning styles. *Educational Leadership.* (Alexandria, VA: Association for Supervision and Curriculum Development), *48*(02), 21–23.

Brunner, R., & Hill, D. (1992, April). Using learning styles research in coaching. *Journal of Physical Education, Recreation and Dance, 63*(4), 26–61.

Bruno, J. (1988). An experimental investigation of the relationships between and among hemispheric processing, learning style preferences, instructional strategies, academic achievement, and attitudes of developmental mathematics students in an urban technical college. (Doctoral dissertation, St. John's University, 1988). *Dissertation Abstracts International, 48,* 1066A.

Bryant, H. W. (1986). *An investigation into the effectiveness of two strategy training approaches on the reading achievement of grade one Native Indian students.* Unpublished doctoral dissertation. Vancouver, CN: University of British Columbia.

Buell, B. G., & Buell, N. A. (1987). Perceptual modality preference as a variable in the effectiveness of continuing education for professionals. (Doctoral dissertation, University of Southern California, 1987). *Dissertation Abstracts International, 48,* 283A.

Buhler, J. (1990). A study of the relationship between selected learning styles and achievement of kindergarten language arts objectives in a local school district. (Doctoral dissertation, University of North Texas, 1990). *Dissertation Abstracts International, 51,* 2978A.

Calvano, E. J. (1985). The influence of student learning styles on the mathematics achievement of middle school students. (Doctoral dissertation, East Texas State University, 1985). *Dissertation Abstracts International, 46,* 10A.

Carbo, M. (1980). An analysis of the relationship between the modality preferences of kindergartners and selected reading treatments as they affect the learning of a basic sight-word vocabulary. (Doctoral dissertation, St. John's University, 1980). *Dissertation Abstracts International, 41,* 1389A. Recipient: Association for Supervision and Curriculum Development National Award for Best Doctoral Research, 1980.

Carns, A. W., & Carns, M. R. (1991, May). Teaching study skills, cognitive strategies, and metacognitive skills through self-diagnosed learning styles. *The School Counselor, 38,* 341–346.

Carruthers, S., & Young, A. (1980). Preference of condition concerning time in learning environments of rural versus city eighth-grade students. *Learning Styles Network Newsletter, 1*(1).

Cattey, M. (1980). Cultural differences in processing information. *American Indian Culture and Research Journal, 7*(4), 51–68.

Cavanaugh, D. (1981). Student learning styles: A diagnostic/prescriptive approach to instruction. *Phi Delta Kappan, 64*(3), 202–203.

Chen, C., & E. Yang, D. (1986). The self-image of Chinese-American adolescents. *Pacific/Asian American Mental Health Research Center Review, 3/4,* 27–29.

Chiu, M. (1993). *Cross-cultural differences in learning styles of secondary school students in Taiwan and the U.S.A.* Unpublished manuscript, Manhasset Public Schools, Manhasset, New York. Semifinalist in 53rd Annual Science Talent Search for Westinghouse Science Scholarships.

Cholakis, M. M. (1986). An experimental investigation of the relationships between and among sociological preferences, vocabulary instruction and achievement, and the attitudes of New York, urban, seventh and eighth grade underachievers. (Doctoral dissertation, St. John's University, 1986). *Dissertation Abstracts International, 47,* 4046A.

Clark-Thayer, S. (1987). The relationship of the knowledge of student-perceived learning style preferences, and study habits and attitudes to achievement of college freshmen in a small urban university. (Doctoral dissertation, Boston University, 1987). *Dissertation Abstracts International, 48,* 872A.

Clay, J. E. (1984). A correlational analysis of the learning characteristics of highly achieving and poorly achieving freshmen at A & M University as revealed through performance on standardized tests. Normal: Alabama A & M University.

Coburn, C. (1992). Stress and trauma compound school problems for immigrants. *New Voices, 2*(3), 1–2.

Cody, C. (1983). Learning styles, including hemispheric dominance: A comparative study of average, gifted, and highly gifted students in grades five through twelve. (Doctoral dissertation, Temple University, 1983). *Dissertation Abstracts International, 44,* 1631A.

Cohen, L. (1986). Birth order and learning styles: An examination of the relationships between birth order and middle school students' preferred learning style profiles. (Doctoral dissertation, University of Minnesota, Graduate Department of Educational Psychology, 1986). *Dissertation Abstracts International, 47,* 2084A.

Cohen, R. A. (1969). Conceptual style, cultural conflict, and nonverbal tests of intelligence. *American Anthropologist, 71*, 828–856.

Coleman, J. S. (1966). *Equality of educational opportunity.* Washington, DC: U.S. Government Printing Office.

Coleman, S. J. (1988). An investigation of the relationships among physical and emotional learning style preferences and perceptual modality strengths of gifted first-grade students. (Doctoral dissertation, Virginia Polytechnic Institute and State University, 1988). *Dissertation Abstracts International, 50*, 873A.

Cook, L. (1989). Relationships among learning style awareness, academic achievement, and locus of control among community college students. (Doctoral dissertation, University of Florida). *Dissertation Abstracts International, 49*, 217A.

Coolidge-Parker, J. A. (1989). A comparison of perceived and objectively measured perceptual learning style modality elements of court reporters and court-reporting students. (Doctoral dissertation, University of South Florida, 1989). *Dissertation Abstracts International, 50*, 1996A.

Cooper, T. J. D. (1991). An investigation of the learning styles of students at two contemporary alternative high schools in the District of Columbia. (Doctoral dissertation, George Washington University, School of Education and Human Development, 1991). *Dissertation Abstracts International, 52*, 2002A.

Cormier, W. H., & Cormier, L. S. (1991). *Interviewing strategies for helpers: Fundamental skills and cognitive behavioral interventions* (3rd ed.). Pacific Grove, CA: Brooks/Cole Publishing.

Cox, C. I. (1982) *Outcome research in cross-cultural counseling.* Unpublished manuscript.

Cramp, D. C. (1990). A study of the effects on student achievement of fourth- and fifth-grade students' instructional times being matched and mismatched with their particular time preference. (Doctoral dissertation, University of Mississippi). *Dissertation Abstracts International, 52* (02A), 407.

Crampton, N. A. S. (1990). Learning style (modality) preferences for students attending private residential alternative schools (at risk). (Doctoral dissertation, University of South Dakota, 1991). *Dissertation Abstracts International, 52*, 407A.

Crino, E. M. (1984). An analysis of the preferred learning styles of kindergarten children and the relationship of these preferred learning styles to curriculum planning for kindergarten children. (Doctoral dissertation, State University of New York at Buffalo, 1984). *Dissertation Abstracts International, 45*, 1282A.

Cross, J. A. (1982). Internal locus of control governs talented students (9–12). *Learning Styles Network Newsletter, 3*(3), 3. St. John's University and the National Association of Secondary School Principals.

Currence, J. A. (1991). High school dropouts as learners: A comparative analysis of schooling experiences and school behaviors, school climate perceptions, learning style preferences, and locus-of-control orientation of persisters and high school dropouts in a rural Eastern Shore county school system. (Doctoral dissertation, University of Maryland, College Park, 1991). *Dissertation Abstracts International, 52*, 2388A.

Curry, L. (1987). Integrating concepts of cognitive or learning styles: A review with attention to psychometric standards. Ottowa: Ontario: Canadian College of Health Services Executives.

D'Antonio, M. (1988). Learning styles: They're not a matter of race, but of individual strengths, experts say. *Newsday*, pp. 1, 3.

Davis, M. A. (1985). An investigation of the relationship of personality types and learning style preferences of high school students (Myers-Briggs Type Indicator). (Doctoral dissertation, George Peabody College for Teachers of Vanderbilt University, 1985). *Dissertation Abstracts International, 46*, 1606A.

Dean, W. L. (1982). A comparison of the learning styles of educable mentally retarded students and learning disabled students. (Doctoral dissertation, University of Mississippi, 1982). *Dissertation Abstracts International, 43*, 1923A.

DeBello, T. (1985). A critical analysis of the achievement and attitude effects of administrative assignments to social studies writing instruction based on identified, eighth grade students' learning style preferences for learning alone, with peers, or with teachers. (Doctoral dissertation, St. John's University, 1985). *Dissertation Abstracts International, 47*, 68A.

DeBello, T. (1990). Comparison of eleven major learning styles models: Variables, appropriate populations, validity of instrumentation, and the research behind them. *Journal of Reading, Writing, and Learning Disabilities International* (New York: Hemisphere Press), *6*(3), 203–222.

DeGregoris, C. N. (1986). Reading comprehension and the interaction of individual sound preferences and varied auditory distractions. (Doctoral dissertation, Hofstra University, 1986). *Dissertation Abstracts International, 47*, 3380A.

Delbrey, A. (1987, August). The relationship between the *Learning Style Inventory* and the *Gregorc Style Delineator*. (Doctoral dissertation, The University of Alabama, 1987). *Dissertation Abstracts International, 49*(02A), 219.

Della Valle, J. (1984). An experimental investigation of the word recognition scores of seventh grade students to provide supervisory and administrative guidelines for the organization of effective instructional environments. (Doctoral dissertation, St. John's University, 1984). *Dissertation Abstracts International, 45*, 359A. Recipient: Phi Delta Kappa National Award for Outstanding Doctoral Research, 1984; National Association of Secondary School Principals' Middle School Research Finalist citation, 1984; and Association for Supervision and Curriculum Development Finalist for Best National Research (Supervision), 1984.

Della Valle, J. (1990, July-September). The development of a learning styles program in an affluent, suburban New York elementary school. *Journal of Reading, Writing, and Learning Styles International* (New York: Hemisphere Press), *6*(3), 315–322.

Douglas, C. (1979). Making biology easier to understand. *The American Biology Teacher, 41*(5), 277–299.

Drew, M. W. (1991). An investigation of the effects of matching and mismatching minority underachievers with culturally similar and dissimilar story content and learning style and traditional instructional strategies. Doctoral dissertation, St. John's University, 1991.

Dunn, K. (1981, February). Madison prep: Alternative to teenage disaster. *Educational Leadership* (Alexandria, VA: Association for Supervision and Curriculum Development), *85*(5), 386–387.

Dunn, R. (1984). How should students do their homework? Research vs. opinion. *Early Years, 14*(4), 43–45.

Dunn, R. (1985). A research-based plan for doing homework. *Education Digest, 9*, 40–42.

Dunn, R. (1987, Spring). Research on instructional environments: Implications for student achievement and attitudes. *Professional School Psychology,* 2(1), 43–52.

Dunn, R. (1988). Commentary: Teaching students through their perceptual strengths or preferences. *Journal of Reading, 31*(4), 304–309.

Dunn, R. (1989a). Capitalizing on students' perceptual strengths to ensure literacy while engaging in conventional lecture/discussion. *Reading Psychology: An International Quarterly, 9*(4), 431–453.

Dunn, R. (1989b). Recent research on learning and seven applications to teaching young children to read. *The Oregon Elementary Principal. 50*(2), 39–32.

Dunn, R. (1989c). Individualizing instruction for mainstreamed gifted children. In R. R. Milgram (Ed.), *Teaching Gifted and Talented Learners in Regular Classrooms* (pp. 63–111). Springfield, IL: Charles C. Thomas.

Dunn, R. (1989d). A small private school in Minnesota. *Teaching K–8* (Norwalk, CT: Early Years), *18*(5), 54–57.

Dunn, R. (1989e). Can schools overcome the impact of societal ills on student achievement? The research indicates—yes! *The Principal* (New York: Board of Jewish Education of Greater New York), *34*(5), 1–15.

Dunn, R. (1989f). Teaching gifted students through their learning style strengths. *International Education* (New Wilmington, PA: Association for the Advancement of International Education), *16*(51), 6–8.

Dunn, R. (1989g). Do students from different cultures have different learning styles? *International Education* (New Wilmington, PA: Association for the Advancement of International Education), *16*(50), 40–42.

Dunn, R. (1990a). Bias over substance: A critical analysis of Kavale and Forness' report on modality-based instruction. *Exceptional Children* (Virginia: Council for Exceptional Children), *56*(4), 354–356.

Dunn, R. (1990b). When you really have to lecture, teach students through their perceptual strengths. *International Education* (New Wilmington, PA: Association for the Advancement of International Education), *17*(53), 1, 6–7.

Dunn, R. (1990c). Teaching young children to *read*: Matching methods to learning style perceptual processing strengths, Part One. *International Education* (New Wilmington, PA: Association for the Advancement of International Education), *17*(54), 2–3.

Dunn, R. (1990d). Understanding the Dunn and Dunn learning styles model and the need for individual diagnosis and prescription. *Journal of Reading, Writing, and Learning Disabilities International* (New York: Hemisphere Press), *6*(3), 223–247.

Dunn, R. (1990e). Rita Dunn answers questions on learning styles. *Educational Leadership* (Alexandria, VA: Association for Supervision and Curriculum Development), *48*(15), 15–19.

Dunn, R. (1990f). Teaching underachievers through their learning style strengths.

International Education (New Wilmington, PA: Association for the Advancement of International Education), *16*(52), 5–7.

Dunn, R. (1990g). Teaching young children to read: Matching methods to learning styles perceptual processing strengths, Part Two. *International Education* (New Wilmington, PA: Association for the Advancement of International Education), *17*(55), 5–7.

Dunn, R. (1991a). Are you willing to experiment with a tactual/visual/auditory global approach to reading? Part three. *International Education* (New Wilmington, PA: Association for the Advancement of International Education), *18*(56), 6–8.

Dunn R. (1991b). *Hands on approaches to learning styles: A practical guide for successful schooling.* New Wilmington, PA: Association for the Advancement of International Education.

Dunn, R. (1991c). Instructional leadership in education: Limited, diffused, sporadic, and lacking in research. *CSA Leadership* (New York: American Federation of School Administrators), 30–41.

Dunn, R. (1992a). Strategies for teaching word recognition to the disabled readers. *Reading and Writing Quarterly* (New York: Hemisphere Press), *8*(2), 157–177.

Dunn, R. (1992b). Teaching the "I-was-paying-attention-but-I-didn't-hear-you-say-it" learner. *International Education* (New Wilmington, PA: Association for the Advancement of International Education), *19*(61), 1, 6.

Dunn, R. (1993a). The learning styles of gifted adolescents in nine culturally-diverse nations. *International Education* (Wilmington, PA: Association for the Advancement of International Education), *20*(64), 4–6.

Dunn, R. (1993b). Learning styles of multiculturally-diverse students. *Emergency Librarian* (British Vancouver, CN: Emergency Librarians' Association), *20*(4), 24–35.

Dunn, R. (1993c). Teaching the . . . "I don't like school and you can't make me like it" learner. *International Education.* (Wilmington, PA: Association for the Advancement of International Education), *20*(65), 4–5.

Dunn, R. (1993d). Teaching gifted students through their learning style strengths. In R. M. Milgram, R. Dunn, & G. E. Price (Eds.), *Teaching and Counseling Gifted and Talented Adolescents for Learning Style: An International Perspective* (chap. 3, pp. 37–67). Westport, CT: Praeger.

Dunn, R. (1993). Chapter 7: Teaching gifted students through their individual learning style strengths. In R. M. Milgram, R. Dunn, & G. E. Price (Eds.), *Teaching and Counseling Gifted and Talented Adolescents for Learning Style: An International Perspective.* Westport, CT: Praeger.

Dunn, R., Bauer, E., Gemake, J., Gregory, J., Primavera, L., & Signer, B. (1994). Matching and mismatching junior high school learning disabled and emotionally handicapped students' perceptual preferences on mathematics scores. *Teacher Education Journal, 5*(1), 3–13.

Dunn, R., Beaudry, J. A., & Klavas, A. (1989). Survey of research on learning styles. *Educational Leadership* (Alexandria, VA: Association for Supervision and Curriculum Development), *46*(6), 50–58.

Dunn, R., & Bruno, A. (1985). What does the research on learning styles have to do with Mario? *The Clearing House* (Washington, DC: Heldref Publications), *59*(1), 9–11.

Dunn, R., Bruno, J., Sklar, R. I., & Beaudry, J. (1990). Effects of matching and mismatching minority developmental college students' hemispheric preferences on mathematics scores. *Journal of Educational Research* (Washington, DC: Heldref Publications), *83*(5), 283–288.

Dunn, R., Cavanaugh, D., Eberle, B., & Zenhausern, R. (1982). Hemispheric preference: The newest element of learning style. *The American Biology Teacher*, *44*(5), 291–294.

Dunn, R., DeBello, T., Brennan, P., Krimsky, J., & Murrain, P. (1981). Learning style researchers define differences differently. *Educational Leadership* (Alexandria, VA: Association for Supervision and Curriculum Development), *38*(5), 382–392.

Dunn, R., Deckinger, E. L., Withers, P., & Katzenstein, H. (1990, Winter). Should college students be taught how to do homework? The effects of studying marketing through individual perceptual strengths. *Illinois School Research and Development Journal* (Normal, IL: Illinois Association for Supervision and Curriculum Development), *26*(3), 96–113.

Dunn, R., Della Valle, J., Dunn, K., Geisert, G., Sinatra, R., & Zenhausern, R. (1986). The effects of matching and mismatching students' mobility preferences on recognition and memory tasks. *Journal of Educational Research* (Washington, DC: Heldref Publications), 79(5), 267–272.

Dunn, R., & Dunn, K. (1972). *Practical approaches to individualizing instruction: Contracts and other effective teaching strategies.* Englewood Cliffs, NJ: Parker Publishing Division of Prentice Hall.

Dunn, R., & Dunn, K. (1978). *Teaching students through their individual learning styles: A practical approach.* Reston, VA: Reston Publishing Company.

Dunn, K., & Dunn, R. (1987). Dispelling outmoded beliefs about student learning. *Educational Leadership* (Alexandria, VA: Association for Supervision and Curriculum Development), *44*,(6), 55–62.

Dunn, R., & Dunn, K. (1992). *Teaching elementary students through their individual learning styles: Practical approaches for grades 3–6.* Boston: Allyn & Bacon.

Dunn, R., & Dunn, K. (1993). *Teaching secondary students through their individual learning styles: Practical approaches for grades 7–12.* Boston: Allyn & Bacon.

Dunn, R., Dunn, K., & Freeley, M. E. (1984). Practical applications of the research: Responding to students' learning styles—step one. *Illinois State Research and Development Journal*, *21* (1), 1–21.

Dunn, R., Dunn, K., & Perrin, J. (1994). *Teaching young children through their individual learning styles: Practical approaches for grades K–2.* Boston: Allyn & Bacon.

Dunn, R., Dunn, K., & Price, G. E. (1977). Diagnosing learning styles: Avoiding malpractice suits against school systems. *Phi Delta Kappan*, *58*(5), 418–420.

Dunn, R., Dunn, K., & Price, G. E. (1989). *Learning Style Inventory manual.* Lawrence, KS: Price Systems.

Dunn, R., Dunn, K., Primavera, L., Sinatra, R., & Virostko, J. (1987). A timely solution: A review of research on the effects of chronobiology on children's achievement and behavior. *The Clearing House* (Washington, DC: Heldref Publications), *61*(1), 5–8.

Dunn, R., Dunn, K., & Treffinger, D. (1992). *Bringing out the giftedness in every child: A guide for parents*. Ne York: John Wiley.

Dunn, R., Gemake, J., Jalali, F., Zenhausern, R., Quinn, P., & Spiridakis, J. (1990, April). Cross-cultural differences in the learning styles of elementary-age students from four ethnic backgrounds. *Journal of Multicultural Counseling and Development, 18*(2), 68–93.

Dunn, R., Gemake, J., Jalali, F., & Zenhausern, R. (1990, January). Cross-cultural differences in learning styles. *Missouri Association for Supervision and Curriculum Development Journal, 1*(2), 9–15.

Dunn, R., Giannitti, M. C., Murray, J. B., Geisert, G., Rossi, I., & Quinn, P. (1990). Grouping students for instruction: Effects of individual vs. group learning style on achievement and attitudes. *Journal of Social Psychology*, (Washington, DC), *130*(4), 485–494.

Dunn, R., & Griggs, S. A. (1988). *Learning styles: Quiet revolution in American secondary schools*. Reston, VA: National Association of Secondary School Principals.

Dunn, R., & Griggs, S. A. (1989a). A quiet revolution in Hempstead. *Teaching K–8* (Norwalk, CT: Early Years), *18*(5), 54–57.

Dunn, R., & Griggs, S. A. (1989b). The learning styles of multicultural groups and counseling implications. *Journal of Multicultural Counseling and Development, 7*(4), 146–155.

Dunn, R., & Griggs, S. A. (1989c). Learning styles: Key to improving schools and student achievement. *Curriculum Report*. Reston, VA: National Association of Secondary School Principals.

Dunn, R., & Griggs, S. A. (1989d). A matter of style. *Momentum* (Washington, DC: National Catholic Education Association), *20*(2), 66–70.

Dunn, R., & Griggs, S. A. (1989e). Learning styles: Quiet revolution in American secondary schools. *Momentum* (Washington, DC: National Catholic Education Association), *63*(1), 40–42.

Dunn, R., & Griggs, S. A. (1989f). A quiet revolution: Learning styles and their application to secondary schools. *Holistic Education* (Greenfield, MA: Holistic Education Review), *2*(4), 14–19.

Dunn, R., & Griggs, S. A. (1990). Research on the learning style characteristics of selected racial and ethnic groups. *Journal of Reading, Writing, and Learning Disabilities* (Washington, DC: Hemisphere Press), *6*(3), 261–280.

Dunn, R., Griggs, S. A., & Price, G. E. (1993a). Learning styles of Mexican American and Anglo-American Elementary School Students. *Journal of Multicultural Counseling and Development, 21*(4), 237–247.

Dunn, R., Griggs, S. A., & Price, G. E. (1993b). The learning styles of gifted adolescents in the United States. In R. M. Milgram, R. Dunn, & G. E. Price (Eds.), *Teaching and Counseling Gifted and Talented Adolescents for Learning: An International Perspective* (pp. 119–136). Westport, CT: Praeger.

Dunn, R., Griggs, S. A., Olson, J., Gorman, & Beasley, M. (in press). A meta-analytic validation of the Dunn and Dunn learning styles model. *Journal of Educational Research*.

Dunn, R., & Klavas, A. (1992). Homework Disk. Jamaica, NY: St. John's University's Center for the Study of Learning and Teaching Styles, 11439.

Dunn, R., Krimsky, J., Murray, J., & Quinn, P. (1985). Light up their lives: A review of research on the effects of lighting on children's achievement. *The Reading Teacher*, *38*(9), 863–869.

Dunn, R., & Milgram, R. (1993). Chapter 1: Learning styles of gifted students in diverse cultures. In R. M. Milgram, R. Dunn, & G. E. Price (Eds.), *Teaching and Counseling Gifted and Talented Adolescents for Learning Style: An International Perspective* (pp. 3–23). Westport, CT: Praeger.

Dunn, R., Pizzo, J., Sinatra, R., & Barretto, R. A. (1983). Can it be too quiet to learn? *Focus: Teaching English Language Arts*, *19*(2), 92.

Dunn, R., & Price, G. E. (1980). The learning style characteristics of gifted children. *Gifted Child Quarterly*, *24*(1), 33–36.

Dunn, R., Price, G. E., Dunn, K., & Griggs, S. A. (1981). Studies in students' learning styles. *Roeper Review* (MI: Roeper City and Country School), *4*(2), 38–40.

Dunn, R., Shea, T. C., Evans, W., & MacMurren, H. (1991). Learning style and equal protection: The next frontier. *The Clearing House* (Washington, DC: Heldref Publications), *65*(2), 93–96.

Dunn, R., & Smith, J. B. (1990). Chapter Four: Learning styles and library media programs. In J. B. Smith (Ed.), *School Library Media Annual* (pp. 32–49). Englewood, CO: Libraries Unlimited.

Dunn, R., White, R. M., & Zenhausern, R. (1982). An investigation of responsible versus less responsible students. *Illinois School Research and Development*, *19*(1), 19–24.

Edelman, M. W. (1987). *The children's time*. Washington, DC: Children's Defense Fund.

Eitington, N. J. (1989). A comparison of learning styles of freshmen with high and low reading achievement in the Community Scholars Liberal Studies Program at Georgetown University. (Doctoral dissertation, Georgetown University, Washington, DC, 1989). *Dissertation Abstracts International*, *50*, 1285A.

Elliot, I. (1991). The reading place. *Teaching K–8* (Norwalk, CT: Early Years), *21*(3), 30–34.

Ellis, A. (1962). *Reason and emotion in psychotherapy*. New York: Lyle Stuart.

Erikson, E. H. (1968). *Identity, youth, and crisis*. New York: W. W. Norton.

Ewing, N. J., & Lan Yong, F. (1992). A comparative study of the learning style preferences among gifted African-American, Mexican-American, and American-born, Chinese middle-grade students. *Roeper Review* (MI: Roeper City and Country School), *14*(3), 120–123.

Fadley, J. L., & Hosler, V. (1979). *Understanding the alpha child at home and at school*. Springfield, IL: Charles C. Thomas.

Ferrell, B. G. (1981). Factor analytic validation of the learning styles paradigm. (Doctoral dissertation, Southern Illinois University of Carbondale, 1981). *Dissertation Abstracts International*, *42*, 3069A.

Fitt, S. (1975). The individual and his environment. In T. G. David & B. D. Wright (Eds.), *Learning environments* (p. 94). Chicago: University of Chicago Press.

Fleming, V. J. (1989, August). Vocational classrooms with style. *Vocational Edu-*

cation Journal (Alexandria, VA: American Vocational Association), *10*(1), 36–39.

Fordham, S., & Ogbu, J. U. (1986). Black students' school success: Coping with the "burden of acting white." *The Urban Review, 18*(3), 176–206.

Freeley, M. E. (1984). An experimental investigation of the relationships among teachers' individual time preferences, inservice workshop schedules, and instructional techniques and the subsequent implementation of learning style strategies in participants' classrooms. (Doctoral dissertation, St. John's University, 1984). *Dissertation Abstracts International, 46,* 403A.

Freeman, D. C. (1979). Ethnic differences in babies. *Human Sociobiology.* New York: Free Press.

French, S. B. (1991). The relationship between congruent and incongruent instructional methods and first-grade reading vocabulary achievement and learning styles. (Doctoral dissertation, University of Southern Mississippi, 1991). *Dissertation Abstracts International, 52*(04A), 1192.

Gadwa, K., & Griggs, S. A. (1985). The school dropout: Implications for counselors. *The School Counselor, 33,* 9–17.

Galvin, A. J. (1992). An analysis of learning and productivity styles across occupational groups in a corporate setting (learning styles, corporate training). (Doctoral dissertation. Boston University, 1992). *Dissertation Abstracts International, 53*(04A), 1027.

Garcia-Otero, M. (1987). Knowledge of learning styles and the effect on the clinical performance of nurse anesthesiology students. (Doctoral dissertation, University of New Orleans, 1987). *Dissertation Abstracts International, 49,* 1602B.

Garcia-Otero, M., & Teddlie, C. (1992). The effect of knowledge of learning styles on anxiety and clinical performance of nurse anesthesiology students. *American Association of Nursing Anesthesiology Journal, 60*(3), 257–260.

Garger, S. (1990, October). Is there a link between learning style and neurophysiology? *Educational Leadership* (Alexandria, VA: Association for Supervision and Curriculum Development), *48*(2), 63–65.

Gardiner, B. (1983). Stepping into a learning styles program. *Roeper Review, 6*(2), 90–92.

Gardiner, B. (1986). An experimental analysis of selected teaching strategies implemented at specific times of the school day and their effects on the social studies achievement test scores and attitudes of fourth grade, low achieving students in an urban school setting. (Doctoral dissertation, St. John's University, 1986). *Dissertation Abstracts International, 47,* 3307A.

Garrett, S. L. (1991). The effects of perceptual preference and motivation on vocabulary and attitude test scores among high school students. (Doctoral dissertation, University of La Verne, CA, 1991). *Dissertation Abstracts International, 53,* 389A.

Geisert, G., & Dunn, R. (1991a). Computer and learning style. *Principal* (Reston, VA: National Association of Elementary School Principals), *70*(4), 47–49.

Geisert, G., & Dunn, R. (1991b). Effective use of computers: Assignments based on individual learning style. *The Clearing House* (Washington, DC: Heldref Publications), *64*(4), 219–224.

Geisert, G., Dunn, R., & Sinatra, R. (1990). Reading, learning styles, and computers. *Journal of Reading, Writing, and Learning Disabilities* (Washington, DC: Hemisphere Press), *6*(3), 297–306.

Giannitti, M. C. (1988). An experimental investigation of the relationships among the learning style sociological preferences of middle-school students (grades 6, 7, 8), their attitudes and achievement in social studies, and selected instructional strategies. (Doctoral dissertation, St. John's University, 1988). *Dissertation Abstracts International, 49*, 2911A.

Glasner, J., & Ingham, J. (1993). Learning styles and literacy. *The Bookmark* (Albany, NY: State Education Department, New York State Library), *50*(111), 218–223.

Glines, D. (1989). Can schools of today survive very far into the 21st. century? *NASSP Bulletin, 73*, 49–56.

Goodlad, J. I. (1984). *A place called school: Prospects for the future.* New York: McGraw-Hill.

Gordon, E. M. (1964). *Assimilation in American life.* New York: Oxford University Press.

Gordon, E. W. (Ed.). (1988). *Report of the New York Board of Regents panel on learning styles.* Albany, NY: State Education Department.

Gould, B. J. (1987). An investigation of the relationships between supervisors' and supervisees' sociological productivity styles on teacher evaluations and interpersonal attraction ratings. (Doctoral dissertation, St. John's University, 1987). *Dissertation Abstracts International, 48*, 18A.

Griggs, S. A. (1983). Counseling high school students for their individual learning styles. *The Clearing House* (Washington, DC: Heldref Publications), *56*, 293–296.

Griggs, S. A. (1984). Counseling the gifted and talented based on learning styles. *Exceptional Children, 50*, 429–432.

Griggs, S. A. (1985). Counseling for individual learning styles. *Journal of Counseling and Development, 64*, 202–205.

Griggs, S. A. (1989, November). Students' sociological grouping preferences of learning styles. *The Clearing House* (Washington, DC: Heldref Publications), *63*(3), 135–139.

Griggs, S. A. (1990). Counseling students toward effective study skills using their learning style strengths. *Journal of Reading, Writing, and Learning Disabilities International, 6*, 281–296.

Griggs, S. A. (1991a). *Learning styles counseling.* Ann Arbor: University of Michigan. Obtainable from Center for the Study of Learning and Teaching Styles, St. John's University, Jamaica, NY 11439.

Griggs, S. A. (1991b). Counseling gifted children with different learning-style preferences. In R. M. Milgram (Ed.), *Counseling Talented and Gifted Children: A Guide for Teachers, Counselors, and Parents* (pp. 53–74). New Jersey: Ablex Publishing Corporation.

Griggs, S. A., & Dunn, R. (1988, September-October). High school dropouts: Do they learn differently from those students who remain in school? *The Principal* (New York: Board of Jewish Education of Greater New York), *34*(1), 1–8.

Griggs, D., Griggs, S. A., Dunn, R., & Ingham, J. (1994). A challenge for nurse educators: Accommodating nursing students' diverse learning styles. *Nurse Educator 19*(6), 41–45.

Griggs, S. A., & Price, G. E. (1980). A comparison between the learning styles of gifted versus average junior high school students. *Phi Delta Kappan, 61* 361.

Griggs, S. A., & Price, G. E. (1982). A comparison between the learning styles of gifted versus average junior high school students. *Creative and Gifted Child Quarterly, 7,* 39–42.

Griggs, S. A., Price, G. E., Kopel, S., & Swaine, W. (1984). The effects of group counseling with sixth-grade students using approaches that are compatible versus incompatible with selected learning style elements. *California Personnel and Guidance Journal, 5*(1), 28–35.

Guild, P. O'R., B. (1980). Learning styles: Knowledge, issues and applications for classroom teachers. (Doctoral dissertation, University of Massachusetts). *Dissertation Abstracts International, 41,* 1033A.

Guinta, S. F. (1984). Administrative considerations concerning learning style and the influence of instructor/student congruence on high schoolers' achievement and educators' perceived stress. (Doctoral dissertation, St. John's University, 1984). *Dissertation Abstracts International, 45,* 32A.

Guzzo, R. S. (1987). Dificuldades de apprenddizagem: Modalidade de attencao e analise de tarefas em materials didaticos. (Doctoral dissertation, University of São Paulo, Institute of Psychology, Brazil, 1987).

Hadfield, O. D., Martin, J. V., & Wooden, S. (1992). Mathematics anxiety and learning style of the Navajo middle school student. *School Science and Mathematics, 92*(4), 171–176.

Hale, J. (1981). Black children: Their roots, culture, and learning. *Young Children, 36,* 37–40.

Hale-Benson, J. (1982). *Black children: Their roots, culture, and learning styles.* Baltimore: Johns Hopkins University Press.

Hanna, S. J. (1989). An investigation of the effects on achievement test scores of individual time preferences and time of training in a corporate setting. Doctoral dissertation, St. John's University, 1989.

Harp, T. Y., & Orsak, L. (1990, July-September). One administrator's challenge: Implementing a learning style program at the secondary level. *Journal of Reading, Writing, and Learning Disabilities International* (New York: Hemisphere Press), *6*(3), 335–342.

Harrison, A. O., Wilson, M. N., Pine, C. J., Chan, S. Q., & Bureil, R. (1990). Family ecologies of minority children. *Child Development, 61,* 347–362.

Harty, P. M. (1982). *Learning styles: A matter of difference in the foreign language classroom.* Unpublished master's dissertation, Wright State University.

Hawk, T. D. (1983). A comparison of teachers' preference for specific inservice activity approaches and their measured learning styles. (Doctoral dissertation, Kansas State University, 1983). *Dissertation Abstracts International, 44,* 3557A.

Hickerson-Roberts, V. L. (1983). Reading achievement, reading attitudes, self-concept, learning styles and estimated high school grade-point average as predictions of academic success for 55 adult learners at Kansas State University. (Doctoral dissertation, Kansas State University, 1983). *Dissertation Abstracts International, 44,* 1295A.

Hill, G. D. (1987). An experimental investigation into the interaction between modality preference and instructional mode in the learning of spelling words by upper-elementary learning disabled students. (Doctoral dissertation, North Texas State University, 1987). *Dissertation Abstracts International, 48*, 2536A.

Hilliard, A. (1976) *Alternatives to I.Q. testing: An approach to the identification of gifted minority students.* Sacramento, CA: Final Report to the California State Department of Education.

Hilliard, A. (1988, June 15). *Black cultural style.* Paper presented at the New York State Education Department Learning Style Symposium, Albany, NY.

Hodges, H. (1985). An analysis of the relationships among preferences for a formal/informal design, one element of learning style, academic achievement, and attitudes of seventh and eighth grade students in remedial mathematics classes in a New York City junior high school. (Doctoral dissertation, St. John's University, 1985). *Dissertation Abstracts International, 45*, 2791A. Recipient: Phi Delta Kappa National Finalist Award for Outstanding Doctoral Research, 1986.

Hong, M. (Ed.). (1993). *Growing up Asian American.* New York: William Morrow & Company.

Hudgens, B. A. (1993). The relationship of cognitive style, planning ability, and locus-of-control to achievement for three ethnic groups (Anglo, African-American, Hispanic). *Dissertation Abstracts International, 53*, 2744A.

Hunt, D. (1979). Learning style and student needs: An introduction to conceptual level. *Student learning styles: Diagnosing and prescribing programs* (pp. 27–38). Reston, VA: National Association of Secondary School Principals.

Hutto, J. R. (1982). The association of teacher manipulation of scientifically acquired learning styles information to the achievement and attitudes of second and third grade remedial students. (Doctoral dissertation, University of Southern Mississippi, 1982). *Dissertation Abstracts International, 44*, 30A.

Ignelzi-Ferraro, D. M. (1989). Identification of the preferred conditions for learning among three groups of mildly handicapped high school students using the Learning Style Inventory. (Doctoral dissertation, University of Pittsburgh, 1989). *Dissertation Abstracts International, 51*, 796A.

Ingham, J. (1990). An experimental investigation of the relationships among learning style perceptual preference, instructional strategies, training achievement, and attitudes of corporate employees. (Doctoral dissertation, St. John's University, 1989). *Dissertation Abstracts International, 51*, 02A. Recipient: American Society for Training and Development National Research Award (1990).

Ingham, J. (1991). Matching instruction with employee perceptual preferences significantly increases training effectiveness. *Human Resource Development Quarterly, 2*(1), 53–64.

Ingham, J., & Dunn, R. (1993). The Dunn and Dunn Model of learning styles: Addressing learning diversity. *The 1993 Annual Developing Human Resources.* London: Pfeiffer & Co.

Ingham, J., & Price, G. E. (1993). Chapter 9: The learning styles of gifted adolescents in the Philippines. In R. M. Milgram, R. Dunn, & G. E. Price (Eds.), *Teaching and Counseling Gifted and Talented Adolescents: An International Learning Style* (pp. 149–160). New York: Praeger.

Ivey, A., & Authier, J. (1978). *Microcounseling: Innovations in interview training.* Springfield, IL: Charles C. Thomas.

Jacobs, R. L. (1987). An investigation of the learning style differences among Afro-American and Euro-American high, average, and low achievers. (Doctoral dissertation, George Peabody University, TN, 1987). *Dissertation Abstracts International, 49*(01A), 39.

Jalali, F. (1988). A cross cultural comparative analysis of the learning styles and field dependence/independence characteristics of selected fourth-, fifth-, and sixth-grade students of Afro, Chinese, Greek, and Mexican heritage. (Doctoral dissertation, St. John's University, 1988). *Dissertation Abstracts International, 50*, 344A.

Jarsonbeck, S. (1984). The effects of a right-brain and mathematics curriculum on low achieving, fourth grade students. (Doctoral dissertation, University of South Florida, 1984). *Dissertation Abstracts International, 45*, 2791A.

Jenkins, C. (1991). The relationship between selected demographic variables and learning environmental preferences of freshman students of Alcorn State University. (Doctoral dissertation, University of Mississippi, 1991). *Dissertation Abstracts International, 92*, 16065.

Jenkins, J. M., Letteri, C. A., & Roslund, P. (1990). *Learning style profile handbook #1: Developing cognitive skills.* Reston, VA: National Association of Secondary School Principals.

Johnson, C. D. (1984). Identifying potential school dropouts. (Doctoral dissertation, United States International University). *Dissertation Abstracts International, 45*, 2397A.

Johnson, J. A., Dupuis, V. L., Musial, D., & Hall, G. E. (1994). *Introduction to the foundation of American education.* Boston, MA: Allyn & Bacon.

Johnston, R. J. (1986). A comparative analysis between the effectiveness of conventional and modular instruction in teaching students with varied learning styles and individual differences enrolled in high school industrial arts manufacturing. (Doctoral dissertation, North Carolina State University, 1986). *Dissertation Abstracts International, 47*, 2923A.

Jordan, J. M. (1991). Counseling African American women: "Sister-friends." In C. C. Lee & B. L. Richardson (Eds.), *Multicultural issues in counseling: New approaches to diversity* (pp. 51–63). Alexandria, VA: American Association for Counseling and Development.

Joseph, C. B. (1984). The child, the family, and the school in English-Haitian education. In C. R. Foster & A. Valman (Eds.), *Haiti—today and tomorrow: An interdisciplinary study* (pp. 351–358). Lanham, MD: University Press.

Kagan, S. (1981). Ecology and the acculturation of cognitive and social styles among Mexican American children. *Hispanic Journal of Behavioral Sciences, 3*(2), 111–144.

Kagan, S., & Buriel, R. (1977). Field dependence-independence and Mexican-American culture and education. In J. L. Martinez, Jr. (Ed.), *Chicago Psychology* (pp. 279–328). New York: Academic Press.

Kahre, C. J. (1985). Relationships between learning styles of student teachers, cooperating teachers, and final evaluations. (Doctoral dissertation, Arizona State University, 1984). *Dissertation Abstracts International, 45*, 2492A.

Kaley, S. B. (1977). Field dependence/independence and learning styles in sixth graders. (Doctoral dissertation, Hofstra University, 1977). *Dissertation Abstracts International 38*, 1301A.

Karlebach, D. G. (1986). *A cognitive framework for deriving and interpreting learning style differences among a group of intermediate grade native and non-native pupils.* Unpublished doctoral dissertation, University of British Columbia, Vancouver, CN.

Kaufman, A. S., & Kaufman, N. (1983). *Kaufman Assessment Battery for Children, interpretive manual.* Circle Pines, MN: American Guidance Service.

Kaulbach, B. (1984). Styles of learning among native children: A review of the research. *Canadian Journal of Native Education, 11*(3), 27–37.

Keefe, J. W. (1982). Assessing student learning styles: An overview of learning style and cognitive style inquiry. *Student Learning Styles and Brain Behavior.* Reston, Virginia: National Association of Secondary School Principals.

Keefe, J. W., Languis, M., Letteri, C., & Dunn, R. (1986). *NASSP Learning Style Profile.* Reston, VA: National Association of Secondary School Principals.

Keefe, J. W., & Monk, J. S. (1986). *Learning style profile examiner's manual.* Reston, VA: National Association of Secondary School Principals.

Kelly, A. P. (1989). Elementary principals' change-facilitating behavior as perceived by self and staff when implementing learning styles instructional programs. Doctoral dissertation, St. John's University, 1989. *Dissertation Abstracts International, 51*, 1852.

Kirby, P. (1979). Cognitive style, learning style, and transfer skill acquisition. Columbia, OH: Ohio State University, National Center for Research in Vocational Education.

Kizilay, P. E. (1991). The relationship of learning style preferences and perceptions of college climate and performance on the National Council Licensure Examination for registered nurses in associate degree nursing programs. Doctoral dissertation, University of Georgia, 1991.

Klavas, A. (1991). Implementation of the Dunn and Dunn Learning Styles Model in United States elementary schools: Principals' and teachers' perceptions of factors that facilitated or impeded the process. Doctoral dissertation, St. John's University, 1991.

Klavas, A. (1993). In Greensboro, North Carolina: Learning style program boosts achievement and test scores. *The Clearing House* (Washington, DC: Heldref Publications), *67*(3), 149–151.

Klavas, A., Dunn, R., Griggs, S. A., Gemake, J. Geisert, G., & Zenhausern, R. (1994). Factors that facilitated or impeded implementation of the Dunn and Dunn learning style model. *Illinois School Research and Development Journal 31*(1), 19–23.

Kleinfeld, J., & Nelson, P. (1991). Adapting instruction to Native Americans' language styles: An iconoclastic view. *Journal of Cross-Cultural Psychology, 22*(2), 273–282.

Kluckholn, C., & Murray, H. A. (1953). Personality formation: The determinants.

In C. Kluckholn, H. A. Kluckholn, H. A. Murray, & D. M. Schneider (Eds.), *Personality in nature, society, and culture* (pp. 335–370). New York: Random House.

Knoll, M. (1994). *Information processing tool box.* New York: Valley Stream Central High School District.

Koester, L. S., & Farley, F. H. (1977). *Arousal and hyperactivity in open and traditional education.* Paper presented at the American Psychological Association annual convention, San Francisco. ERIC Document Reproduction Service No. ED 155 543.

Kohlberg, L. (1976). Moral stages and moralization: The cognitive-development approach. In T. Lickona (Ed.), *Moral development and behavior.* New York: Holt, Rhinehart, & Winston.

Koshuta, V., & Koshuta, P. (1993, April). Learning styles in a one-room school. *Educational Leadership* (Alexandria, VA: Association for Supervision and Curriculum Development), *50*(7), 87.

Kreitner, K. R. (1981). *Modality strengths and learning styles of musically talented high school students.* Unpublished master's dissertation, Ohio State University.

Krimsky, J. (1982). A comparative analysis of the effects of matching and mismatching fourth grade students with their learning style preference for the environmental element of light and their subsequent reading speed and accuracy scores. (Doctoral dissertation, St. John's University, 1982). *Dissertation Abstracts International, 43*, 66A. Recipient: Association for Supervision and Curriculum Development First Alternate National Recognition For Best Doctoral Research (Curriculum), 1982.

Kroon, D. (1985). An experimental investigation of the effects on academic achievement and the resultant administrative implications of instruction congruent and incongruent with secondary, industrial arts students' learning style perceptual preference. (Doctoral dissertation, St. John's University, 1985). *Dissertation Abstracts International, 46*, 3247A.

Krumboltz, J. (1988). The key to achievement: Learning to love learning. In G. Walz (Ed.), *Building strong school counseling programs* (pp. 1–40). Alexandria, VA: American Association for Counseling and Development.

Krywaniuk, L. L. (1974). *Patterns of cognitive abilities of high and low achieving school children.* Unpublished doctoral dissertation, University of Alberta, Edmonton, CN.

Kulp, J. J. (1982). A description of the processes used in developing and implementing a teacher training program based on the Dunns' concept of learning style. (Doctoral dissertation, Temple University, 1982). *Dissertation Abstracts International, 42*, 5021A.

Kussrow, P. G., & Dunn, K. (1992, Summer). Learning styles and the community educator. *Community Education Journal* (Alexandria, VA: National Community Education Association), *19*(4), 16–19.

Kuznar, E., Falciglia, G. A., Grace, A., Wood, L., & Frankel, J. (1991). Learning style preferences: A comparison of younger and older adult females. *Journal of Nutrition for the Elderly, 10*(3), 213–33.

Kryriacou, M., & Dunn, R. (1994). Synthesis of research: Learning styles of students with learning disabilities. *Special Education Journal, 4*(1), 3–9.

LaMothe, J., Billings, D. M., Belcher, A., Cobb, K., Nice, A., & Richardson, V. (1991). Reliability and validity of the Productivity Environmental Preference Survey (PEPS). *Nurse Educator, 16*(4), 30–34.

Lam-Phoon, S. (1986). A comparative study of the learning styles of Southeast Asian and American Caucasian college students of two Seventh-Day Adventist campuses. (Doctoral dissertation, Andrews University, 1986). *Dissertation Abstracts International, 48*, 2234A.

Learning Styles Network Newsletter. (1979–95). Jamaica, NY: St. John's University's Center for the Study of Learning and Teaching Styles, Jamaica, NY 11439.

LeClair, T. J. (1986). The preferred perceptual modality of kindergarten aged children. (Unpublished master's thesis, California State University, 1986). *Master's Abstracts, 24*, 324.

Lee, C. C., & Richardson, B. L. (1991). *Multicultural issues in counseling: New approaches to diversity.* Alexandria, VA: American Association of Counseling and Development.

Lemmon, P. (1985). A school where learning styles make a difference. *Principal* (Reston, VA: National Association of Elementary School Principals), *64*(4), 26–29.

Lenehan, M. (1994). Effects of learning style knowledge on nursing majors' achievement, anxiety, anger, and curiosity. Doctoral dissertation, St. John's University, 1994.

Lenehan, M. C., Dunn, R., Ingham, J., Signer, B., & Murray, J. B. (1994). Learning style: Necessary know-how for academic success in college. *Journal of College Student Development, 35*(6), 461–466.

Lengal, O. (1983). Analysis of the preferred learning styles of former adolescent psychiatric patients. (Doctoral dissertation, Kansas State University, 1983). *Dissertation Abstracts International, 44*, 2344A.

Levy, J. (1979). Human cognition and lateralization of cerebral function. *Trends in Neuroscience*, 220–224.

Levy, J. (1982, Autumn). What do brain scientists know about education? *Learning Styles Network Newsletter* (St. John's University and the National Association of Secondary School Principals), *3*(3), 4.

Lewis, H. (1990). *A question of values: Six ways we make the personal choices that shape our lives.* San Francisco: Harper & Row.

Li, T. C. (1989). The learning styles of the Filipino graduate students of the Evangelical seminaries in metro Manila. Doctoral dissertation, Asia Graduate School of Theology, Philippines, 1989.

Lux, K. (1987). Special needs students: A qualitative study of their learning styles. (Doctoral dissertation, Michigan State University, 1987). *Dissertation Abstracts International, 49*, 421A.

Lynch, P. K. (1981). An analysis of the relationships among academic achievement, attendance, and the learning style time references of eleventh and twelfth grade students identified as initial or chronic truants in a suburban New York school district. (Doctoral dissertation, St. John's University, 1981). *Dissertation Abstracts International, 42*, 1880A. Recipient: Association for Supervision & Curriculum Development, First Alternate National Recognition for Best Doctoral Research (Supervision), 1981.

Martinez, R., & Dukes, R. L. (1987). Race, gender, and self-esteem among youth. *Hispanic Journal of Behavioral Sciences, 9*(4), 427–443.

MacMurren, H. (1992, Spring). Learning style and state law. *Learning Consultant Journal, 13*, 21–24.

MacMurren, H. (1985). A comparative study of the effects of matching and mismatching sixth-grade students with their learning style preferences for the physical element of intake and their subsequent reading speed and accuracy scores and attitudes. (Doctoral dissertation, St. John's University, 1985). *Dissertation Abstracts International, 46*, 3247A.

Madison, M. B. (1984). A study of learning style preferences of specific learning disability students. (Doctoral dissertation, University of Southern Mississippi, 1984). *Dissertation Abstracts International, 46*, 3320A.

Mager, R. F. (1962). *Preparing instructional objectives.* Palo Alto, CA: Fearon.

Mager, R. F., & McCann J. (1963). *Learner-controlled instruction.* Palo Alto, CA: Varian.

Marcus, L. (1977). How teachers view learning styles. *NASSP Bulletin, 61*(408), 112–114.

Mariash, L. J. (1983). *Identification of characteristics of learning styles existent among students attending school in selected northeastern Manitoba communities.* Unpublished master's dissertation, University of Manitoba, Winnipeg, CN.

Martinez, R., & Dukes, R. L. (1987). Race, gender, and self-esteem among youth. *Hispanic Journal of Behavioral Sciences, 9*(4), 427–443.

Martini, M. (1986). An analysis of the relationships between and among computer-assisted instruction, learning style perceptual preferences, attitudes, and the science achievement of seventh grade students in a suburban, New York school district. (Doctoral dissertation, St. John's University, 1986). *Dissertation Abstracts International, 47*, 877A. Recipient: American Association of School Administrators (AASA) First Prize National Research, 1986.

Matthay, E. R., & Associates (1991). *Counseling for college.* Princeton, NJ: Peterson's Guides.

McEwen, P. (1985). *Learning styles, intelligence, and creativity among elementary school students.* Unpublished master's dissertation, State University of New York at Buffalo, Center for Studies on Creativity.

McFarland, M. (1989). An analysis of the relationship between learning style perceptual preferences and attitudes toward computer assisted instruction. (Doctoral dissertation, Portland State University). *Dissertation Abstracts International, 50*, 3143A.

Mein, J. R. (1986). Cognitive and learning style characteristics of high school gifted students. (Doctoral dissertation, University of Florida, 1986). *Dissertation Abstracts International, 48*, 880A.

Melone, R. A. (1987). The relationship between the level of cognitive development and learning styles of the emerging adolescent. (Doctoral dissertation, State University of New York at Buffalo, 1987). *Dissertation Abstracts International, 38*, 607A.

Mickler, M. L., & Zippert, C. P. (1987). Teaching strategies based on learning styles of adult students. *Community/Junior College Quarterly, 11*, 33–37.

Miles, B. (1987). An investigation of the relationships among the learning style sociological preferences of fifth and sixth grade students, selected interactive classroom patterns, and achievement in career awareness and career decision-making concepts. (Doctoral dissertation, St. John's University, 1987). *Dissertation Abstracts International, 48,* 2527A. Recipient: Phi Delta Kappan Eastern Regional Research Finalist, 1988.

Milgram, R. M., & Dunn, R. (1993). Chapter 2: Identify learning styles and creativity in gifted learners: Subjects, instrumentation, administration, reliability, validity. In R. M. Milgram, R. Dunn, & G. E. Price (Eds.), *Teaching and counseling gifted and talented adolescents: An international learning styles perspective* (pp. 25–36). Westport, CT: Praeger.

Milgram, R. M., Dunn, R., & Price, G. E. (Eds.). (1993a). Chapter 9: The learning styles of gifted adolescents in Israel. *Teaching and counseling gifted and talented adolescents for learning style: An international learning styles perspective* (pp. 137–148). Westport, CT: Praeger.

Milgram, R. M., Dunn, R., & Price, G. E. (Eds.). (1993b). *Teaching and counseling gifted and talented adolescents: An international learning style perspective.* Westport, CT: Praeger.

Milgram, R., & Price, G. E. (1993). Chapter 16: The learning styles of gifted adolescents around the world: Differences and similarities. In R. M. Milgram, R. Dunn, & G. E. Price (Eds.), *Teaching and counseling gifted and talented adolescents: An international learning style perspective* (pp. 229–241). Westport, CT: Praeger.

Miller, L. M. (1985). *Mobility as an element of learning style: The effect its inclusion or exclusion has on student performance in the standardized testing environment.* Unpublished master's dissertation, University of North Florida.

Milton Bradley Company (1986). *A question of scruples.* Sandy Hook, CT: Author.

Monheit, S. L. (1987). An analysis of learning based upon the relationship between the learning style preferences of parents and their children. (Doctoral dissertation, Fielding Institute, 1987). *Dissertation Abstracts International, 50,* 395A.

Monsour, S. E. M. (1991). The relationship between a prescribed homework program considering learning style preferences and the mathematics achievement of eighth-grade students. (Doctoral dissertation, University of Southern Mississippi, 1991). *Dissertation Abstracts International, 52,* 1630A.

Moore, A. J. (1984). *Okanagan/Nicola Indian quality education study.* Penticton, CN: Okanagan Indian Learning Institute.

Moore, A. J. (1987). Native Indian learning styles: A review for researchers and teachers. *Journal of American Indian Education, 27*(1), 17–29.

Moore, R. C. (1991). Effects of computer assisted instruction and perceptual preference(s) of eighth-grade students on the mastery of language arts and mathematics (CAI, Perceptual preferences). (Doctoral dissertation, South Carolina State University, 1991). *Dissertation Abstracts International, 53,* 1876A.

Morgan, H. L. (1981). Learning styles: The relation between need for structure and preferred mode of instruction for gifted elementary students. (Doctoral dissertation, University of Pittsburgh, 1981). *Dissertation Abstracts International, 43,* 2223A.

Morris, V. J. P. (1983). The design and implementation of a teaching strategy for language arts at Chipley High School that brings about predictable learning outcomes. (Doctoral dissertation, Florida State University, 1983). *Dissertation Abstracts International, 44,* 3231A.

Moss, V. B. (1981). The stability of first-graders' learning styles and the relationship between selected variables and learning style. (Doctoral dissertation, Mississippi State University, 1981). *Dissertation Abstracts International, 43,* 665A.

Murrain, P. G. (1983). Administrative determinations concerning facilities utilization and instructional grouping: An analysis of the relationships between selected thermal environments and preferences for temperature, an element of learning style, as they affect word recognition scores of secondary students. (Doctoral dissertation, St. John's University, 1983). *Dissertation Abstracts International, 44,* 1749A.

Murray, C. A. (1980). The comparison of learning styles between low and high reading achievement subjects in the seventh and eighth grades in a public middle school. (Doctoral dissertation, United States International University, 1980). *Dissertation Abstracts International, 41,* 1005A.

Naden, R. C. (1992). Prescriptions and/or modality-based instruction on the spelling achievement of fifth-grade students. (Doctoral dissertation, Andrews University, 1992). *Dissertation Abstracts International, 53,* 1051A.

Napier, R. W., & Gershenfeld, M. K. (1973). *Instruction manual groups! Theory and experience.* Boston: Houghton Mifflin.

Napolitano, R. A. (1986). An experimental investigation of the relationships among achievement, attitude scores, and traditionally, marginally, and underprepared college students enrolled in an introductory psychology course when they are matched and mismatched with their learning style preferences for the element of structure. (Doctoral dissertation, St. John's University, 1986). *Dissertation Abstracts International, 47,* 435A.

Natale, S. M., Callan, R. J., Ford, J., & Sora, S. (1992, Winter). Social control, efficiency control, and ethical control in different political institutions: Education. *The International Journal of Applied Philosophy* (NY: International Association of Applied Philosophy), *32,* 25–32.

Nations-Miller, B. R. (1993, February). A profile analysis of the learning styles of tenth- through twelfth-grade at-risk, vocational and gifted students in a suburban Georgia public school. (Doctoral dissertation, Georgia State University, 1992). *Dissertation Abstracts International, 53,* 2784A.

Neely, R. O., & Alm, D. (1992a). Meeting individual needs: A learning styles success story. *The Clearing House,* (Washington, DC: Heldref Publications), (2), 109–113.

Neely, R. O., & Alm, D. (1992b). Empowering students with styles. *Principal* (Reston, VA: National Association of Elementary School Principals), *72*(4), 32–35.

Nelson, B. N. (1991). An investigation of the impact of learning style factors on college students' retention and achievement. (Doctoral dissertation, St. John's University, 1991). *Dissertation Abstracts International, 53,* 3121A.

Nelson, B., Dunn, R., Griggs, S. A., Primavera, L., Fitzpatrick, M., Bacilious, Z., Miller, R. (1993). Effects of learning style intervention on students' retention and achievement. *Journal of College Student Development, 34*(5), 364–369.

Nganwa-Bagumah, M. (1986). Learning styles: The effects of matching and mismatching pupils' design preferences on reading comprehension tests. Bachelor's dissertation, University of Transkei, South Africa, 1986.

Nganwa-Bagumah, M., & Mwamwenda, T. S. (1991). Effects on reading comprehension tests of matching and mismatching students' design preferences. *Perceptual and Motor Skills, 72*(3), 947–951.

Nickerson, E. T., & O'Laughlin, K. (Eds.). (1982). *Helping through action: Action-oriented therapies*. Amherst, MA: Human Resource Development Press.

Nides, A. G. (1984). The effect of learning style preferences on achievement when an advanced organizer is employed. (Doctoral dissertation, Georgia State University College of Education, 1984). *Dissertation Abstracts International, 45*, 1288A.,

Nowicki, S., Jr., & Duke, M. P. (1983). The Nowicki-Strickland life-span locus of control scales: Construct validation. In H. M. Lefcourt (Ed.), *Research with the locus of control construct* (Vol. 2, pp. 13–51). Orlando, FL: Academic Press.

Nudd, A. N., & Gruenfeld, J. W. (1976). Field dependence-independence and social traditionalism: A comparison of ethnic subcultures of Trinidad. *International Journal of Psychology, 11*(1), 23–41.

Oakes, J. (1985). *Keep track: How schools structure inequality*. New Haven, CT: Yale University Press. Ed 274 749.

Office of Pastoral Research of the Archdiocese of New York. (1982). *Hispanics in New York: Religious, cultural, and social experiences*. New York: Author.

Ogato, B. G. (1991). A correlational examination of perceptual modality preferences of middle school students and their academic achievement. (Doctoral dissertation, Virginia Polytechnical Institute, Northern Virginia Graduate Center, 1991).

Orsak, L. (1990a). Learning styles versus the Rip Van Winkle syndrome. *Educational Leadership* (Alexandria, VA: Association for Supervision and curriculum Development), *48*(2), 19–20.

Orsak, L. (1990b). Learning styles and love: A winning combination. *Journal of Reading, Writing, and Learning Disabilities: International* (New York: Hemisphere Press), *6*(3), 343–347.

Ostoyee, C. H. (1988). The effects of teaching style on student writing about field trips with concrete experiences. (Doctoral dissertation, Columbia University, Teachers College, 1988). *Dissertation Abstracts International, 49*, 2916A.

Ott, J. N. (1973). Health and light: The effects of natural light and artificial light on man and other living things. Old Greenwich, CT: Devin-Adair Co.

Parloff, M. B. (1980). *Psychotherapy and research*. Frieda Fromm-Reichman memorial lecture, Washington University School of Psychiatry, St. Louis, MO.

Paskewitz, B. U. (1985). A study of the relationship between learning styles and attitudes toward computer programming of middle school gifted students. (Doctoral dissertation, University of Pittsburgh, 1985). *Dissertation Abstracts International, 47*, 697A.

Paulu, N. (1987). *Dealing with dropouts: The urban superintendents' call to action*. Washington, DC: U.S. Government Printing Office.

Pederson, J. K. (1984). The classification and comparison of learning disabled students and gifted students. (Doctoral dissertation, Texas Tech University, 1984). *Dissertation Abstracts International, 45*, 2810A.

Pena, R. (1989). *Two-of-a-kind learning styles*. New York: Center for the Study of Learning and Teaching Styles, St. John's University.

Perney, V. H. (1976). Effects of race and sex on field dependence-independence in children. *Perceptual and Motor Skills, 42*, 975–980.

Perrin, J. (1990, October). The learning styles project for potential dropouts. *Educational Leadership* (Alexandria, VA: Association for Supervision and Curriculum Development), *48*,(2), 23–24.

Perrin, J. (1984). An experimental investigation of the relationships among the learning style sociological preferences of gifted and non-gifted primary children, selected instructional strategies, attitudes, and achievement in problem solving and rote memorization. (Doctoral dissertation, St. John's University, 1984). *Dissertation Abstracts International, 46*, 342A. Recipient: American Association of School Administrators (AASA) National Research Finalist, 1984.

Pizzo, J. (1981). An investigation of the relationships between selected acoustic environments and sound, an element of learning style, as they affect sixth grade students' reading achievement and attitudes. (Doctoral dissertation, St. John's University, 1981). *Dissertation Abstracts International, 42*, 2475A. Recipient: Association for Supervision and Curriculum Development First Alternate National Recognition for Best Doctoral Research (Curriculum), 1981.

Pizzo, J. (1982, December). Breaking the sound barrier: Classroom noise and learning style. *Orbit, 64* (Ontario, CN: Ontario Institute for Studies in Education), *13*(4), 21–22.

Pizzo, J., Dunn, R., & Dunn, K. (1990). A sound approach to reading: Responding to students' learning styles. *Journal of Reading, Writing, and Learning Disabilities: International* (Washington, DC: Hemisphere Press), *6*(3), 249–260.

Poirier, G. A. (1970). Students as partners in team learning. Berkeley, CA: Center of Team Learning, Chapter 2. (1975) The Rise report: Report of the California commission for reform of intermediate and secondary education. Sacramento, CA: California State Department of Education.

Ponder, D. (1990). An analysis of the changes and gender differences in preferences of learning styles at adolescence and the relationship of the learning styles of adolescents and their parents when matched and mismatched according to gender. (Doctoral dissertation, East Texas State University, 1990). *Dissertation Abstracts International, 64*, 1170A.

Price, G. E. (1980). Which learning style elements are stable and which tend to change over time? *Learning Styles Network Newsletter, 1*(3), 1.

Price, G. E., Dunn, K., Dunn, R., & Griggs, S. A. (1981). Studies in students' learning styles. *Roeper Review*, (MI: Roeper City and Country School) *4*, 223–226.

Price, G. E., & Milgram, R. M. (1993). Chapter 16: The learning styles of gifted adolescents around the world: Differences and similarities. In R. M. Milgram, R. Dunn, & G. E. Price (Eds.), *Teaching and counseling gifted and talented adolescents: An international learning-style perspective* (pp. 229–248). Westport, CT: Praeger.

Quinn, R. (1994). The New York State compact for learning and learning styles. *Learning Styles Network Newsletter* (New York: St. John's University and the National Association of Secondary School Principals), *15*(1), 1–2.

Ragsdale, C. S. (1991). The experiences and impressions of tenth-grade students in a modern European history class designed as a collaborative, heuristic learning environment. (Doctoral dissertation, Union Institute, 1991). *Dissertation Abstracts International, 52,* 796A.

Rahal, B. F. (1986). The effects of matching and mismatching the diagnosed learning styles of intermediate level students with their structure preferences in the learning environment. (Doctoral dissertation, West Virginia University.) *Dissertation Abstracts International, 47*(06A), 2010.

Ramirez, A. I. (1982). Modality and field dependence/independence: Learning components and their relationship to mathematics achievement in the elementary school. (Doctoral dissertation, Florida State University, 1982). *Dissertation Abstracts International, 43,* 666A.

Ramirez, M., & Casteneda, A. (1974). *Cultural democracy: Bicognitive development and education:* New York: Academic Press.

Ramirez, M., & Price-Williams, D. (1974). Cognitive styles of children of three ethnic groups in the United States. *Journal of Cross-Cultural Psychology, 5,* 212–219.

Raviotta, C. F. (1988). A study of the relationship between knowledge of individual learning style and its effect on academic achievement and study orientation in high school mathematics students. (Doctoral dissertation, University of New Orleans, 1988). *Dissertation Abstracts International, 50,* 1204A.

Rea, D. C. (1980). Effects on achievement of placing students in different learning environments based upon identified learning styles. Doctoral dissertation, University of Missouri, 1989.

Reid, J. M. (1987, March). The learning style preferences of ESL students. *TESOL Quarterly, 21,* 87–105. Available to members only: TESP, 1118 22nd Street N. W., Georgetown University, Suite 205, Washington, DC 20037.

Research on the Dunn and Dunn learning style model. (1994). New York: St. John's University's Center for the Study of Learning and Teaching Styles.

Restak, R. (1979). *The brain: The last frontier.* New York: Doubleday.

Review of research on sociological preferences. (1991, Summer). *Learning Styles Network Newsletter.* (New York: St. John's University and the National Association of Secondary School Principals), *12*(2).

Reynolds, J. (1988). A study of the pattern of learning style characteristics for adult dependent decision-makers. (Doctoral dissertation, Virginia Polytech Institute and State University, 1988). *Dissertation Abstracts International, 50,* 854A.

Reynolds, J. (1991, December). Learning style characteristics of adult dependent decision makers: Counseling and instructional implications. *Career Development Quarterly, 40,* 145–154.

Ricca, J. (1983). Curricular implications of learning style differences between gifted and non-gifted students. (Doctoral dissertation, State University of

New York at Buffalo, 1983). *Dissertation Abstracts International, 44* 1324A.

Richardson, B. L. (1991). Utilizing the resources of the African American church: Strategies for counseling professionals. In C. C. Lee & B. L. Richardson (Eds.), *Multicultural issues in counseling: New approaches to diversity* (pp. 65–75). Alexandria, VA: American Association for Counseling and Development.

Ritzinger, F. C. (1971). *Psychological and physiological differentiation in children six to eleven years of age.* Unpublished doctoral dissertation, Washington University, St. Louis, MO.

Roberts, O. A. (1984). Investigation of the relationship between learning style and temperament of senior high students in the Bahamas and Jamaica. Graduate dissertation, Andrews University, 1984.

Rodrigo, R. A. (1989). A comparison of the profiles of the learning styles of first-grade pupils at the Ateneo de Manila Grade School for the school year 1988–1989. Master's thesis, Graduate School Ateneo de Manila University, 1989.

Rodriguez, F. (1988). Minorities and the school system, In R. A. Gorton, G. J. Schneider, & J. C. Fisher (Eds), *Encyclopedia of school administration & supervision* (pp. 172–173). Phoenix, AZ: Oryx Press.

Rowe, W., Bennett, S. K., & Atkinson, D. R. (1994). White racial identity models: A critique and alternative proposal. *The Counseling Psychologist, 22*(1), 129–146.

Sage, C. O. (1984). The Dunn and Dunn learning style model: An analysis of its theoretical, practical, and research foundations. (Doctoral dissertation, University of Denver, 1984). *Dissertation Abstracts International, 45,* 353A.

Santrock, J. W. (1992). *Life-span development* (4th ed.). Dubuque, IA: William C. Brown Publishers.

Selden, C. A. (1989). Reducing adolescent alienation: Strategies for the high school. *NASSP Bulletin, 73,* 77–84.

Shade, B. J. (1982). Afro-American cognitive style: A variable in school success? *Review of Educational Research, 52,* 219–244.

Shade, B. J. (1983). Cognitive strategies as determinants of school achievement. *Psychology in Schools, 20,* 488–492.

Shands, R., & Brunner, C. (1989, Fall). Providing success through a powerful combination: Mastery learning and learning styles. *Perceptions.*(New York: New York State Educators of the Emotionally Disturbed), *25*(1), 6–10.

Shea, T. C. (1983). An investigation of the relationship among preferences for the learning style element of design, selected instructional environments, and reading achievement with ninth grade students to improve administrative determinations concerning effective educational facilities. (Doctoral dissertation, St. John's University, 1983). *Dissertation Abstracts International, 44,* 2004A. Recipient: National Association of Secondary School Principals' Middle School Research Finalist Citation, 1984.

Siebenman, J. B. (1984). An investigation of the relationship between learning style and cognitive style in non-traditional college reading students. (Doctoral dissertation, Arizona State University, 1984). *Dissertation Abstracts International, 45,* 1705A.

Sims, J. E. (1988). Learning styles: A comparative analysis of the learning styles of black-American, Mexican-American, and white-American third and fourth grade students in traditional public schools. (Doctoral dissertation, University of Santa Barbara, 1988).

Sims, J. (1989, Winter). Learning style: Should it be considered? *The Oregon Elementary Principal* (Salem, OR: Oregon Elementary Principals' Association), *50* (2), 28.

Sinatra, C. (1990, July-September). Five diverse secondary schools where learning style instruction works. *Journal of Reading, Writing, and Learning Disabilities International* (New York: Hemisphere Publishing Corporation), *6*(3), 323–342.

Sinatra, C. (1993). The great depression: Don't let it get you down. In R. Dunn & K. Dunn, Teaching secondary students through their individual learning styles: Practical approaches for grades 7–12 (pp. 217–245). Boston: Allyn & Bacon.

Sinatra, R. (1982). Learning literacy in nonverbal style. *Student Learning Styles and Brain Behavior* (pp. 203–211). Reston, VA: National Association of Secondary Principals.

Sinatra, R., de Mendez, E. S., & Price, G. E. (1993). Chapter 10: The learning styles and creative performance accomplishments of adolescents in Guatemala. In R. M. Milgram, R. Dunn, & G. E. Price (Eds.), *Teaching and counseling gifted and talented adolescents: An international learning-style perspective* (pp. 161–174). Westport, CT: Greenwood Press.

Sinatra, R., Hirshoren, A., & Primavera, L. H. (1987). Learning style, behavior ratings and achievement interactions for adjudicated adolescents. *Educational and Psychological Research*, *7*(1), 21–32.

Sinatra, R., Primavera L., & Waked, W. J. (1986). Learning style and intelligence of reading disabled students. *Perceptual and Motor Skills*, *62*, 242–253.

Singleton, N. (1993). Learning style assessment. Doctoral dissertation, University of Portland, 1993.

Slade, M. (1982, October 24). Aptitude, intelligence or what? *New York Times*.

Smith, S. (1987). An experimental investigation of the relationship between and among achievement, preferred time of instruction, and critical-thinking abilities of tenth- and eleventh-grade students in mathematics. (Doctoral dissertation, St. John's University, 1987). *Dissertation Abstracts International*, *47*, 1405A.

Smith, T. D. (1988). An assessment of the self perceived teaching style of three ethnic groups of public school teachers in Texas. (Doctoral dissertation, East Texas University, 1988). *Dissertation Abstract International*, *49* (08-A), 2062A.

Snider, K. P. (1985). A study of learning preferences among educable mentally impaired, emotionally impaired, learning disabled, and general education students in seventh, eighth, and ninth grades as measured by response to the Learning Styles Inventory. (Doctoral dissertation, Michigan State University, 1985). *Dissertation Abstracts International*, *46*, 1251A.

Solberg, S. J. (1987). An analysis of the Learning Style Inventory, the Productivity Environmental Preference Survey, and the Iowa Test of Basic Skills. (Doctoral dissertation, Northern Arizona University, 1987). *Dissertation Ab-*

stracts International, 48, 2530A.

Soliman, A. S. (1993). Chapter 14: The learning styles of adolescents in Egypt. In R. M. Milgram, R. Dunn, & G. E. Price (Eds.), *Teaching and counseling gifted and talented adolescents: An international learning-style perspective* (pp. 211–218). Westport, CT: Greenwood Press.

Spires, R. D. (1983). The effect of teacher inservice about learning styles on students' mathematics and reading achievement. (Doctoral dissertation, Bowling Green State University, 1983). *Dissertation Abstracts International, 44,* 1325A.

Spiridakis, J. (1993). Chapter 15: The learning styles of adolescents in Greece. In R. M. Milgram, R. Dunn, & G. E. Price (Eds.), *Teaching and counseling gifted and talented adolescents: An international learning-style perspective* (pp. 219–228). Westport, CT: Greenwood Press.

Stahlnecker, R. K. (1988). Relationships between learning style preferences of selected elementary pupils and their achievement in math and reading. (Doctoral dissertation, Loma Linda University, 1988). *Dissertation Abstracts International, 50,* 3471A.

Steinauer, M. H. (1981). Interpersonal relationships as reflected in learning style preferences: A study of eleventh grade students and their English teachers in a vocational school. (Doctoral dissertation, Southern Illinois University, 1981). *Dissertation Abstracts International, 43,* 305A.

Stiles, R. (1985). Learning style preferences for design and their relationship to standardized test results. (Doctoral dissertation, University of Tennessee, 1985). *Dissertation Abstracts International, 46,* 2551A.

Stokes, B. M. (1989). An analysis of the relationship between learning style, achievement, race, and gender. (Doctoral dissertation, University of Akron, 1989). *Dissertation Abstracts International, 49,* 757A.

Stone, P. (1992, November). How we turned around a problem school. *The Principal* (Reston, VA: National Association of Elementary School Principal), *71*(2), 34–36.

Streitmatter, J. L. (1988). Ethnicity as a mediating variable of early adolescent identity development. *Journal of Adolescence, 11,* 335–346.

Sue, S. (1977). Community mental health services to minority groups: Some optimism, some pessimism. *American Psychologist, 32,* 616–624.

Sue, S., McKinney, H., Allen, D., & Hall, J. (1974). Delivery of community mental health services to black & white clients. *Journal of Consulting & Clinical Psychology 42,* 594–601.

Sue, D., & Sue, D. W. (1991). Chapter 7: Counseling strategies for Chinese Americans. In C. C. Lee & B. L. Richardson (Eds.), *Multicultural issues in counseling: New approaches to diversity* (pp. 79–90). Alexandria, VA: American Association for Counseling & Development.

Sue, D. W., & Sue, D. (1990). *Counseling the culturally different: Theory and practice* (2nd ed.). New York: John Wiley.

Suh, B., & Price, G. E. (1993). The learning styles of gifted adolescents in Korea. In R. M. Milgram, R. Dunn, & G. E. Price, (Eds.), *Teaching and counseling gifted and talented adolescents: An international learning style perspective* (pp. 175–186). New York: Praeger.

Suinn, R. M. (1982). *The mathematics anxiety rating scale for adolescents.* Fort Collins, CO: Rocky Mountain Behavioral Science Institute.

Sullivan, M. (1993). A meta-analysis of experimental research studies based on the Dunn and Dunn learning styles model and its relationship to academic achievement and performance. Doctoral dissertation, St. John's University, 1993.

Svreck, L. J. (1990). Perceived parental influence, accommodated learning style preferences, and students' attitudes toward learning as they relate to reading and mathematics achievement. Doctoral dissertation, St. John's University, 1990. *Dissertation Abstracts International, 53*, 395.

Swisher, K., & Deyhle, D. (1987). Styles of learning and learning styles: Educational conflicts for American Indian/Alaskan native youth. *Journal of Multilingual and Multicultural Development, 8*(4), 345–360.

Sykes, S., Jones, B., & Phillips, J. (1990, October). Partners in learning styles at a private school. *Educational Leadership* (Alexandria, VA: Association for Supervision and Curriculum Development), *48*(2), 24–26.

Tanenbaum, R. (1982). An investigation of the relationships between selected instructional techniques and identified field dependent and field independent cognitive styles as evidenced among high school students enrolled in studies of nutrition. Doctoral dissertation, St. John's University, 1982. *Dissertation Abstracts International, 43*, 68A.

Tappenden, V. J. (1983). Analysis of the learning styles of vocational education and nonvocational education students in eleventh and twelfth grades from rural, urban, and suburban locations in Ohio. (Doctoral dissertation, Kent State University, 1983). *Dissertation Abstracts International, 44*, 1326A.

Thies, A. P. (1979). A brain behavior analysis of learning style. In *Student learning styles: Diagnosing and prescribing programs*. Reston VA: National Association of Secondary School Principals.

Thrasher, R. (1984). A study of the learning-style preferences of at-risk sixth and ninth graders. Pompano Beach, FL: Florida Association of Alternative Scnool Educators.

Tiedt, P. L., & Tiedt, I. M. (1990). *Multicultural teaching: A handbook of activities, information, and resources*. Third edition. Boston: Allyn & Bacon.

Tingley-Michaelis, C. (1983). Make room for movement. *Early Years, 13*(6), 26–29.

Torres, P. L. (1992). *The identification of second-grade students' learning styles*. Unpublished master's thesis, University of Brasilia, 1992.

Trautman, P. (1979). An investigation of the relationship between selected instructional techniques and identified cognitive style. (Doctoral dissertation, St. John's University, 1979). *Dissertation Abstracts International, 40*, 1428A.

Turner, N. D. (1993). Prescriptions and/or modality-based instruction on the spelling achievement of fifth-grade students. (Doctoral dissertation, Andrews University, 1992). *Dissertation Abstracts International, 53*, 1051A.

Urbschat, K. S. (1977). A study of preferred learning modes and their relationship to the amount of recall of CVC trigrams. (Doctoral dissertation, Wayne State University, 1977). *Dissertation Abstracts International, 38*, 2536A.

U. S. Senate Select Committee on Indian Affairs. (1985). *Indian juvenile alcoholism and eligibility for BIA schools*. Washington, DC: U. S. Government Printing Office.

Vasquez, J. A. (1990). Teaching to the distinctive traits of minority students. *The*

Clearing House (Washington, DC: Heldref Publications), *63*(7), 299–304.

Vaughan, J. L., Underwood, V. L., House, G. L., Schroth, G., Weaver, S. W., Bienversie, N., & Dotson, S. (1992). *Learning styles and TAAS scores: Preliminary results. Research report no. 3.* Commerce, TX: Texas Center for Learning Styles, East Texas State University.

Vaughan, J. L., Weaver, S. L., Underwood, V. L., Bienversie, N., House, G., Durkin, M., & Schroth, G. (1992). *The learning style characteristics of Tohono O'Odham students: An executive summary. Research report no. 1.* Commerce, TX: Texas Center for Learning Styles, East Texas State University.

Vaughan, J. L., Weaver, S. L., Underwood, V. L., & House, G. L. (1992). *A comparison of students' learning styles as determined by the Learning Style Inventory and personal learning power. Research Report No. 2.* Commerce, TX: Texas Center for Learning Styles, East Texas State University.

Vazquez, A. W. (1985). Description of learning styles of high risk adult students taking courses in urban community colleges in Puerto Rico. (Doctoral dissertation, Union for Experimenting Colleges and Universities, Puerto Rico, 1985). *Dissertation Abstracts International, 47,* 1157A.

Vignia, R. A. (1983). An investigation of learning styles of gifted and non-gifted high school students. (Doctoral dissertation, University of Houston, 1983). *Dissertation Abstracts International, 44,* 3653A.

Virostko, J. (1983). An analysis of the relationships among academic achievement in mathematics and reading, assigned instructional schedules, and the learning style time preferences of third, fourth, fifth, and sixth grade students. (Doctoral dissertation, St. John's University, 1983). *Dissertation Abstracts International, 44,* 1683A. Recipient: Kappa Delta Pi International Award for Best Doctoral Research, 1983.

Wallace, J. (1990). The relationship among preferences for learning alone or with peers, selected instructional strategies, and achievement of third-, fourth-, and fifth-grade social studies students. (Doctoral dissertation, Syracuse University, 1990). *Dissertation Abstracts International, 51,* 3626A.

Wechsler, S. (1993). Chapter 13: The learning styles of creative adolescents in Brazil. In R. M. Milgram, R. Dunn, & G. E. Price (Eds.), *Teaching and counseling gifted and talented adolescents: An international learning-style perspective* (pp. 197–210). Westport, CT: Praeger.

Weinberg, F. (1983). An experimental investigation of the interaction between sensory modality preference and mode of presentation in the instruction of arithmetic concepts to third grade underachievers. (Doctoral dissertation, St. John's University, 1983). *Dissertation Abstracts International, 44* 1740A.

Weitz, J. M. (1971). *Cultural change and field dependence in two native Canadian linguistic families.* Unpublished doctoral dissertation, University of Ottawa, Ottawa, CN.

Wegner, W. A. (1980). Opsimathic styles of adults. (Doctoral dissertation, The University of Southern Mississippi, 1980). *Dissertation Abstracts International, 41* (05A), 1898.

Wheeler, R. (1980). An alternative to failure: Teaching reading according to students' perceptual strengths. *Kappa Delta Pi Record, 17*(2) 59–63.

Wheeler, R. (1983). An investigation of the degree of academic achievement

evidenced when second grade, learning disabled students' perceptual preferences are matched and mismatched with complementary sensory approaches to beginning reading instruction. (Doctoral dissertation, St.
John's University, 1983). *Dissertation Abstracts International 44*, 2039A.

White, R. (1981). An investigation of the relationship between selected instructional methods and selected elements of emotional learning style upon
student achievement in seventh grade social studies. (Doctoral dissertation,
St. John's University, 1980). *Dissertation Abstracts International, 42*,
995A. Recipient: Kappa Delta Gamma International Award for Best Doctoral Research Prospectus, 1980.

Wiebe, R. D. (1992). *A learning style profile of physics students in comparison
with non-physics students.* (Master's thesis, Gonzaga University, Spokane,
Washington, 1992).

Wilburn, H. R. (1991). An investigation of interaction among learning styles and
computer-assisted instruction with synthetic speech. (Doctoral dissertation,
University of Texas at Austin, 1991). *Dissertation Abstracts International,
52*, 2398A–2399A.

Wild, J. B. (1979). *A study of the learning styles of learning disabled students
and non-learning disabled students at the junior high school level.* Unpublished master's dissertation, University of Kansas, Lawrence, Kansas.

Wilkins, R. (1994). Free at last? *Modern Maturity, 37*(2), 27, 31–33.

Williams, G. J. (1989). A study of the learning styles of urban black middle school
learning-disabled and non-learning-disabled students. (Doctoral dissertation, Southern Illinois University, 1990). *Dissertation Abstracts International, 51* A.

Williams, G. L. (1984). The effectiveness of computer assisted instruction and its
relationship to selected learning style elements. (Doctoral dissertation,
North Texas State University, 1984). *Dissertation Abstracts International,
45*, 1986A.

Williams, H. S. (1994). The differences in cumulative grade point averages among
African-American freshman college learning styles: A preliminary investigation. *National Forum of Applied Educational Research Journal, 8*(1),
36–40.

Williams, J. (1994). The new segregation. *Modern Maturity, 37*(2), 24–26; 28–32.

Willis, M. G. (1989). Learning styles of African-American children: A review of the
literature and interventions. *Journal of Black Psychology, 16*(1), 47–65.

Wilson, W. J. (1978). *The declining significance of race: Blacks and changing
American institutions.* Chicago: University of Chicago Press.

Wingo, L. H. (1980). Relationships among locus of motivation, sensory modality
and grouping preferences of learning style to basic skills test performance
in reading and mathematics. (Doctoral dissertation, Memphis State University, 1980). *Dissertation Abstracts International, 41*, 2923.

Witkin, H. A., Oltman, P. K., Raskin, E., & Karp, S. A. (1971). *A manual for the
Embedded Figures Tests.* Palo Alto, CA: Consulting Psychologists Press.

Wittenberg, S. K. (1984). A comparison of diagnosed and preferred learning styles
of young adults in need of remediation. (Doctoral dissertation, University
of Toledo, 1984). *Dissertation Abstracts International, 45*, 3539A.

Wittig, C. (1985). *Learning style preferences among students high or low on di-*

vergent thinking and feeling variables. Unpublished master's dissertation, State University of New York at Buffalo, Center for Studies in Creativity, 1985.

Wolfe, G. (1983). Learning styles and the teaching of reading. (Doctoral dissertation, Akron University, 1983). *Dissertation Abstracts International, 45,* 3422A.

Yeap, L. L. (1987). Learning styles of Singapore secondary students. (Doctoral dissertation, University of Pittsburgh, 1987). *Dissertation Abstracts International, 48,* 936A.

Yong, F. L. (1989). Ethnic, gender, and grade differences in the learning style preferences of gifted minority students. Doctoral dissertation, Southern Illinois University at Carbondale, 1989.

Yong, F. L., & Ewing, N. J. (1992). A comparative study of the learning-style preferences among gifted African-American, Mexican-American, and American-born Chinese middle-grade students. *Roeper Review* (Mississippi: Roeper City and Country School), *14*(3), 120–123.

Yong, F. L., & McIntyre, J. D. (1992). A comparative study of the learning styles preferences of students with learning disabilities and students who are gifted. *Journal of Learning Disabilities, 25*(2), 124–132.

Young, B. M. P. (1985). Effective conditions for learning: An analysis of learning environments and learning styles in ability-grouped classes. (Doctoral dissertation, University of Massachusetts, 1985). *Dissertation Abstracts International, 46,* 708A.

Young, D. B., Jr. (1986). Administrative implications of instructional strategies and student learning style preferences of science achievement on seventh-grade students. (Doctoral dissertation, University of Hawaii, 1986). *Dissertation Abstracts International, 48,* 27A.

Zak, F. (1989). Learning style discrimination between vocational and nonvocational students. (Doctoral dissertation, University of Massachusetts, 1989). *Dissertation Abstracts International, 50,* 3843A.

Zenhausern, R. (1980). Hemispheric dominance. *Learning Styles Network Newsletter* (New York: St. John's University and the National Association of Secondary School Principals), *1*(2), 3.

Zikmund, A. B. (1988). The effect of grade level, gender, and learning style on responses to conservation type rhythmic and melodic patterns. (Doctoral dissertation, University of Nebraska, 1988). *Dissertation Abstracts International, 50,* 95A.

Zikmund, A. B. (1992, April). The effects of perceptual mode preferences and other selected variables on upper-elementary school students' response to conservation-type rhythmic and melodic tasks. *Psychology of Music, 20*(1), 57–69.

Author Index

Subject Index

About the Authors

RITA DUNN is Professor of Instructional Leadership and Director of the Center for the Study of Teaching and Learning Styles, St. John's University.

SHIRLEY A. GRIGGS is Professor of Counselor Education at St. John's University.

Both are recognized as outstanding faculty in teaching and research. Dunn and Griggs have coauthored *Learning Styles: Quiet Revolution in American Secondary Schools* (1966) and more than 17 other books as separate authors.